MW01027505

0-07-033783-7   T. Keller

0-07-039825-9   S. Malik   *CSP: A Developer's Guide*
0-07-041984-1   L. Trindell   *NetView: A Professional's Guide to SNA Network Management*
0-07-067175-3   A. Varsegi   *MVS COBOL Application Developer's Toolbox*
0-07-054972-9   J. Savit   *VM and CMS:Performance and Fine Tuning*
0-07-096425-4   M. Gopaul   *IBM Mainframe Programmer's Desk Reference*
0-07-024128-7   F. Graubart-Cervone   *VSE / ESA JCL: Utilities, POWER, and VSAM*
0-07-049654-4   D. Peterson   *ENTERPRISE NETWORK MANAGEMENT: A Guide to IBM's NetView*
0-07-072702-3   Zamir/Ranade   *The MVS JCL Primer*
0-07-002744-7   Archambeault/Gibbs   *CICS / ESA Version 3: Architecture and Problem Determination*
0-07-044309-2   Murphy   *MVS Control Blocks*
0-07-022798-5   Gamble/Merrow   *AS / 400 System Administration Guide*
0-07-035138-4   Kneiling   *DRDA: IBM's Distributed Relational Database Architecture*
0-07-040799-1   Martyn/Hartley/Johnson   *SQL / 400 A Professional Programmer's Guide*

AS/400
System Administration
Guide

AS/400
System Administration
Guide

Jesse Gamble
Bill Merrow

McGraw-Hill, Inc.
New York   San Francisco   Washington, D.C.   Auckland   Bogotá
Caracas   Lisbon   London   Madrid   Mexico City   Milan
Montreal   New Delhi   San Juan   Singapore
Sydney   Tokyo   Toronto

Library of Congress Cataloging-in-Publication Data

Gamble, Jesse.
  AS/400 system administration guide / Jesse Gamble, Bill Merrow.
      p.   cm.
  Includes index.
  ISBN 0-07-022798-5
  1. IBM AS/400 (Computer)   I. Merrow, Bill.   II. Title.
QA76.8.I25919G35   1994
005.4'449—dc20   94-21093
                                                                CIP

1 2 3 4 5 6 7 8 9 0   DOC/DOC   9 9 8 7 6 5 4 3

ISBN 0-07-022798-5

The sponsoring editor for this book was Jerry Papke.

Printed and bound by R. R. Donnelley & Sons Company.

Contents

List of Figures

Preface

Who is this book for?

The title of this book is *AS/400: System Management Guide.* It is designed to provide systems managers of AS/400 systems with information about their operating system. AS/400 is the machine architecture, and OS/400 is the name of the operating system. Because the AS/400 hardware is integrally packaged with OS/400 and the system is actually a combination of the two, we use both terms in this book.

The intended audience of this book is the Technical Support, Operations, and Applications Programming communities. No specific AS/400 or OS/400 expertise is required to make use of this subject matter. Although general data processing knowledge is helpful for reading this book, each new concept is explained when introduced so that DP novices will find value in most sections.

Most of the material applies to OS/400 Version 2.1 and subsequent releases. Special emphasis is placed on the features provided by OS/400 2.2 throughout the book. Many examples are specific to the OS/400 2.2 environment.

An overview of the philosophy and methodology utilized in this book is included to assist the reader. A detailed discussion of the installation and maintenance of OS/400 is provided to aid new AS/400 users. Sample CL and REXX procedures are presented to illustrate the command languages. A separate portion of the book is oriented towards AS/400 recoverability, security, and problem determination. This book contains some basic information on tuning AS/400 systems.

AS/400 systems are often components of larger distributed systems involving mainframes. Basic material on the mainframe

CICS, and VTAM components is included in the distributed processing section of this book. Additional information on CICS may be found in P. Donofrio's book *CICS Programmers Reference* which although written from an MVS standpoint, applies to AS/400 CICS environments.

The structure of this book

This book is comprised of *training* and *reference* chapters. A *reference chapter* provides detailed information on a specific OS/400 component or topic. Thus, the Maintenance chapter is intended to completely describe the system maintenance facilities of OS/400 as well as suggest a preferred approach.

A *training* chapter serves to define the aspects of the OS/400 operating system that we need to understand before we can begin to work with it. The training chapters introduce a subject, then expand it with in depth coverage. The basic structure of each training chapter is:

- An overview of the chapter's contents.
- Technical information in depth.
- Examples (where applicable).

A *technical reference* chapter is concerned with technical details of an OS/400 system component. Each technical reference chapter contains both cookbook data and in-depth information. Each reference chapter contains:

- An overview of the chapter's contents.
- A summary section (key information in overview form).
- In-depth information.
- Examples (where applicable).

The summary sections provided with each reference chapter summarize key topics covered in that chapter. The items listed are each covered in detail in the remainder of the chapter. Any new terms found here will be explained within the body of the chapter.

A *glossary* is provided to define all technical terms used in this book. In addition, each new term is defined within the text when it is first used. The critical definitions are all pinpointed within the index with a secondary "defined" entry under the name of the technical term.

A detailed *index* is provided. If you encounter a technical term and need more information beyond the glossary, then the index will direct you to additional data. A special effort has been made to index each of the AS/400 commands referenced within this book. Where many entries occur for a subject, a sub-entry is provided to help locate where the term is defined, or where detailed information can be found, or to describe associated problems/solutions. A lot of effort has gone into producing the index and the authors are very interested in suggestions and corrections.

About the figures

Figures are used extensively to illustrate the AS/400 hardware and the OS/400 operating system, document command formats, and to show the output of commands. A list of all figures is provided after the table of contents.

The figures in this book depicting storage layouts have the lowest addresses at the bottom and the highest addresses at the top of the diagram. This is consistent with most of the IBM documentation. The space shown in each figure for a specific area of storage is not intended to be strictly proportional to its allocation. Instead, the figures are intended to illustrate the relationships of storage areas.

Every effort has been made to keep figures close to the associated text. However, an occasional reference to a figure in another part of the book is necessary to avoid excessive duplication. Figure numbers take the form *chapter.sequence* where *chapter* is the chapter number and *sequence* is the relative sequence of the figure within that chapter.

Conventions, typesetting and others

Commands used with operating systems or utilities are shown using boldface, such as COMMAND operands. Optional operands are shown surrounded by braces, as in CMD op1{ ,op2} (where op1 is a required parameter and op2 is an optional parameter).

Italics are used to introduce new terms, such as *paging subsystem*, or to set off the title of a book referenced in the text, such as *AS/400: System Management Guide*.

Unless otherwise stated, all numbers used in this book are decimal. Numeric values expressed as "nKB" refer to "n" blocks of 1024 bytes. Thus, 256KB is actually 262144 bytes. Numeric values expressed as "nMB" refer to "n" megabytes of storage. A megabyte is 1024KB. Finally, "2GB" refers to two gigabytes of storage (a gigabyte is 1024MB).

Acknowledgements

A number of unnamed IBM staff also contributed materials, information, guidance, and support to the development of this book. The IBM COMMON and GUIDE user groups provided channels of communication with these and other contributors.

We are sure that we have missed many in this hurried list, and wish to credit them for what is good in this effort. None of them are responsible for what is incorrect or unclear. We are interested in your comments, suggestions, and corrections.

Jesse Gamble
Bill Merrow
Columbus, Ohio

Copyrights and Trademarks

This section is provided to give credit to the copyright and trademark holders whose products are mentioned throughout this book. The authors apologize for any that have been inadvertently omitted from this list.

The IBM Corporation holds trademarks for many terms used herein including IBM™, AS/400™, OS/400™, VSE™, VSE/ESA™, VM/ESA™, CICS/VSE™, ACF/VTAM™, SQL/DS™, DB2™, MVS/XA™, and MVS/ESA™.

Various commercial software packages mentioned within the text are also trademarked including Messenger Plus (by Byteware), and Pilot (by ASC) and possibly others. If any trademark is not properly identified, the omission is unintended.

Introduction to the OS/400 Environment

Part A looks at operating systems in general and OS/400 in particular, the hardware environment that the OS/400 operating system was designed for, as well as the types of users of this operating system. We look at classic mainframe operating systems along with midsize machine operating systems. OS/400 systems can be structured to occupy either position and we review what distinguishes it in each of these roles.

We then discuss the trend towards open systems and the role of the AS/400 in open environments. We include a brief discussion of the features of open systems found in the AS/400 as well as the IBM stated direction for making the AS/400 more compliant with open system standards in the future.

Finally we look at the types of users of the AS/400 found in typical environments and their roles managing/interfacing with the computer. We include both classical data processing roles and the more modern departmental computer roles.

1

Operating Systems and Computer Environments

This chapter describes the OS/400 environment and purpose. We begin by defining the term *operating system*. We then review OS/400 in relation to other current IBM operating systems. Next, we look at the OS/400 mission and briefly at the hardware platforms upon which OS/400 runs (a subsequent chapter gives a more detailed treatment of the AS/400 processor family), and describe the basic functions of the OS/400 operating system. We finish with a quick look at the history of OS/400. Our topics include:

What is an Operating System?
An Overview of IBM Operating Systems
   MVS
   VM
   VSE
   OS/400
   AIX
   PC/DOS
   OS2
The OS/400 Mission
The history of OS/400

1.1   What is an Operating System?

An *Operating System* is a set of software that provides a standard environment for applications. It insulates the application developer from the differences between the various processors and I/O devices encountered in modern data processing shops. An operating system also provides standard services to reduce application development time. These services may be integral to the operating system or provided by more complex subsystem services. Some services that are part of the OS/400 operating system are the *Control Language* (CL) services, the system APIs, the data manager, and the librarian. Examples of more complex services are transaction processing environments such as CICS/400 and languages such as REXX or C/400 or COBOL.

Another key function of modern operating systems is to implement *multiprogramming* and *multitasking*. Although these sound the similar, they are quite different. *Multiprogramming* allows multiple applications to be executed at the same time, sharing the available resources, all without interfering with each other. *Multitasking* is a facility that allows a single process to be divided into a number of separately executing tasks, each of which may communicate asynchronously with the others.

IBM mainframe operating systems have fancy acronym names such as VSE/ESA, VM/ESA, and MVS/ESA. We call these systems VSE, VM, and MVS for simplicity, even though the official name is more complex. For the AS/400, we use the term OS/400 when referring to the operating system as a separate entity, and the term AS/400 when referring to the whole computer system.

Different operating systems have different primary missions and target markets. MVS is designed for large batch workloads and extreme mission critical systems. VM is one of the best Interactive Processing environments. VSE/ESA is an excellent transaction processing system, a midrange batch processing system, and a vehicle for client server application development.

1.2   Types of Operating Systems

Modern computer networks are frequently diagramed with three layers (see Figure 1.1). These three layers involve three very different types of computer systems (from the standpoint of usage

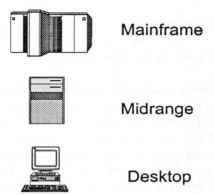

Mainframe

Midrange

Desktop

Figure 1.1   Computer Network Layers

if not for the type of hardware used) and three different types of operating systems:

- Mainframe

- Midrange

- Desktop

These types of systems were historically separated in terms of processor speed, memory size, I/O bandwidth, and similar factors involving *scale.* Technology has advanced to the point that desktop systems can have the speed (MIPs) of mainframes, so these types of measurement are no longer easy to apply. In this book we will use a different view based upon the usage and support requirements of the different types of systems.

1.3   Mainframe Systems

Mainframe systems are large, multiple-user systems that historically have required a controlled environment. Environmental factors include:

- Air conditioning

- Water for chillers

- Special power hookups

- Raised floor with underfloor cabling

Mainframe systems usually involve organization wide use, which means that they are *mission critical.* The unavailability of a mainframe typically has an immediate impact on the entire organization. This means that mainframe systems require dedicated operations and systems support staff and often involve duplicated hardware. Of course, the result is that mainframe systems have a high overhead cost. Mainframes also occupy a relatively small market.

Because of the small size of the mainframe market, mainframe software tends to be fairly expensive. Software is of comparable complexity regardless of execution platform. This, plus the need for a large support staff, results in the high cost per unit of software for mainframe systems.

These factors combine into a general requirement for a central datacenter to house a mainframe system. Often referred to as the *glass house,* such a datacenter has a relatively large fixed overhead cost. This cost must be recovered over a number of user areas to be viewed as cost effective by an individual area. Totally unattended operations are quite rare for mainframe systems used for mission critical tasks. Because unattended operations are not the historical norm for mainframe systems, much mainframe software was designed to be manually operated. This increases the need for a dedicated operations support staff. Mainframe systems have a future so long as mission critical applications require that type of system (it is not clear this is currently true).

MVS and VM are almost exclusively run as mainframe systems. This is a result of the cost of the operating system software, the types of processors used, and the size of the support staff required by these operating systems. VSE/ESA may be run as a mainframe system, but also is increasingly seen in midrange systems. OS/400 may be run in either role, but even in a mainframe environment it requires a smaller staff and can be run unattended for at least a portion of the day.

1.3.1   The MVS Operating System

MVS (*Multiple Virtual Storage*) is a complex operating system designed for the largest processors.   MVS supports large uniprocessors plus multiple-processor ES/9000 systems.   It excels at batch work, and also can be used as a high end transaction processing system. Although MVS *TSO* (*Time Share Option*) offers Interactive processing, MVS is not an efficient interactive processing platform.   This function is gradually moving to cheaper *Programmable Workstations* (*PCs*) from all mainframe systems. MVS is a complex operating system requiring a dedicated staff of systems programmers. MVS is particularly well suited for high-end mission critical applications. In this type of environment, the extra cost in hardware and people resources for MVS is less important than the availability of the systems it supports.

MVS supports *multiprocessing*. Multiprocessing is the simultaneous processing of two or more portions of the same program by two or more processing units or CPUs. At one time, the size of the task, or the critical nature of the workload dictated the use of MVS.

OS/400 also supports multiprocessing.   In general, AS/400 systems are available for the largest tasks. OS/400 contains more and better hardware failure survivability features than MVS. OS/400 also lends itself to operator light and even unattended operations.   There are now no tasks so large as to require the use of MVS except for historical reasons.

1.3.2   VM

VM (*Virtual Machine*) is an operating system as well as an operating environment. As an operating system VM supports *CMS* (*Conversational Monitor System*).   CMS is IBM's premier mainframe interactive environment.   As an operating environment VM allows multiple copies of the MVS, VSE, and other operating systems to share the same processor complex.   VM does this by presenting each guest system with a virtual machine environment. The guest system "thinks" that it has total control of the hardware defined to it by VM.   VM allows real resources to be shared, and also emulates hardware resources that do not exist. Thus, VM can be used to simulate a larger real memory environment than actually exists.   VM adds significant overhead to the systems running under its control, and may be replaced by the PR/SM hardware feature where sharing resources is its only function.

VM supports multiprocessing between separate virtual machines. In fact, VM can emulate multiple processors for a virtual machine and allow testing of large applications in an environment with fewer available processors than are defined.

VM may be used to run both MVS and VSE systems on the same processor complex. VM is often used as a vehicle to facilitate migrations from VSE to MVS, and even the occasional migration from MVS back to VSE. Many users who expected to use VM to migrate from VSE to MVS ended up as permanent VM users because CMS became critical in their environment, or because the decision was made to keep VSE along with MVS.

1.3.3   VSE

VSE/ESA is targeted towards the small to midrange ES/9000 processors.   VSE/ESA is an excellent batch and transaction processing environment. It is also seeing increased use as a file server in distributed processing environments involving AS/400 as well as UNIX-based computers.

VSE/ESA supports all uniprocessors in native mode.   All multiple-processor systems are supported when VSE/ESA runs under VM/ESA or within an LPAR using PR/SM. The lack of native multiple-processor support is the only real growth limiter for VSE/ESA.

Although IBM originally intended that VSE users would grow and migrate to MVS, modern VSE/ESA systems support the largest applications, and VSE-to-MVS migrations are not required. As a result, VSE-to-MVS conversions are relatively rare.

The power of VSE/ESA is best seen in a distributed environment. VSE/ESA supports distributed data and applications across a variety of platforms. SQL/DS supports shared data with VM plus distributed relational databases via DRDA. The VSE/ESA support for distributed CICS allows legacy COBOL applications to be easily downsized into AS/400 and desktop systems while leaving the database and database backup/security/management on VSE/ESA.

Although VSE/ESA is a full function operating system, it does not require a large systems programming staff. In some VSE shops the technical support functions are performed by people with other primary tasks. In terms of service complexity, VSE/ESA is much closer to an AS/400 than it is to MVS.

1.4 Midrange Systems

Midrange systems are multiple-user systems. They also have capacity comparable to mainframe systems. The principle factors separating modern midrange systems from mainframe systems are the environmental and staff requirements. Also, where mainframes usually service the entire company, midrange systems are frequently dedicated to a single division or department. Of course, multiple midrange systems can be combined across a network to service the entire organization. The replacement of large mainframes with multiple midrange systems is often referred to as *rightsizing* or *downsizing*.

Midrange systems, including the IBM AS/400 and RS/6000, usually require a less controlled environment than mainframe systems. Many midrange systems require no unusual air conditioning, are not water cooled, and often run on ordinary power. Their cabling does not usually require a raised floor, except for neatness in very large configurations. Midrange systems are often run within user departments, not in a central datacenter.

Midrange systems usually involve a much smaller support staff than mainframe systems. This is a result of more modern and simpler operating system software, and of the simpler hardware/environmental issues discussed above. The operating systems of midrange computers are designed to run less work at the same time than mainframe operating systems, are simpler to install plus configure, and are also easier to operate. In fact, unattended operations is typical for many midrange systems, at least for a portion of each day.

1.4.1 OS/400

OS/400 is IBM's operating system for the AS/400 processor family. While IBM mainframes have three operating systems, the AS/400 has only a single operating system. This results from the OS/400 operating system being designed integral with the hardware and not after the fact as it was for the old mainframe operating systems. As a result, AS/400 systems are vastly easier to manage and operate than MVS or VM.

AS/400s are often found along with mainframes in dataprocessing organizations of all sizes. Thus, it is not unusual to find an MVS or VSE shop with a number of AS/400 computers in the data center and distributed about the enterprise. Some mainframe shops find it cheaper to migrate to AS/400s and totally eliminate their mainframes along with their complex operating systems. This is often referred to as downsizing.

OS/400 is a more modern operating system than MVS or VSE and incorporates a number of novel features. For example, OS/400 treats almost everything as an *object*. Objects incorporate not only a name for data, but also a description and the various actions supported for that data. An OS/400 user simply names an object and the operating system is able to locate and use it. Another benefit of the object design of OS/400 is that few rules exist as to when something is valid. Thus, a file may be executed without concern as to the source language of the program, or any concern if the file is instead written in the Control Language or REXX.

OS/400 uses a single-level memory model. This means that the operating system is responsible for tracking whether data is in memory or on disk. The user simply thinks of all data as residing in a very large virtual storage address space. Actually, the user does not even have to think of addresses, only the name and desired use of a data item. All storage allocation is done automatically by the OS/400 operating system and all data is immediately available upon request. The only flaw in this design is that a hardware failure can require the recreation of all of the data from backups. The user design and management of a recovery plan is one of the key items in OS/400 systems management.

OS/400 is more flexible than conventional mainframe operating systems. For example, new communications hardware may be attached without regenerating the system, or even telling the system that the hardware was attached. OS/400 automatically determines many characteristics of its hardware environment. Similarly, one may add disk space without major effort. OS/400 will automatically make such space available for growth of existing files without a need to redefine or recreate such files.

OS/400 supports a variety of methods of communicating with other systems. LU 6.2 is supported for communications with IBM systems. The TCP/IP protocol is supported for communications with most systems that do not support the LU 6.2 protocol. PC

LANs can be directly attached to the AS/400 hardware and are fully supported by OS/400. Also, OS/400 supports the AS/400 specific model 5250 cable terminals.

1.4.2   AIX

AIX is the IBM implementation of the UNIX operating system. It is supported on mainframes, but rarely encountered there. AIX is the standard operating system for the RISC System/6000 (often referred to as RS/6000). AIX is also supported on IBM Pcs and is sometimes found there as well. Because IBM's penetration of the PC UNIX market is relatively small, we will concentrate on the RS/6000 implementation here.

The RS/6000 is a powerful desktop system often viewed as competing with the fastest workstations. Large RS/6000 systems have been used to downsize mainframe applications, but are more often seen in desktop or dedicated processing roles for engineering and scientific applications. RS/6000 systems integrate well into large UNIX distributed environments and with reasonable ease into conventional IBM SNA distributed environments.

AIX on the RS/6000 supports a flexible windowed graphical user interface. TCP/IP is the standard communications and client server protocol for this system. Interfacing the UNIX standard of TCP/IP with the rest of the IBM world of SNA is one challenge to working with AIX. The RS/6000 supports both TCP/IP and SNA. It is often chosen as a gateway system to connect the IBM SNA world with non-IBM UNIX systems.

1.5   Desktop Systems

As the name implies, *desktop systems* are usually single-user systems. No special environment is required, and these systems are found throughout modern organizations. Although desktop systems can function in a standalone fashion, more and more we see them connected together.

Desktop systems are interconnected for a variety of reasons. *Local area networks* (*LANs*) are the method used to connect such systems. Let us briefly look at data sharing, hardware resource sharing, and application sharing as applied to LANs.

When a number of desktop system users need access to the same data, the shared data is frequently managed by a LAN file server. A LAN file server can result in hardware savings because it does not need hard disk space to hold a copy of the shared data. More often, the benefit of shared data is that all systems see a current copy of the data, and that updates are available to all systems as soon as they are made.

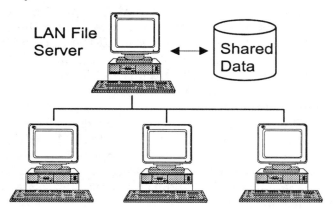

PCs on LAN Sharing Data

Figure 1.2 Desktop Systems Shared Data

Interconnected desktop systems can also share hardware in order to reduce hardware costs. Laser printers, CD-ROM drives or jukeboxes, tape backup systems, and WORM drives are often shared for this reason (see Figure 1.3). Data sharing and hardware cost reduction go hand in hand.

Desktop systems are also interconnected to share application code. This may be done because of the resource requirements of an application, or because of the application's data access/update requirements. When data is shared between systems, it is often easier/cheaper to run related applications on the server that manages the shared data rather than on each individual desktop system. How is this true? Many applications look at much more data than they finally output. Putting the application where the data is reduces the amount of communications traffic between the system requesting the application and the system owning the data. For such applications, a slower LAN (with less bandwidth) will provide acceptable performance when the application resides on the

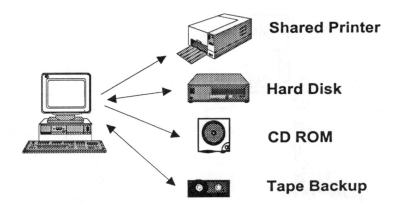

Figure 1.3 Hardware Sharing Example

file server.

If shared data is to be updated, separate applications usually require a complex locking mechanism to ensure that two desktop systems do not interfere with each other's data. When the application and data are on the same system, the locking can usually be done more efficiently, and with a higher degree of data integrity. Shared application design results in simpler application logic that runs faster and is easier to use.

1.5.1 PC/DOS

Microsoft (or IBM) *DOS* (*Disk Operating System*) for the IBM Personal Computer is the most commonly used PC operating system. DOS is frequently run standalone although a large number of its users have added the *Windows* operating environment to the basic system.   DOS machines may function standalone or networked as part of a larger system.   DOS machines may be interconnected using a LAN. DOS systems may also be connected to mainframes using a variety of methods including 3270 emulation cards, asynchronous communications, LAN gateways (such as token ring via a 3174 or 37xx), and VTAM LU6.2 interfaces.

Some mainframe shops have replaced their large computer system with one or more groups of interconnected PCs and/or minicomputers. This is sometimes referred to as downsizing and sometimes as rightsizing. AS/400 systems in combination with PC

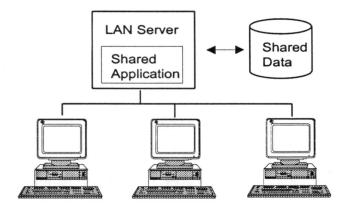

PCs on LAN Sharing Application and Data

Figure 1.4 Desktop Systems with Shared Application

LANs are often chosen as such a downsizing platform.   PC
Support/400 is software that provides a very robust environment for
client server applications using AS/400s and PCs.

A tremendous variety of DOS applications exist.   These applications have become an integral part of many business environments.
This large base of DOS applications ensures that DOS (or DOS
emulation) will be around for a long time.

The principal limitation with DOS is that the PC program
storage cannot exceed 640KB.   At the time DOS was introduced in
1981, this seemed like a great deal of memory.   However, most DOS
applications are now limited by the available memory.   Windows
partially eliminates the 640KB memory limitation, while still
allowing existing DOS applications to execute.   This accounts for
much of the success of Windows.

1.5.2   OS2

OS2 is IBM's choice as the PC operating system of the future.
Although initial OS2 versions had limited success, OS2 Version 2.0
has been making inroads into the installed PC DOS base within the
business world.   Windows (and its follow on Windows/NT) is
Microsoft's answer to IBM's strategic direction and intentions for

OS2. Because Windows is very well established, OS2 is not guaranteed success simply because it is an IBM system.

OS2 supports native OS2 applications and is also capable of emulating most DOS and many Windows applications. OS2 requires a faster processor and more memory than DOS or Windows to achieve the same level of performance. However, OS2 implements true multitasking which is required to effectively run multiple simultaneous applications.

OS2 is also a participant in IBM's *System Application Architecture (SAA)*. SAA is intended to offer a standard environment so that applications can be easily moved between different systems or developed using client server technology across several systems. Although IBM announced SAA with much fanfare, it has little substance or impact in the mainframe world currently. At this time, SAA compliant applications on OS2 are few and far between. It is probable that SAA will not contribute to OS2's success or failure.

1.6 The OS/400 Mission

OS/400 was developed by IBM for the AS/400 processor architecture. It is a comparatively new operating system. As such, it has the advantage of not needing to provide as much compatibility with older system designs as the IBM mainframe systems do. Although OS/400 is new, it is a full functioned operating system that excels in modern distributed environments. And, because older S/38 applications can be easily migrated to the AS/400 it has an enormous breadth of applications available.

OS/400 is an excellent batch engine. As such, it is capable of automatically allocating and controlling a large number of batch tasks. It is also a robust online transaction processing system. The reliable software design and the availability of cost effective RAID DASD make OS/400 suitable for even the most mission-critical applications. The PC Support facility enables even beginning programmers to write distributed applications.

The power of OS/400 is best seen in a distributed environment. It supports distributed data and applications across a variety of platforms. Its broad programming language support makes it an ideal target for downsizing efforts. OS/400 offers a full DRDA implementation and functions as either a SQL client or server with both mainframe and desktop systems.

1.7   A Brief History of OS/400

This section presents a brief history of OS/400, and its predecessors. Origins of various OS/400 features are presented, including those key features that define the current environment. This background information may prove helpful to a fuller understanding of the OS/400 system. Many of the acronyms encountered in modern OS/400 systems are also defined in this section, and are used within the context of other operating system components.

The AS/400 and its operating system OS/400 were introduced in 1988. Although OS/400 is new, its mission is not. The mission of any operating system is to offer high-level services that isolate applications from hardware details, facilitate application development, and implement an execution environment for multiple tasks. OS/400 offers all of these capabilities in a state-of-the-art package. At the same time, OS/400 is a transition vehicle that facilitates migration of older System/36 and System 38 applications to the newer AS/400 hardware.

OS/400 was introduced along with the AS/400 in the late 1980s. It has grown to a customer base of well over 200,000. Although small in comparison to the millions of PCs, the size of the AS/400 user base has resulted in less expensive software than seen on IBM mainframes. This in turn has helped fuel the downsizing and rightsizing trends moving mainframe users to midsize systems.

2

Overview of OS/400 and Open Systems

This chapter is both an overview of OS/400 and a look at the relationship of OS/400 within the modern enterprise. In the previous chapter we looked at the forces driving mainframe systems to migrate to midsize platforms, especially the AS/400. Here, particular emphasis is placed upon the role of the AS/400 with Open Systems standards. The major topics discussed are:

AS/400 and Open Systems
OSI
TCP/IP
DCE
Client Server Support with AIX
Integrated Language Environment

2.1   AS/400 and Open Systems

Open Systems are considered by many to be a requirement for their computing environment. What is meant by this term? *Open System* has come to mean a computer system with a standard set of interfaces that provide a portable environment. Applications using only the features of this environment are portable to other open computing systems. UNIX is the original open system, but various IBM operating systems have been committed to become compliant with the open systems standards.

OS/400 will become compliant with key standards of open systems in future releases. The initial standard to be adopted by it is 1003.1 which defines the operating system interfaces. In addition, a future release of OS/400 will support 1003.2 which specifies characteristics and behavior of the UNIX shell language. And, OS/400 is also committed to support 1003.4 and 1003.4a which specify the operating system interfaces related to real time processing. Figure 2.1 summarizes the open standards currently committed for OS/400.

Standards	Description
1003.1	System Service
1003.2	Shell and Tools
1003.4	Real Time Extensions

Figure 2.1 POSIX Standards Accepted for OS/400

2.2   OSI

OSI is an acronym for *Open Systems Interconnection* which is a standard for communications networking. OSI was defined by the *International Standards Organization* (*ISO*) and has been adopted by CCITT with several standards developed for the OSI model. OSI is based upon a reference model. The purpose of this model is to describe a layered architecture fitting existing communications standards while providing a foundation for future communications standards development. The seven layers described by OSI are:

- Physical layer. Describes electrical, mechanical, and procedural means or establishing, using, and dropping physical connections used for communications. RS-232 and RS-449, RS-422, RS-423 are examples of standards at this layer.

- Data link layer. Describes procedures for establishing, using, and dropping data link connections between network nodes. Examples of standards include HDLC, LAP-B, and LLC.

- Network layer. Describes services for paths between open systems. X.25 is a standard in the network layer.

- Transport layer. Provides services for flow control and recovery. It defines a connectionless transport protocol.

- Session layer. Provides services to organize communications between software units in different open systems within the presentation layer.

- Presentation layer. Offers services to describe data and operations applicable to the data. Facsimile and encryption are elements within this layer.

- Application layer. Provides a means for applications in different open systems to exchange information. Examples of standards in this layer are X.400, X.500 and *FTAM* (File Transfer, Access and Management standard).

The AS/400 supports OSI via OSI Message Services/400. An AS/400 with this software can act as a gateway between OSI and other network types (including SNA and TCP/IP networks). X.400 message traffic can be easily exchanged with TCP/IP systems. Applications written to OSI standards can interface with foreign network applications residing within TCP/IP and SNA networks.

2.3   TCP/IP

TCP/IP is the standard communications protocol for local and wide area networks outside of the IBM world. *TCP/IP* is an acronym for *Transmission Control Protocol/Internet Protocol*. It is especially prevalent within the UNIX world, and is becoming the standard for communicating from PCs to midsize systems. TCP/IP implementations support a general set of functionality. The AS/400 supports TCP/IP as part of its commitment to Open Systems. Note however that the performance of TCP/IP for the AS/400 is poor in comparison to SNA. TCP/IP has been seen to require five to ten times the resources of SNA for the same communications traffic. IBM has committed to address the design flaws causing the poor performance of the current AS/400 TCP/IP implementation in a future release (OS/400 V3). TCP/IP is discussed in more detail in Chapter 13, Communications.

The *TCP/IP File Server Support/400* software provides access to AS/400 folders and files from IBM and non-IBM platforms via TCP/IP. It implements the standard TCP/IP FTP mechanism. FTP is a protocol for file transfer in a client server environment, and is a standard part of all TCP/IP implementations.

TCP/IP networks are easier to administer and manage than SNA networks. This combined with the universal availability of TCP/IP support has driven more and more users to select TCP/IP as their only network protocol. Some IBM mainframes systems have been fairly recently changed to support TCP/IP, but they are often the only area where SNA still prevails in modern shops. The AS/400 can be used to provide a gateway between the IBM SNA world and the TCP/IP world of UNIX and LANs.

2.4 DCE

DCE is an acronym for *Distributed Computing Environment.* DCE is a set of services that facilitate the creation, usage, and management/maintenance of distributed applications across a variety of computing platforms. DCE is a key element of Open Systems. The key components of DCE are,

- Distributed Directory. Identifies location of resources/applications within the network.

- Distributed Security. Defines a user globally to the whole network (supports single logon).

- Distributed Time. Supports synchronization of processes across the network.

- Remote Procedure Call. Supports distributed application code calls across the network.

The DCE/400 Application Toolkit provides standard DCE services for the development of distributed applications within the AS/400 arena. It enables *Remote Procedure Call* (*RPC*) applications and provides client functions for the Directory, Security, and Time services. IBM has also made a statement of direction that it will support the full OSF/DCE Distributed File System for the AS/400 in the future.

2.5 Client Server Support with UNIX

The AS/400 works well with the IBM RS/6000 UNIX-based systems as both a client as well as a server.   The *AS/400 Connection Program/6000* supports both X Windows and ASCII terminal based 5250 emulation access of the AS/400.   File transfer, printer server, and remote command functions are offered via PC Support as well as a separate API interface to SQL and separate file transfer functions.   The interface supports both the SNA and the TCP/IP communications protocols.   IBM has made a statement of direction that this functionality will be extended from the AIX environment to other commonly encountered UNIX systems such as SUN and HP in the future.   The AS/400 implementation of TCP/IP exhibits poor performance in current releases, but this should be corrected in early 1995.

2.6 Integrated Language Environment

The *Integrated Language Environment* (*ILE*) is a new platform for AS/400 application development.   It updates the high level languages supported by OS/400 while still maintaining upward compatibility for existing applications.   It addresses issues for both application development and execution including:

- Faster compiles
- Source debugging
- Faster execution
- Facilitates code reuse
- Enhanced compatibility with other compilers

ILE currently consists of the new C/400 compiler which meets the above goals and is also fully ANSI compliant as well as offering additional data types to C programmers.   IBM has also committed to provide ILE versions of RPG/400 and COBOL/400.   The ILE compilers address a number of deficiencies in the AS/400 languages that often made them unsuitable for large application development.

At the same time they enhance the value of the AS/400 by allowing applications developed for other systems to be more easily ported into the OS/400 environment.

3

OS/400 System Users

This chapter describes the various groups of users that deal with AS/400 computer systems. The different classes of users of the system are reviewed along with their typical responsibilities. The Operations, Application Programming, Systems Programming, and End User views are each analyzed. Their view of the system is described. This is a brief chapter that simply introduces the types of people who make contact with the AS/400 hardware and the OS/400 operating system.

The next chapter takes the structure of a hypothetical AS/400 shop and looks at the roles and responsibilities of those involved with the OS/400 operating system. It is not intended to match any specific shop, but instead to illustrate the type of structure required in a large DP organization. It looks at some of the tasks performed in our hypothetical shop, concentrating on the logistics of these tasks rather than on technical aspects of specific solutions.

3.1 Operations Function and View

The *Operations* area is responsible for the day-to-day operation of data center components. This includes managing the system console, overseeing running jobs, performing tape mounts, operating printers, distributing output, and others. Operations is sometimes divided into components such as Scheduling, Quality Control, Output Distribution, and so on.

Operations interfaces with the AS/400 system through the system console when one is provided (a dedicated terminal) and through other terminals. System operators oversee the status of jobs run by the OS/400 operating system. Equipment operators perform tasks such as tape mounts and loading paper into printers. The operations task is sometimes performed on a 24-hour-a-day, 7-days-a-week basis. Although the AS/400 is capable of automated scheduling and unattended operations, when mission-critical work is involved, an operator is often perceived to be required to handle problems.

A trend exists to minimize the staff required for second shift, third shift, and weekends. OS/400 provides an unattended operations mode. This support includes automated *power off* at a user designated time, with subsequent automatic *power on* and system initialization at a later designated time. A number of shops now run unattended operations for their nonprime periods, and others are attempting to do so.

3.2 Systems Programming

The *Systems Programming* area is responsible for generation and maintenance of the operating system(s) running within the data center. In a small shop, this function may be performed by operations or applications staff or even outside consultants on a part-time basis. However, larger shops typically have dedicated systems staff because the scope of the job greatly increases as the environment becomes more complex.

System Support is another name frequently encountered for this area. This alternate name indicates another area of involvement: support for both technical and nontechnical system staff and users. This support function is sometimes called the *Help Desk*.

Systems programming is usually tasked with operations support, operating system management, problem determination, performance management, and sometimes even applications development and end-user support. In a larger data center with several systems, the network management task is another separate component of the Systems Programming area.

Systems programming typically interfaces with the OS/400 operating system through terminals or through PCs via PC Support/400. The systems programming job includes support for the system at all times it is operating. Because of the growing need for 24-hour support, some shops now provide dial-up access for a systems programming staff that is on call all hours of the day. Such shops may use automated tools that call the support staff at home during periods of unstaffed or *lights out* operation.

3.3 Applications Programming

The *Applications* area is responsible for the development and maintenance of all application software. In some shops, Applications is also responsible for externally purchased applications software. The Applications staff works with the End User community to define requirements for programming systems, develop the application, and then turn the result over to operations for routine processing.

Most AS/400 applications were historically and still are written in RPG. However, more and more applications, especially purchased application systems, are written in a variety of other languages including COBOL, C, and various 4GLs. Although most older application systems were frequently run in batch mode, many modern large applications are complex online transaction processing systems.

Historically, applications interfaced with the OS/400 system through dumb terminals or via PC/Support or CICS or some OEM program development environment.   However, applications programmers are doing more and more of their work directly on PCs. A variety of tools exist that permit applications to be developed and tested on PCs then moved to the host system. For example, Microfocus and CA Realia permit COBOL applications to be totally developed outside of the host computer environment.

It is expected that most program development in the future will occur off of the AS/400. Many applications have PC-based user interfaces and only work with the AS/400 for access to data. The AS/400 is particularly well suited to these client server applications. However, the development of distributed applications has created challenges for the Application development staff.

At many large shops existing mainframe applications are also being moved into a distributed environment where the AS/400 plays a major role.   Such distributed applications are becoming more prevalent as AS/400 systems are adapted to fill the role of a data server and/or client. Mainframe applications staff that are moved into the AS/400 arena face a number of challenges due to the different nature of the OS/400 environment. Retraining combined with some staff replacement is often required when such downsizing occurs.

3.4   End User View of OS/400

End Users are the people who use applications to perform their business related tasks within an organization. Although end users are often not aware of the technical details of a program, they are usually the only group that totally understands the business functions being performed by the programs they deal with.

End users view the system via terminals and PCs. Although some end users function as data entry clerks for online transaction processing systems, more and more users are taking an active role in managing their own workload. Where operations used to initiate work on request, now end users are causing jobs to be run. A number of OEM scheduling systems provide terminal- and PC-based interfaces that allow end users to schedule and manage their own work.

PC Support/400 is often chosen for end users. Although it can be cumbersome and requires more technical skills than most end users appreciate learning, PC Support has a key asset. Being PC based, many End Users already have the hardware needed to access the system, and their basic PC literacy makes PC Support seem more attractive than other options for AS/400 access or management.

OS/400 System Staff
Roles and Responsibilities

It takes a number of individuals to operate and manage OS/400 systems in and out of the data center. This chapter describes these individuals and their functional roles. Although we emphasize the OS/400 related responsibilities, these same tasks are required in all data centers. If you are migrating from a large mainframe environment to departmental AS/400 systems, you still require the individual functions that are described here. In fact, unless care is taken, *downsizing* can actually result in an increase in the size of the staff.

Data centers can vary greatly in size and scope, but are generically described as *small*, *medium*, or *large* operations. These adjectives do not begin to describe the possibilities. A single corporation can utilize multiple data centers with a variety of support structures. Processing can be regionalized, centralized, divided by type or purpose, and interconnected in a variety of ways. For our purposes, we will look at one basic structure. But we will also discuss some of the current issues associated with complex structures and the *rightsizing* of the data center.

We look at roles and responsibilities here in terms of a medium-sized data center, where there is a management structure and specialized professional jobs. In a small operation, the same tasks are performed, but job descriptions must sometimes be altered or expanded beyond traditional roles so that each person fills multiple roles. However, all of the functions described here must be performed, and some are not able to be downsized for mission-critical work. Where an operation is critical without regard to the size of the operation, that is noted, and the minimum requirements of the job are described. This book focuses on system administration functions; extensive references to other chapters in the book are used within this chapter.

We use the term *MIS* (Management Information Systems) to refer to that segment of the corporation providing information through data processing services. Whether MIS is a separate organization or is instead internal staff associated with a departmental system, the same set of roles exist. In our discussion, we look at these roles:

- Front-line Management Positions, i.e., Departmental System Managers, MIS Managers, and Operations Supervisors
- Applications Development positions, including Programmer Analysts and Data Base Analysts
- Computer Operations Roles, including the Computer Operator, the Scheduler, the Report Distribution Clerk, the Media Librarian, the Production Control Analyst, and the Help Desk Representative
- Systems Development Positions, including Systems Programmers and Communications Analysts

We will present a sample organizational chart and view each position in relation to its functional group.

- The Mission of MIS
- Applications Development and the Project Life Cycle
- Computer Operations and Operations Support Positions
- Systems Development

4.1   The Mission of MIS

In today's competitive business world, information availability and the speed of processing data can literally mean success or failure for a corporation. Even in the research and development area, services must be efficient to make the best use of available funds. Where data services directly involve the end client, such as point-of-sale systems, the effectiveness of MIS services can touch an even more valuable and volatile commodity—the customer's opinion of the company. It is no wonder that considerable resources are invested in the management of information services, and that so much is expected in return.

In an environment involving increasing workloads, rapid technological change, and complex problems to be solved, the data processing professional must continue to focus on the MIS mission. That mission is to provide a service or product to the corporation that is consistent and reliable, of a high quality, in keeping with primary company objectives, and provided at the lowest possible cost. If those services are also flexible and easy to use, so much the better.

Most corporations develop very specific mission statements that relate directly to business objectives. These objectives can be translated into a *Service Level Agreement*. The availability and functionality of computer systems has become so important that most MIS groups work under service level agreements that define words like "consistent" and "reliable" in terms of numbers. Acceptable percentages of up time (and conversely down time), system availability schedules, performance level guarantees, processing costs, and other factors critical to company success are carefully spelled out for the benefit of both client and MIS in such agreements.

In order to be successful, MIS must employ professional and well trained people who understand their role in this mission. As a data center grows larger and the scope of responsibility increases, job descriptions become more specialized and specific. Some of these MIS roles are recognized as industry standards. Let's examine some of them now.

4.2   Applications Development

The Applications Development group is responsible for the development and maintenance of all application software. Increasingly, the bulk of this software is purchased externally. The Applications Development group then works with the client community to customize these purchased applications and develop interfaces with existing software. Occasionally, Applications Development is tasked with supporting the End User community once the application enters production. Whether this is done via the Help Desk or less formally, such support often challenges the people skills of the Application staff.

4.2.1   The Manager of Applications Development

The Manager of Applications Development has direct responsibility for providing end-user systems, applications, and computing systems according to approved plans. In today's data center, this responsibility is not restricted to host system processing by the AS/400, but can involve PC processes and interfaces with a variety of information producing sources, such as phone systems or environmental security systems. The integrity of business support processes, and the ultimate satisfaction of the end user are the responsibility of the Manager of Applications Development. This position makes software acquisitions, and is the correspondent on related contract and legal issues.

The Manager of Applications Development insures the success of multiple concurrent project efforts by mandating adherence to documented standards, procedures, and methodologies. Project Leaders generate detailed progress reports for each phase of a project life cycle. This information is critical to management, which is usually facing a backlog of requests, and must juggle resources to accommodate changing priorities.

Applications projects can have a duration of weeks or months, ranging to more than a year in process. Every end user views their needs as high priority, and machine development and testing time is at a premium. Projects must be brought in on time, and data and processing integrity must be maintained. Data security and disaster preparedness must be incorporated in each project effort at the design level. The appropriate and efficient allocation of staff, budget, and resources to meet these demanding requirements is the biggest challenge of the Manager of Applications Development.

4.2.2   The Project Leader

The Project Leader is directly responsible for the performance of the development staff assigned to a project, and for the success of the project itself. Staffing assignments may be permanent, or may change as projects change. The Project Leader may be responsible for more than one project concurrently. All activity is controlled by monitoring life-cycle phases, and reporting against phase activity.

The Project Leader is usually directly responsible for the production of the project requirements document, and takes an active role in the design phase. This individual is responsible for the integrity of the testing environment, and usually creates internal test standards. The project leader often interfaces with end users to get agreement on acceptance test criteria.

The Project Leader also participates directly with any standards committee, and has direct input into OS/400 Command Language standards, coding guidelines, dataset usage, and other related standards. The Project Leader insures that these standards are used in projects under their control. In environments where formal standards do not exist, informal standards quickly evolve.

4.2.3 The Programmer Analyst

The Programmer Analyst analyzes system processes and procedures and develops system specifications. This person writes software code, sets up testing scenarios, prepares CL, conducts tests, debugs software, and prepares documentation. The Programmer Analyst designs conversion plans and creates file conversion programs. The efforts of this person are most critical during the coding, testing, and implementation phases.

Programmer Analysts may be called upon to work with their end user community during the design as well as the production use of their systems. In such cases, people skills often become as important as technical programming skills.

Some Applications Development groups use titles implying seniority or rank within the programming group, such as "senior" or "lead" and the above mentioned responsibilities are then divided according to level of expertise. For small projects, the project leader role is often performed by a senior application programmer.

4.2.4 The Data Base Analyst

With the complexity of systems, data, and interrelationships, the Data Base Analyst (or DBA) plays an important role for data integrity. This person reviews processing schedules, and insures that adequate backups exist for critical files. The DBA analyzes DASD utilization and forecasts future needs. The DBA also reviews new systems and highlights potential data integrity problems. The Data Base Analyst is available to solve complex data base problems, and to participate in the evaluation and selection of data base products and tools.

The DBA role can be especially important in the AS/400 environment because of the integrated nature of the database facility in OS/400. Performance management has been seen to be a key area for DBA involvement in larger AS/400 shops, and performance problems are frequently seen even in carefully defined environments.

4.3 Computer Operations

The mission of Computer Operations is to process all production work as scheduled, and get the output (printout or other product) to the end user on time. Computer Operations is also charged with the maintenance and physical protection of machines and environmental hardware, as well as data storage media.

In a large data center, production processing is usually accomplished in a shift environment, with computer operators and support personnel assigned around the clock. The expense of equipment and the need to secure data requires the computer room to be a physically secured environment with limited access.

The Computer Operations group is generally the first client contact for problem resolution, therefore, the help desk, or client assistance function often resides in Computer Operations, although some help desk functions may be performed within the Applications or Systems Support areas. When AS/400s perform mission critical online services, rapid access to the help desk function, and speedy resolution of problems are key to the success of operations.

4.3.1 The Manager of Computer Operations

The Manager of Computer Operations is responsible for the physical security of all machines and equipment in the data center. This can amount to an annual budget ranging from a few tens of thousands to several million dollars. Equally, this position is responsible for the integrity of the data processed in the data center. The value of the data is usually inestimable. Protecting data stored on tape and disk media, ensuring disaster survivability of data, and ensuring the confidentiality of that data, are primary concerns. Therefore, security, auditability, back-up, recovery, and disaster preparedness are conscious elements of every Operations activity.

Computer Operations is also responsible for any data or media stored or processed in off-site facilities. The Manager must keep an up-to-date disaster preparedness plan, that may incorporate cold site, or hot site facilities. (For more on Disaster Preparedness, see Chapter 20.)

The protection of equipment usually encompasses the machine room environment and support equipment such as air conditioning units, fire suppression systems, power back-up units, and environmental security systems. By default, Operations usually inherits some responsibilities for building facilities due to the unique environmental needs of the data center. The Manager of Computer Operations is the corporate officer in charge of the lease or purchase of equipment, and is correspondent on contracts and associated legal issues. The Manager insures that a regular preventative machine maintenance schedule is followed, and that vendors comply with contractual obligations.

The Manager of Computer Operations is directly responsible for end user satisfaction with production systems availability and output. This person must ensure that the specifics of service level contracts (such as 2-second response time or 97% up time) are met. The Manager insures that the staff creates and adheres to guidelines and methodologies that solve problems, and present systems and output to clients on schedule. The Manager must work constantly with the Applications Development and Systems Development groups to introduce efficiencies in processing that insure commitments are met.

The Computer Operations staff usually works in a shift environment. Batch processing, new software implementation, and machine maintenance usually take place when on-line systems are down. These activities, plus the need to monitor equipment, require staffing beyond normal business hours. It is not unusual to see a high volume data center staffed seven days a week, twenty-four hours a day. For the manager, this creates unique communications and logistics problems, Therefore, most data centers define daily management reporting, and multi-level problem escalation procedures.

Today, the Manager of Computer Operations is faced with great economic pressure to downsize machines, and consequently, staff. While downsizing dramatically improves machine costs, it does not reduce the scope of responsibility for systems availability or output. Reevaluating staffing needs where roles have traditionally been highly specialized becomes an interesting puzzle. Good sizing tools are not yet available. And, not a few companies have downsized machinery for costs savings, and spent more to upgrade when they found their long term assessments of their rate of growth were naive. Pairing the right processing tools with the correct professional support staff is the greatest current challenge for the Manager of Computer Operations.

4.3.2   The Operations Supervisor

The Computer Operations Supervisor is responsible for the day-to-day activities of the Operations staff, for the completion of production work, and for making sure machine room equipment functions properly. The Supervisor is responsible for machine room and physical data security, and is the officer in charge of security policy enforcement.

The Computer Operations Supervisor sometimes manages operators assigned to a shift, and is called a *shift supervisor.*
The focus of a shift supervisor will vary based on assignment. Night shifts will concentrate on processing schedule completion, and may incur more CL, space, and batch errors. Day shifts will concentrate on on-line availability and system performance. They will have more contact with end users and the MIS staff, and consequently more interruptions. Generally, those more familiar with CL and program languages will be assigned to a batch processing shift, but this can vary depending on the type of processing done.

Where batch processing occurs, available processing "windows" are usually tight, yet on-line systems must be brought up on time, and batch output deliverables presented to the client as scheduled. It is the responsibility of operations to meet these goals.

For the Operations Supervisor, maintaining the integrity of the data being processed is a primary mission. Detailed instructions for abend recovery, data re-loads, are restores are critical. The Supervisor insures that operations documentation, or *runbooks*, are kept current and used. The Supervisor makes sure that all problems are properly identified and resolved via *problem logs*, and communicates important information to the next shift through a *shift turnover report.* These documentation tools become an integral part of the *problem management system*. (See Chapter 24, Problem Management.)

4.3.3 The Computer Operator

The Computer Operator submits (or releases) jobs to run, mounts tapes, reviews messages and other output, and performs first level problem resolution for abends or other commonly occurring situations. Operators may own Command Language procedures related to scheduling, controlling, and running jobs. Operators monitor system activity and adjust priorities and multiprogramming levels (within a predesignated scope of authority) to allow for efficient system throughput. As problems occur, they are documented by the operator and submitted through a problem escalation process. This is generally known as an *incident* or *problem reporting system*. These reports are the basis for understanding problem trends.

Computer Operators are charged with completing a production processing schedule for each shift. They may also be involved with running test systems or monitoring security equipment. Shift activities usually involve printing and printer maintenance.

In a large data center, work volumes can be so large that operator functions become specialized. Some operations employ "senior" or "lead" titles for operators with more expertise, or who assist the supervisor in managing the team. Some create specific titles such as "Unit Record Operator" or "Command Language Analyst" for those whose job tasks are highly specialized.

4.3.4 The Scheduler

The Scheduling function is key to the efficient workings of production processing. Although we increasingly see end users performing their own workload scheduling, the functions described here must still be performed. Work must be categorized in terms of priorities, run times, and volumes in order to make efficient use of machine resources. The Scheduler coordinates all system, testing, and production activities to create the production processing schedule. Data is collected on run times to make sure that processing windows can be met. Priorities and run sequences are assigned to job streams, and pertinent information is provided, such as inputs to parameter cards or step recovery procedures. The Scheduler reviews completed schedules and analyzes processing trends and run times for future use.

In some data centers the Scheduler is viewed as a customer liaison, and as such is assigned to the Help Desk or Production Control group. Others view scheduling as an optimizing aid for machine throughput, and assign the Scheduler directly to a shift. Automated scheduling packages exist to expedite this effort, and in some cases the scheduler is a computer operator, submitting work with the aid of on-line tools. In order for automation to be effective, however, processing streams must be clearly defined and repetitive. In general, workload automation requires centralized management of the schedule within the operations area, rather than end user directed scheduling which is unstructured by its nature. Refer to Chapter 9 for details on the Operational Assistant of OS/400.

4.3.5 The Report Distribution Clerk

In some data centers print volumes are so large it is necessary to employ clerks for report printing and distribution. The Report Distribution Clerk prints reports out of the print queue, breaks down output, and routes it to the recipients. This function provides the following benefits:

- The printing process is more efficient, and print output can be produced based on priority.

- There is limited access to negotiable instruments, such as check stock.

- Report delivery insures fewer items are lost.

In some environments the report distribution function is being superseded by automated report delivery systems. Such systems replace reports on paper with online report images. In addition to the savings in staff, such systems often eliminate the bulk of the paper used in a data center and are frequently justified on that basis alone.

4.3.6 The Media Librarian

Data Centers keep a library of tape reels and cartridges. Optical media increasingly are also stored in the media library. Storage media is physically isolated to protect it from damage and to limit access to data. Some data centers use a Media Librarian (sometimes called a Tape Librarian) to control and organize media storage. This provides three main benefits:

- Physical access to stored data is limited. Only the Librarians handle volumes once they are removed from the data center.

- The Computer Operator function is made more efficient. The Media Librarian stages tapes to be used for processing, and removes them when processing is complete, freeing the operators for other functions, and reducing the chance of accidently using the wrong volume.

- Physical volumes are properly stored and cared for, protecting resources and data. Tape reels must be hung in the proper manner to prevent injury, and volumes must be kept in sequence to avoid confusion.

Whether or not you have localized the function in an individual, you must have the media librarian function. The recovery of mission critical applications requires that the media management function be centralized. (See Chapter 20, Recoverability, for a detailed explanation of these requirements.)

In larger data centers, the Media Librarian usually interacts with an automated tape management system that keeps track of data located on specific *volsers*, or volume serial numbers. Use of an automated system requires tape volumes to carry standard labels. The Tape Librarian converts data to standard label volumes as necessary. New volumes are entered into service, and old volumes removed from service, through data transfer.

The Tape Librarian rotates back-up media to the off-site storage facility and keeps a current inventory of that facility. Librarians are usually responsible for maintaining that environment as well. In the event of a disaster, the librarian acquires the required volumes from off-site storage for recovery of the system.

4.4   Operations Support Positions

Because activity in Computer Operations covers twenty-four hours, there needs to be a consolidation point for communications, reporting, and changes. In a large data center, specialized support positions serve this purpose. Maintaining stability in the processing environment involves *controlling change* and *solving problems*. *Change Control Procedures* are used to insure new systems meet standards and have tested properly. *Problem Management Systems* capture data and report trends. Both processes are necessary for continued data integrity.

We will examine these processes in more detail in Chapter 24. For our purposes here, let's look at the individuals who administer these systems in Computer Operations.

4.4.1   The Production Control Analyst

The Production Control Analyst is the focal point for problem resolution in the data center. The PC Analyst collects all problem logs or reports of incidents. Problem Reporting is usually not limited to Computer Operations, but encompasses all of MIS.

Once collected, the PC Analyst categorizes problems by *type* and *severity*. They are assigned a tracking code or reference number, then routed to the appropriate group or person for resolution. The PC Analyst follows up on progress, and closes the problem log when the incident is solved. The Production Control Analyst produces a *trend analysis* of problems, and makes recommendations to management for procedural, system, or policy changes.

The Production Control Analyst also administers the MIS *Change Control Procedure* via reviews of all planned changes. Proposed changes are reviewed to insure their compliance with standards. The purpose of the Change Control review is to insure that new applications will run properly in the production environment. Therefore the PC analyst may review test results, plus resource, output distribution, documentation and scheduling requirements. Upon completion of the review, the PC Analyst will move the new system into the production environment.

Use of a Problem Management and Change Control system yields positive results:

- In general, problems become less severe and take less time to solve.

- The processing environment is stable, and processing time is used more efficiently.

- The end user's opinion of MIS is more favorable, because problems and interruptions are less frequent.

The Production Control Analyst plays an integral part in maintaining data integrity and processing stability.

The PC Analyst also performs other tasks for Computer Operations that are not easily done in a shift structure. Large data centers often employ an entire Production Control group to handle systems management tasks. Often the Scheduler and Help Desk Representative are included in this group.

4.4.2   The Help Desk Representative

The Help Desk serves the client community by answering calls immediately, responding to requests, and following up to ensure end user satisfaction. The Help Desk Representative is a customer service agent who receives client calls to MIS. With the proliferation of PCs inside the end user community, the scope and complexity of the Help Desk task has increased dramatically.

End users will have varying needs, and varying degrees of technical expertise. The Help Desk Representative must be able to accurately assess the need, document the nature of the call, and assign an action to the proper group or person in MIS for response where immediate assistance (such as answering a question) does not solve the problem or is not possible. The Help Desk Representative will also ensure the customer is ultimately satisfied.

As with the Problem Management System, client requests or comments must be documented and assigned a tracking designator. Where an automated system is used, the Help Desk will most likely use the same mechanism, opening a problem or incident log to document the user call, and closing it when it is complete. This way problems reported to the Help Desk automatically become part of the Problem Management process.

MIS can publish one number for a Help Desk, and funnel calls to one central point. This has many advantages:

- Clients are less frustrated, because their calls are answered immediately and professionally.

- The MIS professional staff has fewer calls, and therefore fewer interruptions.

- Documenting and tracking client requests insures that their needs are addressed.

- MIS knows the number of client calls by type, and can make improvements to lessen the number of requests.

- MIS calls are answered by a trained customer service staff, providing a professional business image.

4.4.3   Systems Development

The mission of the Systems Development group is to maintain all system software and ensure that systems perform efficiently. System software is purchased or leased from vendors, therefore the Systems Development group must meet vendor guidelines for software installation and maintenance, and, conversely, must ensure that the vendor meets all contractual requirements.

The Systems Development group enforces standards and security requirements by setting system parameters and access authorities to augment MIS policies. They also maintain a systems disaster preparedness plan.

Increasingly, the Systems Development group is also charged with responsibilities for communications equipment, lines, and software. In some instances, this includes LANS and PC connectivity software.

4.4.4   The Manager of Systems Development

The Manager of Systems Development is directly responsible for the integrity and workings of machine operating systems and associated program products. Of equal responsibility is the security and recoverability of these systems. The Manager of Systems Development protects systems integrity by mandating adherence to standards, procedures, and security practices. As with application changes, system changes occur through a Change Control methodology. The Manager ensures that Systems Programmer responsibilities are logically divided to create a "checks and balance" situation, so that no one individual has access to all system files and functions. The group also maintains a disaster preparedness plan that encompasses situations from one pack lost all the way to complete system recovery.

The Manager of Systems Development ensures the efficiency of systems by monitoring the appropriate system *measurements*. Creating appropriate reports and monitoring system performance at correct intervals is critical to the system tuning process. The Manager must translate system performance criteria into measurements that relate to user resource needs. Systems Development must project resource use against long term business plans and make recommendations for system changes.

The Manager's scope of responsibility usually extends into communications systems and hardware. Even where separate communications groups exist, the initial responsibility for network equipment probably started in the Systems Group. In today's data center, this responsibility has evolved to often include PC networks, particularly *WANS* (*Wide Area Networks*). Today's networks become complex because of the variety of equipment hooked to them and the increasing demand for total *connectivity*. This complexity demands that the Systems Development group not only administer communications software systems, but have involvement in the physical wiring scheme.

4.4.5 The Systems Programmer

The mission of the Systems Programmer is to make the most efficient use of machine resources by properly maintaining and *tuning* the system. Tuning requires an understanding of how the operating system works and how each component interrelates with the others. Changes in one area may impact performance in another. Transaction volume increases or decreases, and changes in hardware, applications, the operating system, and procedures all have an impact on system performance. Therefore, the Systems Programmer must constantly measure activity against pre-determined thresholds and performance standards, and make adjustments.

The Systems Programmer is also the guardian against system integrity loss, and indirectly, data loss. Critical files and packs must be backed up at appropriate intervals to ensure that the system can be restored in case of disaster. System Programmers must also plan for less dramatic but very real problem scenarios, such as DASD volume damage from head crashes.

The Systems Programmer performs the OS/400 system installation, applies maintenance, maintains program products, and sometimes codes CL commands, as well as common subroutines and exits. As in Applications Development, a Change Control Methodology is used in the Systems Development group. Maintenance activity such as parameter changes are also documented and double checked. Changes at the system level, while sometimes simple in execution, can have a far reaching effect. The Systems Programmer must keep attention to detail and test all changes.

4.4.6   The Communications Analyst

In today's data center, *connectivity* between hardware resources has created a complex environment. With an ever increasing demand for shared resources, most data centers have evolved *hybrid* networking systems. Hybrid systems involve multiple connecting architectures, and can involve all of the following aspects:

- Multiple devices and similar devices of various types requiring the ability to share resources, particularly PCs and printers.

- Host computers connected with terminals and local peripheral equipment, but also connected to external processing sites.

- Voice and data phone lines providing the ability to send and receive data, such as "lock box" transmissions.

- Multiple communications protocols including SNA, TCP/IP, and IPX, each with its own unique terminology/configuration.

Systems must be designed to meet all of these connectivity needs, which must be accomplished with optimal bandwidth utilization at the lowest possible cost. Many data centers employ a Communications Analyst to oversee this important and dynamic environment.

The Communications Analyst plans the communications network, and monitors network use and efficiencies. This requires a thorough knowledge of communications hardware, Local Area Network software, Network Control Programs (NCP), and various network performance measuring tools.

The Communications Analyst is responsible for the *Logical* communication system, i.e, the signal flow and the connecting architectures. In some instances, this individual may be responsible for the physical network components as well, i.e., the ports, cables, and connectors.

The Communications Analyst creates standards for the communications environment. But the biggest problem faced today is the lack of standards involving the purchase of PC hardware and software. Many networks become more complex because of the incompatibility of hardware or the inequity of PC operating systems that require emulation bridges or other hardware and software devices to allow them to communicate.

In fact, the PC boom has created so many issues related to connectivity, security, and even hardware repair, that some corporations simply turn the entire responsibility over to MIS. This is good for establishing standards, but creates enormous stress on MIS resources. Some data centers have opted for *service contracts* with outside vendors to handle first level problem resolution as well as end user training. This option is workable, but can be costly. Most opt to assign responsibilities within the corporation, with the Communications Analyst playing a key role in keeping the PC LANS efficient and functional.

Part

B

AS/400 Hardware Components and Design Issues

Part B looks at the AS/400 hardware environment. The material is specific to the OS/400 operating system, although we do concentrate upon the information from a hardware viewpoint. We cover the AS/400 processor family, I/O architecture, general I/O devices, and DASD. Because of the critical nature of DASD with respect to failure survivability, we include a separate chapter on how DASD evolved to where it is now, and how it works as part of the I/O subsystem. Finally, a chapter describing the architected system limits of the AS/400 is provided to assist in determining the maximum capacity of a given set of hardware.

Chapter

5

Processors

This chapter describes the AS/400 processors and the hardware modes supported by the OS/400 operating system. We begin with a look at the architecture of IBM computers in general then move into the specific characteristics of the AS/400. This will allow us to place the AS/400 in comparison to other systems, as well as give us a better appreciation of the unique characteristics of the AS/400 object oriented architecture. We finish with a look at the characteristics of the different processor models of AS/400 systems.

5.1 IBM Computer Architecture

IBM and most other manufacturer's computer systems all exhibit certain common characteristics. In this section we will look at the architectural features common to most systems. We cover number systems, addressing, and virtual/real storage usage and mapping. We also briefly look at how computers perform I/O to communicate with the outside world.

5.1.1 Binary and Hexadecimal Number Systems

All digital computers employ a base two (binary) numbering system rather than the base ten (decimal) system we humans are accustomed to using. IBM computers also employ another numbering system called hexadecimal (base sixteen). Hexadecimal is actually just a compact version of binary, but both binary and hexadecimal numbers are encountered. Here, we will look at both binary and hexadecimal systems.

The decimal system we are all familiar with uses ten digits, i.e., the numbers zero through nine. We form larger numbers by specifying multiple digits in a series. The right-most digit is the units count. The digits to the left of the units digit specify powers of ten. Thus, the number 142 is actually one times ten to the second power plus four times ten to the first power plus two.

The *binary* number system uses only two digits, zero and one. We can form all of the same numbers in binary that we can in decimal by specifying multiple digits representing powers of two. Thus, the decimal number 142 becomes 10001110 for two to the seventh power plus two to the third power plus two to the second power plus two to the first power. We can see that binary numbers can be used to represent any decimal number but that binary numbers become large quickly. Hexadecimal was developed as an abbreviated form of binary numbers.

The hexadecimal number system uses sixteen digits. These are zero through ten plus A though F. These digits represent the decimal values of zero through fifteen. Additional digits represent powers of sixteen. In hexadecimal notation, the decimal number 142 is recorded simply as 8E (eight times sixteen plus fourteen).

Hexadecimal is an abbreviation of binary rather than a new numbering system. This is seen in our table (Figure 5.1). Note that each hexadecimal value corresponds to four binary digits. Thus, a binary number is converted to hexadecimal by marking off groups of four binary digits and replacing each group with the corresponding hexadecimal digit. Thus, 10001110 (binary for 142 decimal) becomes 1000 and 1110. These become the hexadecimal digits 8 and E, or 8E.

A hexadecimal number is converted to binary by replacing each hexadecimal digit with the four binary digits shown in our table. Thus, C4 becomes 1100 plus 0100. This may be displayed as an eight digit binary string (called a byte) of 11000100.

IBM computers employ these number systems internally. We normally deal with decimal numbers, but may see the computer's binary and hexadecimal systems. We will not have to use them on a day-to-day basis. We may see them in some operating system error messages, storage dumps, and in some diagnostic displays. We may also have to specify parameters such as unit names or addresses to the operating system using hexadecimal numbers.

Hexadecimal Number	Binary Number	Decimal Value
0	0000	0
1	0001	1
2	0010	2
3	0011	3
4	0100	4
5	0101	5
6	0110	6
7	0111	7
8	1000	8
9	1001	9
A	1010	10
B	1011	11
C	1100	12
D	1101	13
E	1110	14
F	1111	15

Figure 5.1 Hexadecimal Numbers

5.1.2   Data and Addressing

Computers deal with several types of data. Two types of data that influence the design of the hardware are characters and numbers. Characters are often accessed and/or referred to as *bytes*. Numbers are often manipulated as units referred to as *words*. A word is an integral number of bytes and we sometimes refer to the word size in bytes. Data can be stored in processor registers or in main storage. The size of a processor register is usually the *word size*. A register is very fast storage that is part of the processor.

The AS/400 architecture insulates the applications from the details of addressing data through the use of *objects*. An *object* is an abstract reference to data along with a set of tools to manage the data that is independent of the location in memory, format, or size of the data. AS/400 instructions reference data using *space objects*. The pointer used to reference AS/400 data occupies 128 bits. 64 bits of this represent an address in virtual storage. Current AS/400 models only use 48-bit addressing so 16 bits are reserved for the operating system. In addition, 32 bits of each pointer are reserved for address expansion. Thus, the AS/400 architecture can be extended to support 96-bit addresses without any changes to existing applications.

Computers access data using a number called an *address*. The smallest unit of data accessible is determined by the hardware design. Some computers resolve addresses to the word level and are often called *word addressing* machines. Such machines are better suited towards numerical processing than towards character processing.

Current IBM mainframes as well as the AS/400 employ *byte addressing*. Each address uniquely references a single character of data. IBM processors are able to access single or multiple bytes of data at a given address. Single-byte addressing is used for character manipulation which is frequently required for business processing. Some multiple-byte addressing modes may be used to manipulate groups of characters. The other multiple byte addressing modes are used to access numbers. Numbers are frequently dealt with in scientific or engineering work. IBM computers are often classified as *general purpose* machines as they can deal with numbers as easily as they can deal with characters.

The size of a number in bytes determines the range of integers that may be stored within a numeric field. Binary fields are the simplest (and usually the most efficient) form of numbers. A binary field can store a numeric value in a range determined by the number of bits provided. Thus, 2-byte fields can store numbers in the range of plus or minus 2^{15}-1 (or +/-32767), while 4-byte fields store numbers in a range of plus or minus 2^{31}-1 (or +/-2147483647).

The AS/400 supports decimal numbers stored as binary values, as well as special packed decimal and floating point data formats. The AS/400 allows access and manipulation of numeric data without regard to the internal format. Thus, a packed number may be added to a binary number. And, a floating point number may be compared with a binary constant. The object oriented architecture of the AS/400 hides the details of instruction execution from the programmer. This eliminates one of the most common types of problems seen in prior computer systems where mixing data types resulted in bad output or a program failure. It also simplifies programming of the AS/400. One need only worry about the algorithm used to solve a particular problem, and not get involved in the details of converting different types of numeric data. Efficiency is effected by the type of data used. The most efficient form of a number is usually a binary value, and for this reason binary numeric data is used within many system objects.

Addresses are a special form of a binary number used to reference storage. The maximum value of an address determines the amount of memory that can be accessed by a machine. The address size is usually the same as, or smaller than, the register size (word size). The AS/400 supports a 48-bit address which can reference 2^{48}-1 characters (roughly 280GB). Each user on the AS/400 has a private 16MB address space for their own use as well as access to objects stored within the 280-trillion-byte address space of the system. Lets look at how storage addressing schemes accomplish this in the next section.

On IBM mainframe computers the word size is 32 bits and the address size is either 24 bits or 31 bits. A 24-bit address can reference up to 2^{24}-1 characters which is somewhat more than 16 million bytes (the actual value is abbreviated as 16MB). A 31-bit address can reference up to 2^{31}-1 characters which is somewhat more than two billion bytes (the actual value is abbreviated as 2GB). It is interesting to note that the AS/400 can address vastly more data than the *large* mainframe systems.

5.2 Storage

In this section we look at how processor storage is organized. We will discuss virtual and real storage, look at address spaces, and see how storage protection makes a multitasking operating system possible. Before we begin, let's discuss the meaning of *storage*.

Computer storage is used to hold programs and data. Computer storage is referenced using addresses. A program must be loaded into storage in order to be executed. And, data being processed by a program must also be resident within storage.

The storage on modern processors is made up of random access memory chips. Although each chip may hold four million or more bits, a very large number of chips may be required for the main memory of a computer system. These memory chips are often the principal source of heat within a modern computer system and may well the largest single cost of that system.

5.2.1 Virtual and Real Storage

Even though a computer may be capable of addressing many gigabytes of memory, that total amount of storage is usually not present. Furthermore, the actual amount of storage provided on a given computer varies a great deal. If programs had to be designed for the smallest amount of storage supplied on any supported computer, they would be greatly restricted in function. Virtual storage reduces or even eliminates this design issue.

The amount of memory present on a given system is called the machines *real* memory size. The maximum amount of memory addressable of a given program is the *virtual* memory size and is usually much larger than the real memory size. The AS/400 is unique in that the processor hardware maps virtual addresses into references to real storage, without constant interruptions of the OS/400 operating system. Virtual storage management can be done efficiently because a program usually only references a small amount of data at a time. Only the data currently being used is maintained in real memory. The AS/400 manages real memory in units of 512 bytes.

Virtual memory that is not mapped to real memory is called nonresident and must be stored someplace. Nonresident memory is written to disk (auxiliary storage) in units called *pages*. The AS/400 page size is 512 bytes. Data that has been written to disk is said to have been *paged out*. When nonresident data is required, it is read into real memory (*paged in*). This process is diagrammed in Figure 5.2.

When we discuss storage addresses in this book we are referring to virtual addresses unless stated otherwise. When we design programs we generally do not concern ourselves with the amount of real memory present, nor with the management of the real memory. Real storage management is a function of the AS/400 hardware and of the OS/400 operating system. Our programs deal in virtual storage addresses and allocate/manage virtual storage.

The AS/400 hardware presents a single level of storage where all memory is virtual, with the system automatically managing the real memory and DASD subsystems. Although we can think of the AS/400 as having a single level of storage, data is paged in and

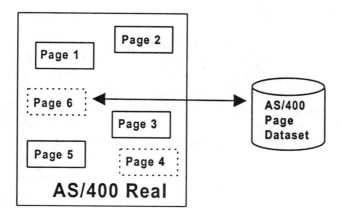

Figure 5.2 Virtual Storage Paging

paged out, so system performance is highly dependant upon the amount of real memory installed on a given computer system. Let us now look at the object architecture of the AS/400 that hides the details of virtual storage addressing.

5.2.2   Private User Storage

Each user of the AS/400 has a unique 16MB address space that is hardware protected. Because no other user has access to this storage, no special locking mechanism is employed for it. This 16MB is virtual storage, and the user is unconcerned about how much real memory is being used at any time in order to manage it. All object accesses are indirect and performed using reference information stored within the user storage area. The actual objects manipulated by a program need not occupy the user storage area. Only object descriptors and work space is usually part of the private storage area so the 16MB limit is not typically restrictive.

The separation of reference and object control information decouples a user from object implementation details and also strengthens the overall security system. A user can reference an object that is not currently available. If this is done, the object will be automatically allocated to the requesting user, then deallocated when no longer needed. The allocation process involves locks to ensure that two users do not attempt to alter an object at the same time. The object allocation process also involves security checks to determine that the user is authorized for the type of access requested.

The separate object reference and object instance also improves the security of objects by not making visible any of the security attributes of an object nor even permitting the object header to be seen. In fact, on the AS/400 no system object is ever visible to a user program. Thus, the AS/400 combines extreme flexibility within the user private storage with a totally secure environment for the system, while ensuring acceptable performance.

5.2.3 Single Level Storage

As indicated earlier, the AS/400 offers a single level storage system. This means that all system data is viewed as being resident within a single large virtual address space. This address space is referenced using 48-bit addresses which are adequate for 280 trillion bytes of data. The system architecture actually supports 64-bit addresses which would suffice for 64,000 times 256GB. This *single level storage* system offers a number of advantages to the AS/400.

The first advantage is one of simplicity. Neither the operating system nor applications are concerned about whether data is resident within real memory or is on DASD. Data management is performed by the hardware at a level below the OS/400 operating system. This means that tracking data validity at the buffer level is not a software responsibility.

This leads us to the second advantage of the shareability of programs and data. If a program is used by two or more jobs on the AS/400, only a single copy of the program is needed. The hardware tracks which programs are resident and who is using each program. This hardware controlled sharing extends to data, even to database records. Thus, the application need not be concerned about having an old copy of data, such as is required for the classic mainframe systems. Only a single copy of any database record exists within the AS/400, and all programs are guaranteed to access the latest version of each record.

The third advantage of the storage system is one of performance. With only a single copy maintained within storage of each object, the AS/400 is capable of supporting very large transaction processing environments. The system overhead of creating the single-level storage system is more than compensated for by the economies of scale that come into play for large numbers of users using the same programs to access the same data.

5.3   AS/400 Object Architecture

Although the AS/400 implements virtual storage in the same fashion as other IBM computer systems, it has a different means of referencing storage that is unique among IBM systems. In a conventional IBM system, data is directly referenced via an address. In the AS/400 system, data is referenced using an object name. The object encapsulates the data address, so the user need not be aware of data addresses for normal system usage.

An *object* is comprised of data and the operations supported for this data. Thus, each object includes a description of how to handle the associated data. For example, a numeric object contains the value of its associated number as well as information on how to perform relational and arithmetic operations on the number. This permits numbers in different formats to be compared and added. Thus, a binary object can be added to a decimal object, then the result compared to a floating point number. On the AS/400 these operations will all work as desired, because the hardware automatically does any conversions needed. On older conventional computer systems, each data type would have to be manually converted by the program before arithmetic or a comparison would be possible.

Each object has a 128-bit descriptor associated with it. This *space object* descriptor contains a 64-bit field which is the virtual address of the object data. Current AS/400 systems only implement 48-bit virtual addresses, but new systems could be introduced using the full 64-bit address and all existing AS/400 software would be supported without change. In addition, 32 bits of each descriptor are reserved for address expansion. Thus, the AS/400 architecture can be extended to support 96-bit addresses without any changes to existing applications. The remaining 32 bits of the object descriptor contain access control information. All AS/400 objects contain integrated security information and the AS/400 system is capable of B-level security at the hardware level.

All references to programs or data in the AS/400 are performed via objects. Each file is an object. Each program is an object. The Command Language (called CL) is a high-level interface to the AS/400 in which commands are applied to objects. In addition, the data manipulated by user programs is made available via references to object names.

To use or reference an object you only need the object descriptor. However, like other computer systems, the AS/400 cannot perform operations upon an object unless the object is resident in real storage. The system automatically moves objects from auxiliary storage into main memory as they are referenced, and moves them from main memory back to auxiliary storage when they are no longer needed.

5.3.1   Storage Pools

Although the details of virtual storage addressing are hidden by the AS/400, the system administrator often must manage real storage. The AS/400 frequently runs more than a single job at a time. A single large job could monopolize all real memory and impact processing of other jobs. OS/400 implements *Storage Pools* to allow the system administrator to subdivide main storage. Each storage pool can be reserved for a given job or group of jobs to ensure that no single job can occupy all storage.

A storage pool is used to reserve an amount of main storage. This storage need not be contiguous. It is managed as a series of 1KB blocks of memory. These blocks may be located anyplace within main storage, and are automatically managed by the AS/400.

All real storage is not available for allocation to storage pools. Some real storage is occupied by *system control objects.* These objects are loaded when the system is started and are not paged in and out. System control objects reduce the amount of main storage available for suballocation into storage pools.

Another class of storage is used for *shared objects.* A single object may be referenced by a number of programs. If multiple copies of an object were required, then the amount of storage used when many jobs are run would be large. A shared object is able to be used by multiple jobs at the same time. The system loads the object the first time it is referenced and tracks the number of simultaneous users so that the object is not removed from main memory while a job using that object remains active. If required, the system also synchronizes access to shared objects. Shared objects reduce the amount of paging in large systems, and also provide a means of communication between jobs.

5.4 Types of Objects

All blocks of storage, programs, and files used on an AS/400 are objects. When a program is executed, the program object is loaded into main memory. When a file is referenced it is made available in memory.

An object may contain an executable program, the source for a program, CL statements, components of the operating system, or other data. Each object is identified by a name. The user determines the name of the object, the system manages the storage occupied by the object. Figure 5.3 lists the various types of objects.

Type	Use
Library	Groups Objects
Folder	Groups Objects
Files	Holds Records
Programs	Contains Code
Command Definitions	Reference Programs
Queues	List of Objects to Process
User Profile	Describes User

Figure 5.3   Object Types

An object is comprised of a set of attributes and a value. The attributes include the library containing the object, the object name, type, size, creation date, as well as a short description of the object. In order to secure an object, one describes the access privileges required for the object. An object is identified using the object name and type. The name of an object need not be unique. Several objects having the same name but different types may be present within a single AS/400 library. Within a single library, the object name and type must be unique. Several objects of the same name and type may exist within different libraries of a single AS/400 system.

Many CL commands operate upon only a single object type. For such commands, the object type need not be included as part of the command as it will be defaulted to the required type. When an object type is specified for a command, it must be valid for the command type. Thus, the CALL command requires an object of type program to be specified and will fail if another type of object is present.

The value of an object is the set of data stored within the object. For example, the value of a file is the collection of records contained by the file. And, a program object's value is the code making up the program. It is important to note that any object can contain any value. Other types of computer systems often store different types of data in different types of containers. The AS/400 can store anything in any object.

An object can be comprised of other objects. Thus, a program can contain its own code plus references to other objects. These other objects could contain additional code or data used by the program. The AS/400 system includes a number of simple objects that are frequently used in building larger and more complex objects.

5.4.1   Libraries

A *library* is an object used to group other objects. Thus, a library is a directory. Although the objects in a library are usually related in some fashion, no relationship need exist. The objects in a library need not be of the same type. For example, a library may contain programs, files, and even other groups of objects.

Objects required for a single functional area or task are frequently grouped into a library. This allows easy backup and restore of all job related information with a single command. Although no architectural limitation exists for the maximum number of objects present in a library, you should keep each library smaller than about 8000 objects for efficiency in the SAVE operation.

In a secured system, it is common to group objects requiring the same access rights into a library and to then secure access to the library. This greatly simplifies the security administration task. When this is done carefully, the objects grouped for security reasons are also grouped according to their functional area.

All objects are contained within a single library. The library name is used to qualify the name of an object and thus to uniquely identify each object. When a library name is used in conjunction with the name and type of an object, the object is said to be *fully qualified*. Again, this simply means that the object has been uniquely identified.

When an object is specified in a command, the library name of the object may be explicitly stated or omitted. An explicit library specification uniquely identifies the object and no search is required. When the library name is omitted the AS/400 performs a library search to locate the object. A list of libraries, called a *library list* is searched in the order named. The first library containing the named object is the one used to access the object, and the remaining libraries in the library list are not searched. The system creates a library list for each job when it is defined. Information may be supplied in the job header to customize the library list for each job.

Although an object may not be present in two different libraries at the same time, an object can be moved from one library to another. The object is not actually moved in storage, but the object ownership is transferred between libraries. Many object types may also be renamed and copied between libraries. The AS/400 is unique among IBM systems in that the object characteristics (including its security attributes) travel with an object that has been renamed or copied or otherwise moved within the system. This feature is a key element of B level security and also greatly enhances the user friendly nature of the AS/400.

5.4.2 Folders

A folder is a named object used as a label or name for a group of objects. For those familiar with PCs, folders perform the same function as do PC DOS directories. Just as a PC directory may contain files or directories, a folder may contain other folders as well as data and programs. Thus, for the AS/400, folders are used to logically group objects within libraries.

As we indicated above, the folder structure is logically equivalent to the PC hierarchical directory structure. This is not a coincidence. When PC Support/400 is used to access an AS/400 system from a PC, then the AS/400 and PC files are mapped together into folders. AS/400 data may be accessed as though it was resident upon the PC, by treating the folder names as though they were PC directory names. This concept is explained in Chapter 16, PC Support.

5.4.3 Files

A file is an object containing either a set of records or a stream of data. A database is an example of a file containing records. A *stream* is a single variable length record treated as a series of characters. A text file such as a document is an example of a stream. A file is the lowest level of data managed as an object.

Files may be easily created by AS/400 programs (which are in turn themselves simply special types of files). All program output and input takes the form of files. Input and output file names may be associated with data queues and message queues.

5.4.4 Programs

A program is an object containing instructions. Programs may be either compiled or interpreted. For compiled programs, the program source was previously processed by a compiler specific to the source language which generated the program object. Compiled objects are directly processed, and are the most efficient type of program.

Only objects of the program type may be executed. The CALL command verifies that the type of the object to be executed is program and fails if it is not valid. Thus, you cannot accidently issue the CALL command for a file or other data object. But, you can issue a CALL for an object which, although of the program type, requires special processing.

One benefit of the object architecture is that the type of an object is always known. This means that OS/400 knows how to process each program given the object header information, without the user being required to specify this information. Thus, interpreted programs (such as REXX) contain the program source which is not itself executable, but which is implicitly processed each time the program is executed.

Note that only a single copy of a program object is needed, even if the program is being used by 100 different jobs. The AS/400 hardware tracks who is using which objects, when they are done with them, and automatically handles any required locking. When a program object is no longer in use, the hardware is aware that the storage used for the program can be reclaimed.

5.4.5   Command Definitions

Command Definition objects contain the description of a command and identify the program used to perform the command. The system provides a number of commands, but the user may also define their own commands. The command definition statements are used within a command definition object to add user commands to the system.

The user may also change existing system commands. For example, parameter values can be restricted on a system command to prevent accidental modification or loss of critical data. A command definition may also be used to alter command defaults, perform additional security checks, and even change the name of existing commands.

Separating programs from command definitions is a powerful capability of the AS/400. It allows a program to be treated as a resource or tool that can be applied as needed. Any existing AS/400 command can be referenced by a command definition. This allows commands to be treated as resources by providing default parameter values, and by ensuring that all user parameters are valid before being processed by the command.

5.4.6   Queues

A *queue* is a list of objects to be processed. The AS/400 uses queues to manage lists of jobs, output, messages, and data. Each of these data types has its own type of queue. Each type of queue has its own rules.

A *job queue* is used to manage batch requests submitted by users. The user determines the priority of work in the queue by determining the order of the jobs. Jobs may be entered into the queue the desired order of execution, or the order of a job queue may be altered once it is created.

An *output queue* is a type of queue managed by the system. An output queue contains program output waiting to be printed. As with the job queue, the contents of an output queue may be rearranged to determine the priority of printout. An output queue may be directed to a device such as a printer, or it may be processed by another program. An example of the second user of an output queue would be a file transfer program that automatically sends data placed in its queue to other computer systems.

A *message queue* contains messages. All communication between programs, users, and jobs occurs using messages. When a message is sent to a program or a user it is placed in a queue associated with the target program or user. A user or program obtains the message by *receiving* it. Message queues provide a mechanism to facilitate the use of jobs as services shared by all system users. Using message queues to pass information about work to be done between programs also ensures that no requests are lost just because the target program is currently busy. They can also be used to save requests in the event that the target program is not currently active.

A *data queue* is used to pass data between programs and users. Data queues function similarly to message queues. Like message queues, data queues facilitate the creation of general purpose system services. Classical system design often dictated that the output of one program was passed to the next program via a temporary file. The use of data queues allows the same flexibility in design, but without the cost of the I/Os to write, then read a temporary file.

5.4.7   User Profiles

A *User Profile* object is used to identify a particular user or a group of users to the AS/400 system. A user is known to the system by the user profile name. When a user signs on, the sign on name is used to locate a specific user profile. The user profile contains the password required to complete the sign on.

Once a user has signed on, the user profile determines the security authorization levels of the user. This information determines which objects the user is able to see, access, and alter. Thus, menus on the AS/400 are tailored dynamically in response to the user profile information. Each user can see a different menu for the same program, where only the authorized commands are visible.

Chapter

6

I/O

Computers are of no use without a way of communicating with the outside world. The Input and Output hardware is the computers means of communication. This chapter discusses the various types of Input and Output hardware. These are often referred to as *I/O devices*. We will look at how I/O devices are attached to the computer and how I/O is performed.

We will review the organization of the IBM AS/400 I/O system and discuss the functions of the processor, the system bus, I/O processors, and devices when performing I/O. The I/O devices supported by OS/400 are reviewed. The general functions, operational characteristics, and performance issues of each will be briefly covered. DASD devices will be covered in detail in the next chapter. Here, we look at:

> System Bus, I/O Processors, and Devices
> Unit Record Devices
> Printers
> CRTs
> Magnetic Tape
> Backup Devices
> Communications Support
> LAN Support

6.1   System Bus, I/O Processors, Cables, and Devices

With few exceptions, I/O devices are not attached directly to the AS/400 processor. Just as a city's suburbs are connected to the city via roads which carry the traffic, each I/O device is connected to the processor by the *System Bus*. The function of a bus is to carry the traffic between the processor and the I/O device. This traffic is comprised of both control information and data. Refer to Figure 6.1 for a diagram of the processor and system bus.

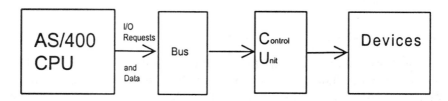

Figure 6.1   I/O Bus and Processor Relationship

A bus may be in use by several different I/O requests simultaneously. An AS/400 processor always has one system bus, but that single bus supports simultaneous communications with a number of devices. An arbitration mechanism determines which device has priority to access the bus at any given time. This mechanism ensures that data is not lost by fast devices such as DASD monopolizing the entire bus.

AS/400 processors may have more than a single bus. The 9402 and 9404 processor families support either one or two busses. The 9406 family has models with from one to seven busses. Multiple busses increase the total amount of data that may be transferred at a time. They also can improve the reliability of the system by providing a redundant path for I/O should one bus fail.

Most I/O devices have complex functionality. In order to reduce the cost of the individual devices, this functionality is often implemented in two different places. The actual I/O device is often just a vehicle for reading and writing data. The complex logic to drive the device is performed by an *I/O processor*. Thus, the instruction processor communicates with the outside world via a bus connected to an I/O processor connected to the actual I/O device.

An I/O processor (sometimes called I/O processor controller or IOP in IBM documentation) is a processor that is loaded with instructions by the system processor. The I/O processor instructions perform self test diagnostics, test the actual I/O devices, and direct the I/O process including any device-specific error recovery. The I/O processor is loaded with licensed internal code stored with the OS/400 system and shipped plus maintained as part of the AS/400 package.

6.2 Cables

If the system bus is within the processor and I/O processors and devices are outside, the two need to be connected to each other. Cables are used to pass the signals from the bus to the I/O processors and devices. Various types of cables are used by the AS/400. One that is pretty much unique to the S/3x and AS/400 world is the *twinaxial* cable used to connect terminal devices such as the 5250. Various types of coaxial cables as well as twisted pair wiring are also encountered in AS/400 systems, especially when LANs or individual PCs are attached.

6.3 Unit Record Devices

What is a *Unit Record Device*? As the name implies, it is a device that deals with a one record at a time. Card readers and punches, as well as line printers, are all examples of unit record devices. Remember card readers? You say you do not even know what a *card* is! Well, cards were those rectangular pieces of cardboard with holes punched in them (by a card punch of course), that were used as the primary source of data on some of the original computers. Cards were invented in the 1890s and used through the early 1980s. Early S3X computers supported cards, and many programs converted from that environment still contain references to logical cards. Modern computers do not use cards, but the 80-byte records we may use for RPG/400, and for many data files are in fact logical images of those original 80-column cards.

However, we still do use some unit record devices. Printers are one of the few types of unit record devices still used by modern computer systems. Let's look at printers in more detail, followed by CRTs.

6.3.1 Printers

The classic 1403 printer used heavy print trains comprised of metal slugs containing the character images. The 1403 was replaced by band printers where a continuous metal band contained the embossed character images. These early printers used wide *ribbons* to carry the ink. A small hammer was used to transfer the ink from the ribbon to the paper using the character shaped in metal as the pattern. These old *impact line printers* were as noisy as they were messy. Later, low-end printers that employed pins to print using a dot matrix representing characters came into play. These slow lower quality printers were complemented with even slower letter quality printers that used print wheels or balls containing the type.

The ribbon, hammers, pins, and even the old messy ink are now gone from many shops. Most modern printers use ink jets, laser xerography, and other techniques to apply the page text and graphics images directly onto the paper. Such modern printers also often have no physical representation of the characters but instead draw characters using drops of ink or tiny particles of toner as directed by their own local controller.

The old style printers could use a single character set at a time. In order to change the character set, you had to physically change the print chain or band. Modern printers use electronic descriptions of character sets, and supporting a new character set is as simple as loading the definition of the characters into your processor.

Early printers had fixed length lines of 120 or 132 characters. These printers were also fixed pitch — the characters they printed were all of the same width. Although they were well suited to producing columnar data, such as accounting reports, text could be hard to read. Modern printers have variable length lines and also support character sets with fixed or variable widths. Modern laser printers can produce camera ready copy that bypasses the need for a separate photo-typesetter in the production of manuals and other published material.

Until fairly recently, printers were large, expensive, pieces of I/O gear that resided only within the data center. It would take a while for our report to be separated from all of the other printouts and delivered to our office. This is no longer the case. Many of us have a small printer on our desk top, or a printer close to us, shared by the people within our department. Our reports and other printouts are delivered to our work area by virtue of being printed where we work.

Of course, the OS/400 operating system still supports a variety of printers. All of these printers are supported as system printers. A *system printer* is a printer capable of supporting the large volumes of output produced by batch jobs. These printers are usually driven by OS/400 using output previously prepared from batch jobs.

6.3.2 CRTs

Many of us use a *Cathode Ray Terminal* (or *CRT*) as our primary interface to a computer system. Be it a PC, an AS/400, or even a large ES/9000, we talk to computers using a keyboard and CRT. CRTs became the standard computer interface for programmers and end users in the 1970s. Early CRTs were bulky, hard to read, and very, very expensive.

The standard terminal family for AS/400 systems is the 5250. The 5250 uses the unusual *twinaxial* cable for connection to the controller on the host AS/400 system. PC Support/400 is an example of software that permits a PC to emulate a 5250. Increasingly often, 5250 terminals are being replaced by PCs in some shops.

Modern 3270 style terminals are the standard IBM mainframe interface. Of course, many of us simply emulate a 3270 terminal on a PC sitting on our desk top. 3270 terminals have lines that are usually 80 characters long. This is a result of emulating cards on the terminal. An alternative terminal line size is 132 characters. This is a result of emulating the standard size print line on a terminal.

3270 terminals are each connected to a control unit, and the control unit is connected to the processor using a bus or channel cable. Each terminal is connected to the control unit using a coaxial cable. Coaxial cable is relatively large and expensive. For this reason, many companies simulate coaxial cable by using a ballen and twisted pair wire. Thus, ordinary phone wire can be used to connect 3270 terminals to a control unit.

6.4   Magnetic Tape

Magnetic tape is one old form of data storage that has survived into modern times. We are all familiar with magnetic tape used to record sound (cassette tapes for our car) and video (video tapes for our VCR or camcorder). Tapes used by computer systems are physically similar, although usually of a higher quality.

Magnetic tape may be wound on a reel (often called *round tape*) or packaged within a cartridge (sometimes called *square tape*). Tape cartridges are now common for mainframe computers, but are also seen as a low cost media for PCs and midrange computers. Tape cartridges have been replacing the old tape reels and may soon probably be the only surviving tape media. However, reels and cartridges are not quite totally compatible. For example, note that the AS/400 supports extending files on tape reels where this is not supported for tape cartridges. The types of magnetic tape supported by the AS/400 include:

- 1/2-inch reel

- 1/2-inch cartridge

- 8-mm cartridge

- 1/4-inch cartridge

The capacities of these tape devices range from 40MB to over 2GB. Although we still refer to magnetic tape, what we are talking about has changed a great deal over time. Changes include the speed of I/O, the density of the data, and the physical tape media being used. The early reel type tape drives wrote seven tracks of data at densities of 200, 556, and 800 bits per inch (BPI). Later versions could read and write nine tracks of data at densities of 1600 BPI and later yet at 6250 BPI. The larger density tapes stored more data and were faster. Higher data densities resulted in a faster data transfer rate for the same speed of moving the tape through the drive.

Modern tape drives use higher densities yet (up to 76,200 BPI) and also record more data tracks. A series of cartridges may be pre-loaded into an input stacker so that operator intervention is minimized for multiple tape jobs. The latest tape devices incorporate hardware data compression to reduce the amount of space taken to store a given amount of data by another factor of two. However, as we will see when we talk about DASD, magnetic tape has barely kept pace with the growth in disk capacity in terms of the number of tapes it takes to backup DASD data.

6.4.1 Sequential Data

Magnetic tape was originally introduced as a primary data media. That is, data was stored on tape and processed directly from tape. A data center would receive data on tape, and frequently ship tapes to other data centers. All of this tape data was stored sequentially. A tape has a *begin*, and an *end*. All tape I/O starts at the beginning, and proceeds through the tape to the end. Thus, a tape is like a book that must be read from beginning to end. Although one can quickly skip to a desired page in a book, the same is not true of a tape. It takes roughly the same amount of time to skip to the halfway point of a tape file as it does to read down to that same halfway point.

Magnetic tape is referred to as a *sequential media*. It is ideal for storing a file that is rebuilt as a whole. Originally, most computer data files were sequential. For example, an employee payroll master file was a list of employees recorded in employee number sequence on a magnetic tape reel. In order to add a new employee, the entire file was read from the old employee master tape recreated on a new tape that became the current employee master.

For most modern systems, this approach is no longer used. It takes a long time to read and rewrite large sequential files. And modern systems are processing larger and larger files every day. Also, modern systems present data to online users as they request it. Magnetic tape is not acceptable for storing data that must be retrieved and presented randomly. Such files are now stored on Direct Access Storage Devices (DASD or disks for short). But, you say, we still have tape drives. What are they being used for?

6.4.2 Backup Data

Magnetic tape efficiently stores and accesses data sequentially. We need to periodically backup our large disk master files so that our data is protected. Magnetic tapes are easily shipped between data centers. And, magnetic tapes can be stored for long periods in a vault, with confidence that the data will still be good when needed. Thus, tape is still an ideal backup media.

Magnetic tape can also be used to record critical data as it is generated. Thus, magnetic tape is used to save laboratory data, seismic data, and even space mission data. It is also used in some data centers to save *journals* of online system transaction data. Tape journal data can be used to recover the state of disk master files should they be lost. This is accomplished by restoring the disk master from the last full tape backup, then repeating the current transactions from the tape journal record. Both of these uses exploit the sequential nature of magnetic tape.

6.4.3 Magnetic Tape Devices

The AS/400 supports a number of IBM tape devices and features. Refer to Figure 6.2 for a complete list of the supported tape devices. In general, the cartridge devices have much lower error rates than the reel devices and are the preferred devices for backups and for software installation. Unfortunately, no single standard exists for tape cartridges across the line of AS/400 processors. This can complicate movement of tape data between different-sized AS/400 systems.

A number of vendors now support automated tape libraries (often called *silos*). A tape silo accesses and loads the desired cartridge automatically without operator intervention. OS/400 supports the IBM devices and various OEM vendors have supported their own special purpose tape silo hardware on the AS/400.

6.5 Communications Support

Communications hardware supports access to data on systems that are not connected directly via channels. It can also be used to support devices that are too far away to be channel attached. Modern communications hardware supports both asynchronous and synchronous communications.

Device	Type
3422	1/2-inch Reel
3430	1/2-inch Reel
3480	1/2-inch Cartridge
3490	1/2-inch Cartridge
6342	1/4-inch Cartridge
6347	1/4-inch Cartridge
6366	1/4-inch Cartridge
7208	8-mm Cartridge
9348	1/2-inch Reel

Figure 6.2 AS/400 Supported Magnetic Tape Devices

6.5.1 Asynchronous Communications

Many of us have used asynchronous communications, although we may not know it. Using a modem to dial a bulletin board or to access your mainframe system from your PC at home is typically an *asynch* connection. *Asynchronous communications* is characterized by a lack of a common clock (or time base) between the sender and the receiver. The units of data are bracketed by *stop bits*.

In asynchonous communications, the sender and receiver periodically exchange signals that indicate the status of the data transfer. These signals facilitate error identification and recovery. Exchanging signals involves changing the direction of communications. Changing the direction of communications introduces a relatively long delay. When communications occur over long distances, this need to exchange control signals can greatly slow down the effective data transfer rate. One perverse example of this slowdown is encountered when using a dialup phone service where the data passes through a satellite. The stop bits also reduce the amount of usable data that can be transmitted since they occupy communications bandwidth.

It is relatively cheap to build an *asynch* modem and many PC systems now include such modems. For this reason, most bulletin board systems, and services like **Compuserve** and **Prodigy** use asynch communications. However, error recovery, and extremely fast data transmission are complicated for asynch communications.

6.5.2 Synchronous Communications

Synchronous Communications is characterized by the use of a common clock (or time base) between the sender and receiver. This allows units of data (characters or bytes) to be assembled as they are received. It also facilitates error recovery. Synchronous communications can also be more efficient over large distances since status signals are not exchanged as often. It sounds like synchronous communication is better, why is it not used exclusively?

Synchronous modems are more complex to make than asynch modems and therefore, more expensive. It is also more difficult to program synchronous communications protocols than it is to program asynch protocols. Lastly, asynch hardware and protocols were standardized before synchronous hardware and protocols were standardized. Essentially all asynch modems can talk to each other (at some speed). The opposite is true for most synchronous modems, even when purchased in the same country.

OS/400 implements SNA which directly supports synchronous communications with many mainframe and midsize systems. Asynch communications are generally supported via gateways or as options on communications control units.

6.6 Local Area Network Support

A *Local Area Network* (*LAN*) is a group of interconnected PCs that share disk space and files. Individual PCs may have their own hard disks, but also have shared access to the common disk files. A LAN includes a server PC which owns and manages the shared disk space. Requests for this shared disk are passed from the nodes of the LAN to the server which handles the requests.

It is common for LANs to be interconnected with other LANs and also with mainframes. Widely separated LANs may be interconnected via a *Wide Area Network* (*WAN*). A LAN is often connected

to a mainframe via a terminal control unit. In this case the
individual LAN nodes usually look like terminals. OS/400 permits
PCs to be emulated as either 3270 devices or as 5250 terminals.

LANs are supported by modern mainframes via gateway
adapters on communications control units. LANs may also be
locally attached to a mainframe through an adapter for a terminal
control unit. For example, the 3174 local controller permits a LAN
to be attached via a token ring interface. Such a LAN can be
shared by the mainframe and the AS/400 system. Various manu-
facturers also provide boards for an individual PC that make the
PC appear as a single 3270 terminal. Many 3270 emulation boards
also support LU6.2 communication via a DFT connection. In
general, such emulation boards are not useful for attaching PCs to
AS/400 systems.

Boards are also available for a LAN server that make the LAN
server appear as a local or remote terminal control unit to the
mainframe. One advantage of this type of connection is that the
details of the LAN configuration need not be known directly by the
mainframe world. Additional terminals may usually be added to
such a LAN without altering data center definitions.

7

DASD

DASD is an acronym for *Direct Access Storage Device*. This simply means that all data can be accessed with roughly equal cost in terms of time, and contrasts with sequential storage where an entire set of data must be read to find any particular piece of data. Although we usually think of disk drives when we think of DASD, this term encompasses floppy disks, optical storage, and solid-state devices as well. Thus, the term DASD spans several types of rotating media read magnetically or optically and even extends to devices with no moving parts.

The DASD devices employed by modern computer systems are covered in this chapter. A brief history of DASD is presented to help our understanding of current technology, how it evolved, and where it may be going. Diagrams of possible configurations are included. Some statistics on capacity, device models, performance, and features are included. The key topic of Recoverability is separately covered in Chapter 20.

DASD are complex devices. This discussion is by necessity an overview. For details on how to attach DASD to the AS/400 refer to the IBM manual *AS/400: Physical Planning Guide* (GA41-9571). For information on the DASD capacities of individual AS/400 models refer to the IBM manual *AS/400: Product Specifications* (SA41-9983). For a more complete treatment of mainframe DASD devices refer to the book *DASD: IBM's Direct Access Storage Devices* by Robert Johnson and Daniel Johnson. Although this book has a mainframe orientation, it is the most complete treatment of DASD the author has encountered and is highly recommended.

7.1 DASD at a Glance

DASD is usually the first level of storage outside of the processor. It offers medium speed random access to large amounts of data. This is in contrast to magnetic tape which offers relatively slow sequential access to extremely large amounts of data, and to processor memory which offers high-speed random access to small amounts of data.

We might ask, "Why use tape anymore?" DASD is moderately expensive storage compared to magnetic tape. We usually have to select what data is maintained on disk, as opposed to tape. The low cost of tape media ensures that tape will continue to be used into the next century at least as a backup media.

The effective management of the DASD resource is a key part of managing a modern data center. Deciding what data to put on disk, how long to keep it there, how often to back it up to tape, and whether or not a permanent archival copy is needed are questions we answer each and every day.

Modern systems support two general types of DASD. These are Count Key Data and Fixed Block Architecture. *Count Key Data* (or *CKD*) DASD is an older architecture dating from the 1960s which is seen only in mainframe operating systems. *Fixed Block Architecture* (or *FBA*) is a newer DASD architecture similar to that used by PCs, many UNIX systems, and our AS/400 systems. IBM's highest performance and capacity DASD use the CKD architecture. Larger mainframe shops tend to use only CKD DASD. Because the AS/400 is often part of distributed systems that include CKD DASD we discuss both types of DASD here.

DASD hardware is complex to program. Operating systems provide a simple interface (*Input Output Control System* called an IOCS) that maps logical files to the physical DASD such that a programmer does not have to be aware of the details of I/O programming. The IOCS also provides a device independent layer so that a program need not be rewritten just because a new type of DASD is being installed. OS/400 operates at a high level where all storage is viewed as a single series of addresses that cross physical DASD boundaries. The IOCS function is incorporated within the base structure of OS/400.   OS/400 automatically performs file allocation within pools of DASD.

7.2   DASD Structure and Terminology

In this section we will look at just what DASD are, what they are made up of, and their associated terminology. We look at both the CKD and FBA DASD architectures and discuss the advantages and disadvantages of each. Although the AS/400 does not utilize CKD addressed DASD directly, the AS/400 is often used to access mainframe resident data that is stored on CKD DASD, and the FBA style of DASD often encountered on AS/400s is itself simply a logical mapping of the same architecture as used by CKD DASD units. For this reason, we look at both types of DASD. We will also look at how we choose our DASD configuration, and why we make the selections we do.

Modern DASD have evolved over twenty five years, so we will briefly look at their history in the next sections. DASD of different times are usually divided into several generations. This helps us to better understand how modern DASD were developed.

7.2.1   Physical Characteristics

A disk drive is made up of a series of circular platters that each spin under a read/write *head*. Each platter is logically comprised of a series of concentric circles of data. The read/write head is positioned to the desired circle of data. Each circle of data is called a *track*. Each track holds the same amount of data. The vertically aligned tracks on all of the platters are referred to as a *cylinder*. The whole assembly is called a *DASD volume*.

The capacity of a DASD volume is determined by the size of a track, the number of tracks in a cylinder, and the number of cylinders. Each different DASD model has a different track size, cylinder size, cylinder count and thus, a different capacity. The DASD capacity relationship can be expressed mathematically as:

$$Capacity = TrackSize * TrksPerCylinder * Cylinders$$

Equation 1   DASD Capacity

Disk drives are attached to a processor via bus paths (sometimes called channel paths). Actually the disk control unit is attached to the processor via the bus and the disk drives attach to the control unit. Figure 7.1 illustrates the relationship of the bus, control unit, and disk drives. A processor may have multiple busses, and each bus may have multiple control units. Our diagram illustrates the simplest system, one with a single bus and a single control unit.

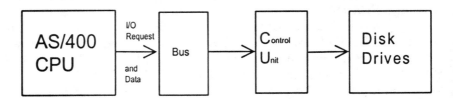

Figure 7.1   CPU, Bus, Control Unit Relationship

Disk drives are grouped together into *strings*. One or more strings of DASD units may be attached to a single control unit. Figure 7.2 illustrates the relationship of DASD strings to the control unit. A control unit is attached to the processor by one or more data transfer paths (each of which is called a *bus* as discussed above). The group of all DASD in a computer system is often referred to as the *DASD subsystem*.

7.2.2   CKD

CKD is an acronym for *Count, Key, and Data*. As we have seen above, a CKD disk records data on tracks. A physical block must be wholly contained within a single track. Each physical block (the *Data*) is preceded by a Count field, and optionally by a Key field. The sequence on disk is count, followed by key, followed by data, hence, the term Count-Key-Data.

The *Count* field is an eight-byte identifier for the block. It contains the address and length of the block as CCHHRKLL where:

CC   is the two-byte cylinder number.

HH   is the two-byte head number. Although modern DASD have only a small number of tracks per cylinder (15 for 3380/3390), the DASD hardware architecture supports up to

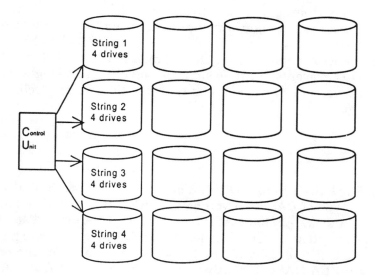

Figure 7.2 Strings of DASD

2**16-1 or 65,535 tracks.

R   is the one-byte record number. Record numbers range from
     0 to 255. Mainframe access methods use record zero to keep
     track of available space on a track and not for user data.

K   is the one-byte key length. The key length is zero if no key
     is present which is typical for all modern access methods.

LL   is the two-byte block length. The maximum block length is
     thus, 2**16-1 or 65,535 bytes.

The Count field is followed by a gap, the key field (optional), a
second gap, then the data. The function of the count field is to
assist the hardware in identifying the desired block. In the distant
past when CKD DASD were designed, the disk drive hardware
could not locate a block automatically and the count field was
required to facilitate locating the desired block among several
recorded upon a track. The *search count equal* command is still
used to located a data block on a CKD DASD.

The *Key* field is optional and is little used. Its original purpose was to support a tag up to 255 bytes for each block. The hardware supports *search key equal* commands that allow selecting a block based upon its key value. This search is considered to be a data transfer operation and keeps the channel and DASD control unit busy. This prevents multiple simultaneous I/Os to a single control unit and was one of the reasons that key field usage declined 20 years ago.

7.2.3 FBA

Fixed Block Architecture (FBA) disks are the newest and also the simplest type of DASD. If you have a PC, you have a disk similar to an FBA disk. AS/400 DASD are all of the FBA type. Each FBA drive is viewed as a series of fixed-length 512-byte blocks. The first block is block zero, followed by block one, and so on for the entire disk. An FBA DASD logically appears as a series of fixed blocks, but is really physically a CKD device with physical blocks recorded on tracks that are organized into cylinders.

Although the physical structure of the disk is actually the old head, track, and cylinder layout, the software needs no knowledge of the actual size of a track nor the number of tracks in a cylinder. FBA disks are preformatted into 512-byte blocks so no hardware low-level format is required. The FBA hardware translates each logical block number into the actual physical location of the block.

Disk allocation on an FBA volume simply involves mapping a file to a sequence of 512-byte blocks. Each FBA file is a series of blocks that is defined by the first block number and the count of blocks. The operating system IOCS automatically maps records into the fixed-length FBA blocks. Note that the fixed size of 512 is a lower limit on the amount of space that can be efficiently allocated/managed as a unit. We see this unit at various points within the OS/400 design. One place is the virtual storage page unit of 512 bytes.

Because any file can be defined by its starting block and length in blocks, DASD file protection is easy to implement for FBA. The FBA controller hardware contains a built-in mechanism to ensure that any FBA I/O program is restricted to the file it is allowed to update. For the AS/400, the hardware manages storage so no access outside of a file is possible. Within OS/400, storage protection is a basic component of the operating system. No direct addressing of disk storage is possible for any normal AS/400 program, and thus no corruption of files can result from an application software fault.

We have seen that FBA DASD are easier to manage than CKD DASD. Yet, FBA DASD are usually used only by PCs, AS/400s, and the smaller VSE shops in the mainframe arena. If FBA is better, why is it not used in all mainframe shops? FBA was never supported by the large mainframe MVS operating system, only limited FBA models were delivered by IBM, and the most cost effective disks on a cost-per-megabyte basis are still the largest CKD DASD. However, FBA is the standard type of DASD for the AS/400.

7.3 DASD Futures

Although we first think of magnetic disk storage when we hear the term DASD, other DASD types are currently available. In addition, a number of options are available to improve the reliability and performance of the existing magnetic media. In this section we look at the emerging DASD technologies as well as some possible future directions.

7.3.1 DASD Subsystems

Although we often think of magnetic DASD in terms of single drives, modern magnetic auxiliary storage is often part of a total storage subsystem. DASD subsystems involve multiple drives and occasionally multiple types of storage. High-end DASD subsystems include their own I/O controllers, actually special purpose computer systems dedicated to I/O management.

Magnetic DASD subsystems may offer built-in recoverability via RAID (Redundant Array of Inexpensive DASD) technology. They may incorporate large caches of memory that can dramatically improve read and even write performance. These cached subsystems sometimes include their own battery backup to ensure that no data is lost in the event of a power loss. Modern memory caches usually have their own local process to determine which data is kept in cache for optimum performance.

7.3.2 Optical Media

Optical storage is currently available for the AS/400. Optical DASD employ a LASER to read and write information. The recording media is typically much more durable than that of magnetic DASD. This is a result of no possible physical contact between the LASER read/write head and the media as well as improved resistance to magnetic fields, heat, and contamination. Optical media are usually much cheaper in cost-per-megabyte than magnetic media. However, read/write optical disk drives are currently more expensive and slower than magnetic DASD. Three basic types of optical DASD currently exist. These are:

- Read only (CD/ROM)
- Write once, read mostly (WORM)
- Read/Write

The CD/ROM DASD is generally available at a low cost. Each CD/ROM disk stores about 600MB and is cheaply reproduced using the same methods employed for audio CDs. CD/ROM is relatively slow, with access times of about 300 milliseconds (nearly 1/3 of a second!). CD/ROM is commonly used now for distribution of software and online documentation. It is also seeing increased use as a way of distributing read-only databases. When used with caching software, the performance of CD/ROM DASD is acceptable for many online query applications.

WORM drives are much more expensive than CD/ROM units with purchase prices starting over $1000. The performance of WORM drives is comparable to that of CD/ROM with the exception that writing data is typically a relatively slow process. The capacity of WORM drives varies from 100MB to over 1GB. WORM drives can be used to write data a single time. Once the entire WORM drive volume is filled, a new one must be used. The normal use for WORM DASD units is for the logging or archiving of data. WORM drives also make good backup devices, although they are much more expensive than magnetic tape.

Read/Write optical DASD are currently the most expensive. These units usually have a relatively slow write time with faster read times. Read rates are comparable to or better than those for CD/ROM or WORM drives. Large numbers of Read/Write optical media volumes may be managed by a *jukebox* mechanism with one or more read/write stations. Such data jukeboxes can have total capacities in the terabyte range! Once a volume has been loaded into a read/write station, its performance is comparable to that of any other optical unit. A jukebox is often a standalone DASD subsystem with its own processor and fairly large amounts of locally managed cache memory that result in average access times approaching that of magnetic DASD. For these reasons, optical jukeboxes are increasingly replacing magnetic DASD for some applications.

7.3.3 Hybrid Subsystems

Modern DASD subsystems are beginning to employ a mixture of media. Thus, a magnetic DASD subsystem may include cache memory on the front to improve access and large optical media on the rear to greatly increase the capacity of the unit at a relatively lower cost. Back end optical media can also be used to automatically create backups of data stored on the magnetic DASD units of the subsystem.

An additional type of hybrid storage system involves the use of magnetic tape along with DASD. In these systems, the tape is used for back and archival storage. When a file that is only resident on tape is accessed, it is automatically loaded to DASD. This results in very slow access time for some data, but allows very large files to be accessed. This type of storage is being replaced by optical solutions as optical media are much faster than tape as well as being very inexpensive on a cost-per-megabyte basis for large storage sizes.

For very large total storage capacities (over a tera-byte), magnetic tape juke boxes will still be used as a part of hybrid storage systems. This is a result of the very low cost of magnetic tape media, the reliability of magnetic media in longer term storage, as well as the increased density and performance characteristics seen in the newer tape cartridges.

8

AS/400 Limits

Any computer system has a capacity based upon the speed and amount of hardware present. Thus, the amount of DASD present determines an upper limit on the size of a database. And, the speed of the processor determines the maximum number of online users that can be serviced with acceptable response time. However, a computer architecture also contains designed in limits that cannot be exceeded no matter how much hardware you purchase. In this chapter we look at the architectural limits of AS/400 computer systems. For additional information on the hardware limits of individual AS/400 models refer to the IBM manual *AS/400: Product Specifications* (SA41-9983).

8.1   Database Limits

The maximum amount of data in bytes and records is an important limit for any computer system. Database size limits were increased in Version 2 Release 2 Modification 0 of OS/400 as follows:

- Data Space (file) size from 2GB to 256GB. Note that this is dramatically better than most mainframe computer systems.

- Number of records in a data space from less than 16 million records to less than 2 billion records.

- Size of a Save File was increased from a maximum of 3GB to 255.99 GB (the same limitation as the database).

• Index Size from 1GB to 4GB. Maximum index entries
supported is approximately 2GB.

• Length of Index Key from 120 bytes to 2000 bytes. Maximum
number of key fields is still 120.

8.2   Save/Restore Limits

• 32KB limit removed from SAVDLO.

8.2.1   DASD Limits by Model

The actual maximum DASD space available varies by AS/400 model
as well as by the type of DASD unit used in a configuration. In this
section we look at the capacity of several processor models and
DASD types. It must be noted that the actual storage usable is
dependant upon a number of factors, but will always be less than
what is listed. For example, if your DASD are organized as a
RAID-5 array, then some DASD space is used for redundant storage
of data. Likewise, any storage needed for the operating system,
program libraries, and journals is not included and reduces space
available for storage of your database.

DASD Unit	35/45	50	60/70	80/90
9332-400	12.8	22.4	35.2	50.0
9332-600	19.2	33.6	52.8	75.0
9335	27.3	47.8	75.2	106.8
9336-010	15.0	26.3	41.4	67.8
9336-020	27.4	47.9	75.4	123.4

Figure 8.1 DASD Capacity

8.3 Processor Models, Capacities, and Limits

This section discusses the characteristics of the AS/400 processor models. The most important characteristic of the AS/400 family, is that all software and data is portable across the entire line. Applications written for the smallest "x02" model will run on the largest "x95" series. The extreme degree of portability is a consequence of the design of the AS/400 which hides the hardware implementation details. The customer is precluded from writing applications at the hardware level, which further ensures the portability of all applications.

On the other hand, the many processor models cover a wide range of memory sizes, processor speeds, and DASD sizes. Thus, extremely large applications will not run on the smallest systems. However, all applications will generally prove to be upwardly compatible. And, when the volume of activity for a given application increases beyond the capacity of your current system, you can easily and safely add memory or DASD to your current processor or nearly as easily upgrade to a larger processor model.

8.3.1 9402 Models

The smallest AS/400s occupy a box similar to a tower PC and are designed to sit beside a desktop. The three processor models are the F02, F04, and F06. The basic memory for each of these is 8MB, but expansion memory is supported. A 1.2GB tape cartridge is part of the standard support, and a 1.2MB 5.25-inch floppy disk drive is optional. Best of all, the 9402 models use standard wall power, and require no special environmental controls.

The 9402 models support fairly limited expansion, which limits the size of application they can support, as well as the number of users that can be physically attached. These systems are suitable for a small number of users, perhaps as many as a dozen. However, they are even seen in moderately large single-user applications.

Note that the minimum memory of 8MB is usually not adequate for even the simplest applications. For example, we observed serious performance problems running small REXX programs on an F02 with 8MB. As few as two to three users doing nothing except editing also resulted in poor performance. An upgrade to 24MB of memory immediately corrected most performance problems. The F02 is limited by its processor to development use or for a small number of users of small applications.

8.3.2   9404 Models

The 9404 is the middle size AS/400. The three models are the F10, F20, and F25. The largest storage size is 72MB or 80MB, in conjunction with the faster processor, this system is suitable for many departmental sized applications. The 9404 can be plugged into a standard wall outlet, which makes it functional for office environments. The box that the 9404 models are packaged in is only a little larger than that of the F0x models and resembles that of the S/36 series.

All of the 9404 models have two separate I/O busses. This provides for generous expansion including large amounts of DASD (up to 15GB). These models are frequently seen as front-end processors for larger systems, but are also used for large single-user applications. In general, an F25 is suitable for complex applications with up to fifty users.

8.3.3   9406 Models

The 9406 is the largest size AS/400. The models are comprised of one or more rack enclosures. The components of the system you request are packaged into standard racks. System expansion is accomplished by adding new components to an existing rack or by adding additional racks to a system. Seven predefined racks are available to design your initial system. These include a System Unit rack, the System Unit Expansion rack, the Bus Expansion rack, the General Purpose I/O rack, two different DASD racks, plus the I/O Card Expansion rack.

The smallest models can be fit into a single rack, while larger systems can cover many racks. In general, the 9406 models require a controlled environment, and benefit from a UPS system. These systems are suitable for the largest applications, including those considered the domain of so called *mainframe* systems. Thus, large applications with upwards of 1000 users are considered feasible for the larger AS/400 systems.

8.3.4   Capacity

The different models of the AS/400 each have a different capacity
for work. We discussed some of the typical uses of the various
processor groups above. The range in processing capacity from the
small F02 to the largest F95 is more than thirty to one. The F95
includes four processors which greatly increases the number of
users and the total amount of work. And, the range in DASD sizes
is more than one hundred to one.

It is difficult to make general statements about which processor
model or configuration is suitable for a given application. However,
IBM has performed extensive benchmarks and provides relative
capacity figures. These values can be used to project the transaction volume and number of users that a given system can support
and the capacity increase for system expansion if the equivalent
values for your current environment are known. Refer to the IBM
manual *AS/400: Product Specifications* (SA41-9983) for tables on
the relative processor, bus, main memory, and auxiliary storage
capacities of the different AS/400 models.

Part

C

Software Capabilities

Part C takes a detailed look at the OS/400 operating system management tools, programming languages, and subsystem capabilities. The material covered is intended to be useful for operations, systems programming, applications, and even end users. Our emphasis is on OS/400 batch support, with online and distributed processing covered in Part D.

Chapter 9, Workload Scheduling, looks at workload management and automated job scheduling. Chapters 10 and 11 explain the Command Language and the AS/400 programming language capabilities. Finally, Chapter 12 provides information on AFP printing.

9

Workload Scheduling

9.1 Job Scheduling Tools

This chapter looks at the workload scheduling and system automation capabilities of OS/400. Some of these facilities are discussed in detail in other chapters of this book and will just be briefly mentioned here.

9.1.1 Operational Assistant

One important recurring system maintenance issue with OS/400 is managing journals and logs. Left alone, these files will gradually fill all available auxiliary storage. In any production environment, it is a requirement to periodically archive and/or purge such files. The Operational Assistant automates this process. This is described fully in Chapter 22.

9.1.2 Managing Available Disk Space

In order to run any unit of work, it is important to first ensure that adequate auxiliary storage (disk space) is available. Needless to say, if you encounter cases where your important work runs for three hours and then fails because of a lack of disk space, you will soon wish to develop a method to ensure that the space needed is available *before* starting the work. Fortunately, OS/400 includes a tool to easily analyze available space. This tool is provided from the DISKTASKS menu (simply key go disktasks from any command line). You should perform this process on a regular basis. The frequency of use is determined based upon your workload, and should be just often enough to prevent problems. In a busy environment this could mean weekly use, while more typical systems can manage with monthly usage.

The DISKTASKS menu gives you a choice as to frequency. Select option 1 to display the job scheduling menu. This display may be manually accessed via the RTVDSKINF command. You have three options for performing the data collection function:

- Specific date/time of collection. Select 1 and specify the desired date and time (key * CURRENT for the current date/time). The job name will be QEZDKSPDT.

- Weekly collection. Select 2 and specify the day and time during each week that collection is to be performed. The job name will be QEZDKWKMTH.

- Monthly collection. Select 3 and specify the day of the week, the week position, and the time for collection. The job name will be QEZDKWKMTH.

Note that the job submitted cannot gather data on objects that are in use. Thus, you should ensure that the disk information is gathered during a low use period. Because it can take several hours to analyze a large system, this can be difficult. Large systems may have to settle for monthly execution if the necessary idle period is not available during each week. In especially complex environments, you may have to manually select the idle period for data collection based upon your knowledge of the system. The first collection option is provided for such cases. Whenever possible, periodic automated disk space usage collection is encouraged.

Figure 9.1 is an example of a portion of a disk space usage report. The percent of library and size columns are zero for objects found to be in use or damaged objects. Such objects occupy space that is not reported upon. Damaged objects should be repaired, replaced, or deleted. You should gather data when the system is idle to ensure that the minimum possible number of objects are active.

```
              Disk Space Report
        Library and Objects Information
 Library/                   % of      Size in    Last      Last
 Object    Type    Owner    Library   1000 Bytes Change    Use       Description

 QDOC      *LIB    FARLEY             122.7      10/03/91  01/24/92  My Library
 ODDATA    *FLR             00.00     00.0                           LOCKED
 EVEDATA   *FLR             00.00     00.0                           DAMAGED
```

Figure 9.1   Disk Space Usage Report

The OS/400 system job scheduling facility is used to manage the disk space information gathering jobs. The job names used are QEZDKSPDT for specified date/time and QEZDKWKMTH for the weekly/monthly jobs. These names should not be used for your own work, and you should not alter them using the job scheduler.

Once data has been collected, you can generate reports at various different levels. The generation of reports can take a great deal of time, but does not need to be scheduled when the system is otherwise idle. The system summary information should also be produced. Based upon what is seen in this, other reports may also be desirable. These reports can be used to identify what is using up your available disk space. Automatically producing these reports does not correct any shortage conditions. However, they can be used to determine if your production can be run in the available space. You will need to take action to regain space required for your production work.

9.2 Job Submission

You can run AS/400 jobs on demand or at a designated date/time in the future when you submit them. Enter the SBMJOB command and press F4 (Prompt). Next, on the Submit Job display, enter into the *Command to run* field the command you wish to run as a batch job. To run a program, you type CALL followed by the program name. Thus, CALL PAYROLL will run the program named payroll as a batch job. If you wish to run a CL command, simply enter the name of the command. In order to enter parameters associated with your CL command, press F4 after entering the name of the CL command to receive the command prompt screen. When you press the Enter key, the command is submitted as a batch job.

To have the command submitted at a future date/time, provide the Schedule Date (SCDDATE) and Schedule Time (SCDTIME) parameters of the SBMJOB command. When these parameters are omitted (as above), the job is submitted immediately, otherwise the command is submitted at the designated date and time.

The SCDDATE parameter supports the following options:

- * CURRENT is the current date (this is the default).

- * MON - * SUN is the next occurrence of the day named.

- * MONTHSTR is the start of the month (first day).

- * MONTHEND is the end of the month (last day).

The SCDTIME parameter supports * CURRENT (the default) for the current time, or any specific time value as hh:mm:ss. When the time is specified, the colon may vary based upon the current system separator character specification.

Once submitted for a future time, the job status will show as * Scheduled until the designated date/time, when it will change to * Released. The SBMJOB command is used to submit a job once. In order to run a job repeatedly, we use the job scheduler.

9.3 Job Scheduler

The AS/400 supports a built-in job scheduler. The job scheduler is fully documented within the *AS/400: Operator's Guide* manual. The job schedule (CQDFTJOBSCD) is managed using a series of panels we will look at in this section. The job schedule can be globally managed from the Work with Job Schedule Entries display. The WRKJOBSCDE command accesses this control screen, from which all of the individual functions may be easily selected. The functions available for existing entries are Change, Hold, Remove, Display, and Release. New entries may also be added.

9.3.1 Creating Job Schedule Entries

You can add entries to the job schedule using the ADDJOBSCDE command. You can also get to this screen via F6 (add) from the work with job schedule entries display. Enter the job specifications

```
                      Work with Job Schedule Entries    SYSTEM01
                                                 01/10/92 15:20:21
Type options, press Enter.
2=Change        3=Hold      4=Remove      5=Display details    6=Release
8=Work with last submission               10=Submit immediately

                                                                   Next
                           -----Schedule------        Recovery   Submit
Opt  Job         Status    Date       Time     Frequency  Action   Date
 __  TEST        SCD       12/12/99   14:47:05 *ONCE   *SBMRLS   12/12/99
 __  QEZDKWKMTH  SCD       *FRI       10:00:00 *WEEKLY *NOSBM    01/17/92
 __  SAVE        SCD       *ALL       02:20:00 *WEEKLY *NOSBM    01/11/92
 __  RESTORE     SCD       *ALL       02:10:00 *WEEKLY *NOSBM    01/11/92


                                                            Bottom
     Parameters or command
===>  _____
```

Figure 9.2   WRKJOBSCDE Panel

(date, time, frequency). By default, a job will be scheduled to run once, at which point the job entry will be deleted. If you want to preserve a job schedule entry that specifies ONCE, provide the *Yes for the SAVE parameter on the ADDJOBSCDE command. Job schedule entries that specify weekly or monthly as their frequency are automatically saved by the job scheduler.

Note that even when a job is scheduled, it may not run. In order for a scheduled job to actually run, you must ensure that the job queue is allocated, it is not held, and the maximum jobs are not already active. If a job you schedule does not run, look at each of these areas and fix the problem. Once the problem is corrected, the job will automatically run.

9.3.2   Updating the Job Schedule

To change an existing job schedule entry, use the Change Job Schedule command (CHGJOBSCDE) or select option 2 (Change) from the WRKJOBSCDE screen. Note that changes made affect future executions of the job but do not alter any already submitted. If the job has already been submitted, you may end it via the WRKUSRJOB command, then manually reschedule it.

You may Hold a job schedule entry via option 3 (Hold) from the WRKJOBSCDE screen or via the Hold Job Schedule Entry (HLDJOBSCDE) command. When the date/time to schedule the job arrives, the entry is ignored. If the Hold option is specified *after* the job has been scheduled, it has no effect until the next date/time arrives. Use the WRKUSRJOB command to affect jobs that are already scheduled.

Once a job schedule entry is held, the job will not be submitted until the entry is released. To release a held job schedule entry, use option 6 (Release) from the CHGJOBSCDE screen or issue the RLSJOBSCDE command. If a schedule entry is released after its date/time has arrived, the previously held jobs are not submitted, but a warning message is produced indicating that jobs were missed. If the release is performed before the date/time arrives, then the job will be scheduled normally.

9.3.3 Removing Job Schedule Entries

You can remove a job schedule entry from the WRKJOBSCDE panel or via the RMVJOBSCDE command. If the job in question is already submitted and you do not wish it to run, you must end it manually via the WRKUSRJOB command.

To delete the scheduler definition, use option 4 (Remove) from the WRKJOBSCDE panel and select the desired line in the display. With the RMVJOBSCDE command, specify the desired entry to be removed as a parameter. Once it is removed, you will have to reenter the schedule command to restore it.

Chapter

10

Control Language

This chapter looks at the Control Language (CL) of OS/400. *Control Language* (referred to as simply *CL*) is used to define commands. CL is used for both IBM supplied commands as well as user commands. The purpose of this chapter is to illustrate certain CL features of use to the AS/400 system administrator. To accomplish this task, we look at a number of CL features in some detail, as well as several of examples of CL programs. However, this chapter is not intended to teach the programming of CL commands. Refer to the IBM manuals *AS/400 Programming: Control Language Programmer's Guide* and *AS/400 Programming: Control Language Reference* for a complete discussion of the use of CL.

10.1 Altering Supplied CL Commands

Many of the commands provided with OS/400 are written in CL. One of the most powerful tailoring options for the AS/400 programmer is to alter or extend the supplied commands. Alterations can consist of relatively simple modifications to default parameters, the addition of environment specific security checks, or even major changes in command syntax. We will discuss examples of each of these types of modifications, so that you will be able to make similar changes with confidence. In each case, you are encouraged to place your altered command in your own library located ahead of QSYS in the system search chain. Doing so preserves the original command definitions as well as ensures that future system maintenance does not overlay your own customized CL commands.

You may use the SEU utility to create your customized command files, or any other utility that can produce a file type compatible with the CRTCMD command. SEU is the standard OS/400 source entry utility, and is preferred for CL editing because it supports an integrated CL syntax checker. The CRTCMD command is used to create a command object. CRTCMD reads the command definition statements from its input file, validates and compiles the command, and writes the command definition object to its output file. You may execute CRTCMD in either batch or interactive mode. The command objects created by CRTCMD may also be executed in either batch or interactive mode.

10.2   CL Command Performance

Because CL commands are compiled, their execution is relatively fast. Specifically, CL command execution is much faster than REXX execution on the AS/400. This is a result of REXX being interpreted as well as the AS/400 having an especially poorly performing REXX implementation. CL is usually preferred over REXX because AS/400 users must learn CL, while knowledge of REXX is optional. Why learn two languages when one will do just fine?

10.3   Validity Checking

The system performs some automatic validity checking for all commands. However, it is not unusual to require additional validity checking beyond what the system does by default. You may include your own validity checking logic in the command source or you may package the validity checking separate from the command and specify the name of the validity checking program when CRTCMD is executed via the VLDCKR parameter.

When you are altering existing commands to add environment specific security or validity checking, it can be advantageous to do this through a separate validity checking program. In this case, the original command remains unaltered, and your new command object is output by CRTCMD when the original command source is processed in combination with your validity checking program. Note that any user of the command must have read authority for the library containing your version of the command object as well as any validity checking program object. It is best to place the validity checking object in the same library as the command object if this is feasible.

The validity checking program need not exist when CRTCMD is executed, but must be available in order to execute the associated command. If *LIBL is specified as the library qualifier, then the validity checking program may reside anyplace within the library list, otherwise it must occupy the same library as the associated command. A single validity checking program may be shared by several CL programs, so long as the parameters to be checked are identical for each of these programs.

All parameters of the associated command are passed to the validity checking program exactly as they were passed to the command. Note that a validity checking program is only invoked after all parameters of the command have passed syntax checking. This simplifies the task of the program. Refer to Figure 10.1 for an example of a validity checking program which uses the DCL command to define the variable PARM01.

```
PGM PARM(&PARM01)
DCL VAR(&PARM01) TYPE(*CHAR) LEN(8)
IF COND(&PARM01 *EQ 'ERROR' ) THEN(DO)
SNDPGMMSG MSGID(CPD0006) MSGF(QCPFMSG) +
        MSGDTA(' 0000 diagnostic message from user +
        validity checker for invalid PARM01' ) +
        MSGTYPE(*DIAG)
SNDPGMMSG MSGID(CPD0002) MSGF(QCPFMSG) MSGTYPE(*ESCAPE)
```

Figure 10.1 Validity Checking CL Program

10.4 CL Program Components

As indicated earlier, CL is a programming language. Although it is a procedural language (one where the programmer determines the logic flow), CL programs are made up of various pieces. In this section we look at the role of each of the parts of a CL program in the order these parts are normally encountered. We look at examples of simple programs using the various CL components and finish with a look at a few working CL programs.

10.4.1 PGM Command

The PGM command is optional. It is used to define the start of a CL program and identify any parameters received when the program is invoked. We suggest that you always provide a PGM command for each CL program. You should also include with this PGM command a comment that briefly describes the purpose of the command. If you use revision logs in your business applications, you should also include comments documenting the date and reasons for recent changes to the CL program. Revision logs are generally a good idea even in a single-person shop as even the best CL programmer often forgets what was changed last. They are usually mandated in larger shops to coordinate work between individuals, as well as to ensure that problem determination can be easily done.

10.4.2 DCL Command

The DCL command is required whenever a CL program uses variables. The DCL command is otherwise omitted. It is used to declare all variables used by a CL program. Declare each variable name referenced by a CL program along with its type.

If no variables are used by a CL program, then the DCL command is not needed. Our simplest example (see Figure 10.2) does not include a DCL command as it uses no variables. Refer to Figure 10.1 for an example of a validity checking program which uses the DCL command to define the variable PARM01.

10.4.3 CL Processing Commands

A CL program may contain calls to other CL programs. This may be done by simply using the CL program name as a command. Many CL commands are provided for the purpose of facilitating the writing of CL programs. Examples of such commands are CALL, RETURN, and OVRDBF. Some commands can only be used within

CL programs and are otherwise invalid. Some examples include CHGVAR, TFRCTL, PGM, and ENDPGM.

Some CL commands may not themselves be used within CL programs. These commands are documented in the CL reference manual. The CL reference manual contains detailed documentation on all IBM supplied commands.

10.4.4 Logic Control Commands

Any procedural language requires a means of determining the flow of program logic. The *logic control commands* allow the CL programmer to test data, conditionally perform statements, and loop to repeat sections of a CL program. Examples of such commands are IF, THEN, ELSE, DO, ENDDO, and GOTO.

The IF/THEN/ELSE construct provides a mechanism to test a relational expression and to perform a different command for success or failure of the test. The operand of THEN and ELSE may be a single CL statement. However, note that DO/ENDDO may be used with a THEN or ELSE clause to conditionally perform a block of commands. Refer to the THEN(DO) block in Figure 10.1 for an example of conditionalization of a block of commands.

10.4.5 Built-in Functions

The CL built-in functions provide character and numeric manipulation capabilities and are used within arithmetic, logical, and relational expressions. The command language built-in functions include %SUBSTRING, %BINARY, and %SWITCH.

The built-in function %SUBSTRING (abbreviated as %SST) is used to access a substring of an existing character string. The substring function may be used anyplace in a CL program that a character string may be used. Thus, you may code the command CHGVAR &TGT %SST(&SRC 4 8) to place character positions four through thirteen of &SRC into &TGT.

The built-in function %BINARY (abbreviated as %BIN) is used to manipulate 2- and 4-character values as binary numbers. Use %BIN in conjunction with the CHGVAR command to read or alter binary data. Thus, the command CHGVAR &DEC %BIN(&CHAR) treats the character variable &CHAR as a binary value which is in turn assigned as a decimal value to the &DEC variable. And, the CL command CHGVAR %BIN(&CHAR) &DEC converts the decimal value in the variable &DEC into a binary number which is then stored within the character variable named &CHAR.

10.4.6 Program Call Commands

The *Program Call Commands* allow the CL programmer to pass control to other programs, including other CL programs. The CALL and RETURN commands are used to invoke another program then return to the statement after the invoking call. The TFRCTL command is used to simply transfer to another program with no return possible.

One of the simplest types of CL programs consists only of calls to other CL programs. This type of grouping simplifies scheduling and reduces the chance of errors. Thus, if you frequently need to run CL program ONE followed by another CL program named TWO, then you can create a command called BOTH that calls these two programs then exits. Refer to Figure 10.2 for an example of such a program.

```
PGM   /* this program calls ONE then TWO */
CALL PGM(ONE)
CALL PGM(TWO)
ENDPGM   /* end of program BOTH */
```

Figure 10.2 CALL Sample CL Program

10.4.7 End Program

The ENDPGM command is optional. It is used to end a control language program. Our example above (refer to Figure 10.2) used the ENDPGM statement to improve readability. If the ENDPGM statement is not used, the physical end of the CL source file marks the end of the program. Although this command serves no purpose, we suggest that you always code the ENDPGM statement to improve the readability and maintainability of your own CL programs.

10.5 Predefined Values

OS/400 makes much use of predefined values (or reserved terms with a built-in meaning). In CL all predefined values are identified by a leading asterisk. Thus, *PGM and *LIBL are each predefined values. Although the most common predefined values are those used for operands, some predefined values are used by CL as operators in expressions. Examples include *EQ and *AND. In CL, predefined values perform much the same function as do the reserved words in other languages.

The predefined value term *N has a special meaning of a null parameter, and is treated like a zero length string. CL sets the value of omitted parameters to *N. When the value of a variable is *N when its program is run, the value is treated as a null. Note that *N is different from a numeric zero.

10.6 CL Command Names

All CL commands have names in the form of verb + object. All commands have a spelled out descriptive command name as well as the short command name you use to invoke the command. IBM uses a standard set of verb names of three characters and object names also usually of three characters so that command names are consistent.

The same verb name is used with all of the object names to which it applies. A given verb will usually apply only to a subset of all possible objects. Different verbs may be valid for different sets of objects. The common or important verbs include:

- ADD adds definitions or entries

- CLR clears queues, libraries, and members

- CPY copies information

- CRT specifies attributes and creates an object

- CHG changes the contents or attributes of an object

- DLT deletes an object

- DSP displays the contents of an object

- EDT edits data

- END ends actions or data

- PRT prints objects

- RMV removes objects

- RNM renames objects

- RTV retrieves data

- STR starts a process

- WRK works with the attributes or contents of an object

The verbs are applied to an object. Thus, for a class, the commands to create, display, and delete are CRTCLS, DSPCLS, and DLTCLS. And for objects some of the available commands are CRTOBJ, CHGOBJD, and WRKOBJ, to create, change, and work with objects. Object names are usually three-character abbreviations but may be prefixed with a modifier that further describes the type of object. Thus, the command CRTCLPGM creates a CL program. (CL is the modifier of the object type program.)   And, the command STRPGMMNU is used to start a programmer menu.

Less consistency occurs in the names used for objects and modifiers, but several common ones are worth looking at. In any case, you should attempt to develop and follow standards for your own names. Some common IBM object names and ones you are encouraged to follow are:

- AUT is a security/authority modifier

- CLPGM refers to a CL program

- CLS refers to a class

- CMD refers to a command

- CTL refers to a controller

- DEV refers to a device

- DOC refers to a document

- DTA refers to data

- DTAQ refers to a data queue

- JOB refers to a job

- JRN refers to a journal

- LIB refers to a library

- MOD is a mode modifier

- MSGF refers to a message file

- MSGQ refers to a message queue

- NAM is a name modifier

- OBJ refers to an object

- PGM refers to a program

- SYS refers to the system

Programming Languages/SAA

This chapter looks at the languages supported by the OS/400 operating system. The position of the AS/400 in the IBM System Application Architecture (SAA) is discussed as are all of the SAA languages supported by the AS/400. The issue of POSIX compliance is analyzed. The curious predominance of RPG/400 is discussed.

Before we begin, let us note that the AS/400 was a follow on for the popular S/38 midrange computer. As such, much of the AS/400 language support and system philosophy comes directly from the S/38. Examples of this include the AS/400 SEU and RPG which were based directly on the S/38 facilities as well as the Control Language philosophy.

11.1 System Application Architecture (SAA)

The *System Application Architecture (SAA)* was developed by IBM to ensure interoperability and portability of applications across the entire line of IBM computers from ES/9000 mainframes through midsize systems such as the AS/400 down to desktop PCs. SAA defines common communications (via APPC), command programming (via REXX), user interfaces (on graphics terminals and PCs), and application development languages (including C, RPG, COBOL, FORTRAN, and PL/I).

SAA is viewed by many as the last major initiative on IBM's part before it lost dominance of the computer industry. SAA was an attempt to provide alternatives to the open system initiatives that came into being in the late 1980s and early 1990s. As such, SAA is a failure. However, SAA does help ensure that applications developed for one IBM system can be more easily ported to other IBM systems. It also helps in the creation of IBM system-based client/server applications.

11.2 Source Entry Utility (SEU)

The *Source Entry Utility* (*SEU*) is the standard text entry tool on the AS/400. It is used to create program source members for essentially all AS/400 supported languages. SEU is a full screen editor allowing lines of a member to be copied, moved, inserted, changed, or deleted. It also supports the usual search commands of other IBM editors.

SEU goes beyond conventional IBM editors in that it contains prompters for languages that offer online access to help on language syntax and usage. SEU also contains an interactive syntax checker that detects many common programming errors before a compiler is invoked. This additional support is provided for some of the AS/400 high-level languages as well as for the Command Language.

In spite of its benefits, SEU is an older technology editor more suitable to the late 1970s than the 1990s (in fact SEU comes from the old S/38 facility). It is usually far easier to prepare program source using your favorite PC editor and upload it to the AS/400 than it is to use SEU. The one exception is RPG program source where the SEU prompter and syntax checker are a real asset.

11.3 CL

The AS/400 Control Language (CL) is not a general purpose programming language. However, it is a very powerful Command List (or CLIST) language and is extensively used by IBM and users of the AS/400 system. Because most supplied IBM commands are written in CL, the general AS/400 user who wants to tailor the system soon learns CL. CL is compiled (using CRTCMD) so its performance is better than most other CLIST type languages.

IBM mainframe operating systems use a *Job Control Language (JCL)*. Mainframe JCL languages control batch job execution and contain limited conditional capabilities to alter the job flow based upon runtime conditions and user parameters. CL performs most of the functions of mainframe JCL, but is generally much more powerful. Although sometimes cumbersome, especially for string parsing, CL can even be used for simple programming. CL is described in some detail in its own chapter (refer to Chapter 10), so it will not be further discussed here.

11.4 RPG

RPG (an acronym for *Report Program Generator*) is an old language dating back into the 60s. Once nearly dead, RPG is the standard applications development language for the AS/400. How can this be? RPG is relatively easy for beginning programmers to learn, and yet particularly well suited to report generation tasks. Existing mainframe RPG programs are easily ported to the AS/400 as are S/38 RPG programs. The many S/38 customers who migrated to the AS/400 generally moved their existing RPG applications, and maintained RPG as their principal application development language. Also, RPG as implemented on the AS/400 is a much enhanced language with powerful database access capabilities as well as excellent integration with the OS/400 operating system. The performance of RPG programs on the AS/400 is usually far better than that of any other language.

RPG is an SAA language. However, the SAA RPG is a subset of the full AS/400 implementation. Generally, the issue of portability of RPG applications is outweighed by the ability/desire to use the AS/400 unique RPG facilities. One major area of incompatibility of SAA RPG and the full AS/400 RPG is the SAA specification's lack of the database interface including the commit and rollback commands as well as the keyed file extensions.

Note that the RPG language is not generally available on any open systems implementation including UNIX. If you may wish to move your applications to a UNIX platform in the future then RPG is a poor choice for applications development. Even where RPG is available on other platforms, programmers familiar with it are not generally available outside of the AS/400 community.

RPG source programs are entered using the SEU utility. SEU fully supports automatic syntax checking and online reference for

RPG programs, and its use is a good idea for the old fixed format RPG. The newer RPG FREE (free format RPG) is more readable and is generally encouraged. To compile your RPG source program and create an executable use the CRTRPGPGM command.

11.5 COBOL

COBOL was the standard business programming language for most computer systems until recently, when higher level languages and development environments integrated with databases have begun to supplant some of its traditional uses. The COBOL implementation on the AS/400 is fairly good, although it does lack the mainframe VS COBOL II extensions. This lack can complicate porting of mainframe COBOL applications. You should consider defining standards that preclude the use of the mainframe extensions for any applications you may wish to port to the AS/400 in the future. CICS/400 only supports COBOL for command level transaction development, so if you are considering the use of CICS/400 you will be using COBOL for your online applications.

COBOL is a frequently used language especially for porting and downsizing of mainframe applications. The high availability and relatively low cost of COBOL programmers and of COBOL applications indicate that COBOL will be an important language well into the future for business systems in general, and the AS/400 in particular. You should consider the use of COBOL in addition to, or in place of, RPG as your standard applications development language. The AS/400 RPG language is not generally portable to other platforms, and programmers who know RPG are difficult to find for any other platform. However, you should note that COBOL performance on the AS/400 often falls well short of that of RPG, especially when a lot of external calls are used in the COBOL program. This performance impact is especially visible for entry level AS/400 systems but can be an important factor for large batch applications on any AS/400 model.

Enter COBOL source programs using the SEU utility with a type of CBL. The CBL type specification enables full SEU syntax checking as well as online reference to COBOL information. IBM supplies a prototype file named QCBLSRC you can use or copy to hold your COBOL source programs. Use the CRTCBLPGM command to compile your source program into an executable object.

11.6 PL/I

PL/I is an IBM language popularized in the 1970s for engineering work. PL/I was also adopted by a few mainframe shops for business programming. The AS/400 has a complete PL/I implementation. The AS/400 PL/I is little used and performs fairly poorly. Its principal use is in porting S/38 and mainframe PL/I applications to facilitate downsizing.   The benefits of porting existing PL/I applications must be weighed against the issue of limited availability of PL/I programmers, especially PL/I programmers familiar with the AS/400 as well as the limited future for this language.

You enter PL/I programs using your favorite text editor (SEU can even be used for this).   The default location for PL/I source members is QPLISRC. Use the CL command CRTPLIPGM to compile the PL/I source.   If the source is not a member of QPLISRC, use the SRCFILE parameter to specify the name and location of the source file member.   CRTPLIPGM compiles the program outputting an object. The compiled object can be executed like any other program.

The AS/400 PL/I is significantly extended in comparison to the S/38 PL/I implementation. Portability of S/38 PL/I applications is ensured through a compatibility option that directly supports the more limited S/38 PL/I compiler subset. The CL command CALL QCL enters the S/38 compatible environment. PL/I programs entered and executed in this mode operate as though they are run on a S/38.

11.7 PASCAL

PASCAL is a language developed to teach structured programming to computer science students by Niklaus Wirth at the technical university of Zurich. It is a high-level language with strong typing and excellent diagnostics. PASCAL originally was only used in the university environment but was popularized by the Borland Turbo PASCAL implementations for a whole generation of programmers. As a result, PASCAL is widely known and is used on many platforms. The AS/400 PASCAL implementation meets the ANSI83 PASCAL standard, but includes some IBM extensions to the language. Note that AS/400 PASCAL is little used although it can be useful in porting PC applications.

You enter PASCAL programs using your favorite text editor. SEU can be used for PASCAL source. The default type for PASCAL programs is PAS. When a file in QPASSRC is edited, the PAS type is assumed by SEU. No syntax editor is provided for PASCAL so no benefit exists from using SEU beyond the default program typing.

Use the CL command CRTPASPGM to compile the PASCAL source. If the source is not a member of QPASSRC, use the SRCFILE parameter to specify the name and location of the source file member. CRTPASPGM compiles the program outputting an object. The compiled object can be executed like any other program.

11.8 FORTRAN/400

FORTRAN is one of the oldest computer languages supported by the AS/400. The name *FORTRAN* is actually an acronym for *FORmula TRANslator*. FORTRAN is still frequently used for numerical processing and engineering work. The AS/400 implementation is based upon the FORTRAN 77 as well as the SAA FORTRAN standards. A number of extensions provide support for AS/400 datatypes and system facilities.

A sample source file named QFTNSRC is placed in the QGPL library when FORTRAN/400 is installed. You can use this for your source or better yet copy it to a file in your own library using the CRTDUPOBJ command. Use a source member type of FTN for your FORTRAN programs. Using a type of FTN ensures that SEU will perform FORTRAN specific syntax checks as well as present FORTRAN reference information via the SEU index search function.

The FORTRAN syntax is not similar to that of modern languages, and can be especially difficult for business programmers to learn. FORTRAN does not support good diagnostics which complicates debugging. It also is ill-suited for character string processing. However, FORTRAN is supported by essentially every computer system, and FORTRAN applications are usually easily ported to other platforms.

If the primary use for your AS/400 is business data processing, then FORTRAN will most likely not be used. One possible exception is in the area of decision support systems and statistical applications. Some of these systems make use of FORTRAN subroutine libraries. If this use is hidden from your staff, it is perfectly acceptable.

Most business programmers are not familiar with FORTRAN. You should avoid situations where you may have to maintain or modify existing FORTRAN applications. Do not accept *free* applications that use FORTRAN unless your staff is already familiar with the language. One exception to this rule is the case where the FORTRAN application must run on a variety of platforms, where only one is your AS/400. In this case, the portability of FORTRAN outweighs any support and management issues of the language.

11.9 BASIC

BASIC is another very old computer language. Like PASCAL, BASIC was created to teach computer programming in a university environment. Also like PASCAL, BASIC gained a following in the PC arena and is known by many programmers. AS/400 BASIC implements the language but it is little used and will not be discussed in any detail in this book.

11.10 C/400

C is a language developed by Bell Labs that has become the standard system development language for UNIX and PCs. C is generally accepted to be a key component of open systems, since most open system software is written in C. However, the IBM version of C for the AS/400 is an especially bad implementation from the standpoint of performance as well as that of usability. Essentially all OEM software that is developed in C is written using one of the non-IBM compilers. Very few customers use C for native AS/400 applications development, although more and more are porting standard applications from other environments to the AS/400 using C.

IBM has stated an intention of expanding the functionality and usability of their C compiler. Note that IBM does not currently offer a C++ implementation. This lack is serious as more and more portable applications are being developed using C++. The AS/400 is one of the few modern computer systems not supporting C++ at this time.

You use the CRTCPGM command to compile C source members. The resulting executable object can be run like any other program. Note that calling IBM C/400 programs from other languages is especially poorly performing and should be discouraged unless the program is invoked very few times or unless it is preinitialized. However, even preinitialized C programs perform very poorly when called by RPG or COBOL programs.

One case where C may be the language of choice for your environment is that of applications developed for UNIX that also must run on the AS/400. Although COBOL is also available for UNIX systems, many UNIX applications are written only in C. Also, applications involving complex data structures may be best written in C. If you have this situation, you should carefully benchmark the ported C application on your AS/400 as the performance of C applications is currently often poor in comparison to the original UNIX system.

11.11 REXX

REXX is a language developed by IBM and used as the command list language for IBM's SAA strategy. As such, REXX is available for mainframes, midsize computers such as the AS/400, as well as desktop PCs. Some platforms support REXX as both interpreted for speedy development as well as optionally compiled for improved performance. The AS/400 version of REXX is only available as an interpreter which impacts performance, and is an especially poorly performing implementation of the language.

REXX on the AS/400 is so poorly performing as to make it nearly useless on the smaller systems, and should not be used for frequently executed programs in general. The performance of REXX programs is best when the source type is REXX. In this case, the REXX interpreter saves a copy of the internal form of the program, which somewhat improves subsequent execution speed. Even in this case, REXX is a distant second in comparison to other AS/400 programming languages and is best used for one time only tasks or where REXX language portability is important. One recent benchmark of a simple REXX program that issued a CL command and displayed the output ran 28 seconds while a C version of the same program completed in about 16 seconds on an F02 system.

Although faster systems reduce the relative performance factor, REXX as currently implemented is the slowest way to solve any task across the entire AS/400 family.

Because Command Language (CL) can be used to perform most of the usual REXX CLIST type tasks, and because users must know CL anyway, many AS/400 users tend not to bother learning REXX. Of course, CL is also compiled and runs far far faster than REXX. Some OEM products do exploit REXX, primarily because of its portability across IBM platforms.

REXX members reside in QREXSRC by default and may be entered using any available system text editor. Although SEU may be used to enter the source for REXX programs, it does not contain support for either REXX prompting or syntax checking, so little benefit exists for using the cumbersome SEU. Users often find it easier to create REXX source programs on a PC, then move them to the AS/400 via PC support.

What is AFP, and what is it good for? *AFP* is an acronym for *Advanced Function Printing*. Advanced function printing is a facility that allows programs to print text and images on a printer in graphics mode. AFP output is accomplished using the *All Points Addressable* (*APA*) printer feature. AFP is not required to print the various fonts built into your printer on a page, but is required to support downloaded fonts. AFP is also required to include graphic images such as logos, line art, and half tone pictures.

12.1 AFP at a Glance

Let us start by looking at what AFP does, then move on to answering the question "When and why do I need to use AFP?" In this section we look at the features AFP provides, as well as the hardware and software setup required to use AFP. In the next section we look at business requirements for AFP by answering a brief questionnaire.

AFP printing supports:

- Printing form overlays (the printer file OVERLAY keyword)

- Printing boxes or lines in any position on the page

- Printing logos or images in any position on the page

● Printing downloadable fonts

To use AFP,

1. select a printer capable of printing IPDS data streams;

2. change the printer device description to AFP(*YES);

3. have forms created as an overlay object (via an OEM vendor or AFP utility, only needed for forms creations); change or override the printer file in your program to specify the overlay;

4. increase the amount of memory for the printer spool writer by 3MB (three megabytes).

12.2   AFP Key Issues

AFP is not a single thing. Instead it is a facility that solves a number of problems, and is supported by hardware with a wide range of functionality. To determine whether you need AFP, and which AFP features are needed, answer the following questions:

● Will the printer resident fonts or the AS/400 compatibility fonts be adequate? **No.** Install AFP Fonts/400 (5738-FNT).

● Will images, logos, or creation of forms overlay be needed? **Yes.** Install AFP Utilities/400 (5738AF1) or an OEM vendor product such as FORMS XPRESS.

● Is a 3816 printer fast enough for the anticipated print volume? **No.** Install 382X or 383X printers.

● Will it take longer to print non-AFP reports on an AFP printer? **Yes.** Change the printer file device to DEVTYPE(*AFPDS). This will eliminate one conversion step for each file defined as DEVTYPE(*IPDS) and two conversion steps for each file defined as DEVTYPE(*SCS).

- Will copying or displaying of an AFP spool file be needed? **Yes**. Sorry, your normal display and copy spool file commands will not work on AFP data streams.

12.3   Important AFP Printing References

The information required to effectively use AFP is spread throughout a number of manuals. This book gathers together much of this information. You may also wish to reference the following:

- *Guide to Programming for Printing* SC41-8194

- *About Type: IBM's Technical Reference for 240-Pel Digitized Type* S544-3516. The newest version of the manual is harder to use than Version 2 (Third Edition, July, 1989). This manual is very important as it assists in deciding on the character set, coded font, and code page name for the fonts you will be using.

12.4   Printer File Keywords

All printed output is associated with a *printer file*. The printer file defines keywords that control the printing process. The following are the AFP related printer file keywords:

- **DEVTYPE(*AFPDS)** This must be specified to use any of the following: FRONTMGN,   BACKMGN,   FRONTOVL, BACKOVL, FNTCHRSET, CDEFNT, and IGCCDEFNT. Note that an *AFPDS Spool file cannot be displayed or copied.

- **PAGRTT(*AUTO, *DEVD, *COR, 0, 90, 180, 270)** Overlay rotation is determined at creation time, not by the PAGRTT keyword. This parameter only affects text orientation. On the 3831 and 3835 when printing in landscape mode (horizontal on the paper), rotation is in the counterclockwise direction instead of the usual clockwise direction.

- **FIDELITY(*ABSOLUTE, *CONTENT)** Code * CONTENT to allow printing to automatically continue after errors are found. If a specified font is not available, a font substitution occurs. Code * ABSOLUTE to have printing stop when errors are found. Font substitution is not performed in this case.

- **FRONTOVL & BACKOVL** Contain the name of the object and the offset down and across for printing the front and back side of the page. The offset is in *Units Of Measure* (abbreviated as UOM) and is a quantity of either Inches or CMs. Use the offset to position the overlay to a different point on the page.

- **FRONTMGN & BACKMGN(*DEVD,0,NNNN)** Define offset down and across printed text in the UOM on the printed page.

- **UOM(*INCH,*CM)** Specifies that the Units Of Measure are either inches or centimeters.

- **FNTCHRSET(*FONT, [Font Character Set, Code Page])** Specifies a downloadable font consisting of a character set and code page. Using this parameter causes downloading of the font to a printer. The printer must support the downloadable font feature.

- **CDEFNT(*FNTCHRSET, Coded Font Name)** Specifies a downloadable font. Using this parameter causes downloading of the font to any download capable printer.

- **FONT(*CPI, *DEVD, [FGID, Point Size])** Specifies the font identifier and point size to be used with the printer file. If FNTCHRSET or CDEFNT is not specified, then this parameter determines the font to be used for printers supporting printer resident fonts. If the font identifier is not supported on the printer, then font substitution occurs if the FIDELITY keyword is *CONTENT. For printers that only use host resident fonts such as 3831 and 3835, font substitution also occurs if the FIDELITY keyword is *CONTENT.

12.5   Issues Concerning 3831 and 3835 Printers

When creating the printer device description, use F1C10110 for the form definition (FORMDF) keyword. The recommended setup for 3835 is to not allow RPM (the Remote Print Manager) to notify the AS/400 printer writer of intervention-required conditions at the printer. These conditions occur at end of form or for a stacker error. In such cases, the printer sounds an alarm and the RPM program displays the following message: *Operator intervention is required at the printer.*

To allow RPM to notify the AS/400 about intervention-required conditions, specify the RPM inactivity parameter. The RPM inactivity parameter value is a number of seconds, and must be set to a value less than 9999. This is the number of seconds that elapse before a message is sent to the AS/400. Currently, the result on the AS/400 could be a *device not available* message or a cancel writer performed by the system. Clearly, canceling the writer usually is not what is desired. Even if the AS/400 generates the correct error message, your response to the message may give you unexpected results if any of the spool files are in a "PRT" status.

12.6   Understanding "PRT" Status

When a report has finished printing on the 3835, it goes to "PRT" status. This status means that the last page of the report has passed the print head but it is not currently in the stacker. It will remain in "PRT" status until the 3835 notifies the AS/400 that the report is in the stacker. This notification is only done when the printer is not actively printing. Therefore, the last report remains in "PRT" status until one of the following actions occurs at the AS/400:

- The printer writer is canceled. This should be a control cancel so that the AS/400 can cause an NPRO function on the 3835. An immediate cancel will cause the spool file output to go to "RDY" status, which would cause the report to reprint the next time the writer is started for that output queue.

- The printer writer is changed to a different output queue or form type.

- The print request timer expires (specified via the PRTRQSTMR keyword on the CRTDEVPRT command). This causes an NPRO function on the 3835. If you do a manual NPRO function on the 3835, the AS/400 will not be notified until the print request timer expires. If this value is *nomax, the spool file will remain in "PRT" status until the writer is either canceled or changed or a new report is printed.

As of OS/400 Version 2 Release 2, IBM software does not directly support HP printers as AFP capable. If you want to use your HP printer as an AFP printer, you must buy an OEM interface to make the HP printer look like an IPDS printer to the AS/400. OEM vendor products such as FORMS XPRESS also allow you to create forms for HP printers (these are not standard AFP Forms), then merge the data from a spool file and print it on your HP printers. This function is not an AFP data stream and does not support multiple font changes in the spool file.

12.7   AFP Printing Data Flow

When a program generates a spool file, the device type parameter determines the format of the data (*SCS, *IPDS, *AFPDS). For AFP (* NO) devices, if the type of the spool data is different from the actual printer, the printer writer converts SCS data streams to IPDS format during the printing process. * AFPDS data streams cannot be sent to non-AFP devices. For AFP (* YES) devices, the spool file data is converted to IPDS format before it is passed to the PDJ job. PDJ performs the actual printing on the device.

AS/400 Output Queue

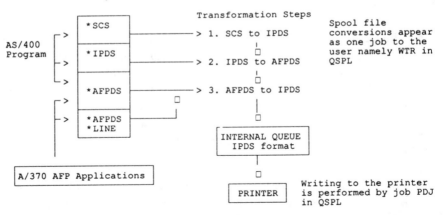

Figure 12.1   AFP Printing Data Flow

If the spool file is in IPDS format, it must be first converted to AFPDS, then back to IPDS. When the writer converts the spool file, the file has a status of PND. It stays in PND status until PDJ starts printing the spool file. Spool file parameter PRTCVT(*YES) allows PDJ to start printing before it has completed conversion.

12.8   Boxes, Lines, and Font Changes Using DDS

Normally, preprinted forms are created as overlays and added to the print file so that the system can merge the overlay data and the program data at print time. For the example in Figure 12.2, we have added boxes and line commands to demonstrate the capability of DDS. Only the font change commands are normally found in the DDS source. Images, page segments, lines and boxes are included in an overlay object which can be specified with the overlay keywords in DDS or on the create printer file command.

```
         COMPANY NAME
         COMPANY ADDRESS
         COMPANY CITY STATE


12345 ITEM DESCRIPTION      1   $25.60    $25.60
12345 ITEM DESCRIPTION      2   $25.60    $51.20
12345 ITEM DESCRIPTION      3   $25.60    $76.80
12345 ITEM DESCRIPTION      4   $25.60    $102.40
12345 ITEM DESCRIPTION      5   $25.60    $128.00
12345 ITEM DESCRIPTION      6   $25.60    $153.60
12345 ITEM DESCRIPTION      7   $25.60    $179.20
12345 ITEM DESCRIPTION      8   $25.60    $204.80
12345 ITEM DESCRIPTION      9   $25.60    $230.40
```

Figure 12.2   Using DDS with a complex form

```
CRTPRTF    FILE(MYLIB/AFPDDS) SRCFILE(MYLIB/AFPDDS) DEVTYPE(*AFPDS) +
           FNTCHRSET(COSOPR12 T1VI0037) FRONTMGN(0 .5)
```

A	R TOPBOX			BOX(1.0 0.5 10.0 7.0 .03)
A				BOX(1.2 0.7 4.0 6.8 .02)
A	R LINE			LINE(4.5 1.0 6.0 *HRZ .01)
A				LINE(5.0 1.0 6.0 *HRZ .01)
A				LINE(5.5 1.0 6.0 *HRZ .01)
A				LINE(6.0 1.0 6.0 *HRZ .01)
A				LINE(6.5 1.0 6.0 *HRZ .01)
A				LINE(7.0 1.0 6.0 *HRZ .01)
A				LINE(7.5 1.0 6.0 *HRZ .01)
A				LINE(8.0 1.0 6.0 *HRZ .01)
A				LINE(8.5 1.0 6.0 *HRZ .01)
A	R HEAD			
A	NAME	35		POSITION(2.0 2.0)
A	ADDR	35		POSITION(2.2 2.0)
A	CITYST	35		POSITION(2.4 2.0)
A	R DETLIN			
A	ITEMNO	5		POSITION(&LN 1.0)
A	ITEM	35		POSITION(&LN 1.5)
A				FNTCHRSET(COD0GR10 T1V10037)
A	QTY	5	0	POSITION(&LN 4.0)
A				EDTWRD(' 0')
A	COST	9	2	POSITION(&LN 4.5)
A				EDTWRD(' $0. ')
A	XCOST	9	2	POSITION(&LN 5.5)
A				EDTWRD(' $0. ')
A				CDEFNT(X0GBE1)
A	LN	5	3P	

```
Default font will be COSOPR12 (Prestige 9 point 12 pitch)
ITEM font will be COD0GR10 (Gothic Reverse 10 point 10 pitch)
XCOST font will be X0GBE1 (Gothic Bold 9 point 12 pitch) same as COD0GB12
     with code page T1V10037
```

Figure 12.3   DDS Source for AFP Printing

The FRONTMGN keyword moves the printed data one half inch to the right. The default font or *CPI value is very important for alignment of data if the position keywords are not specified in the DDS source. In this example (Figure 12.3), the absolute position is determined by adding the margin to the position specified.

12.9   Understanding AFP Resources

The following are objects (resources) needed to perform Advanced Function Printing (AFP):

● Form Definition

● Font

```
FAFDDS  O   E                         PRINTER
I                ' COMPANY NAME          ' C        CO
I                ' COMPANY ADDRESS       ' C        COADR
I                ' COMPANY CITY STATE    ' C        COCITY
I                ' ITEM DESCRIPTION      ' C        ITEMDS
C                  WRITETOPBOX
C                  WRITELINE
C                  MOVELCO              NAME
C                  MOVELCOADR           ADDR
C                  MOVELCOCITY          CITYST
C                  WRITEHEAD
C                  Z-ADD4.3             LN
C        LOOP      TAG
C                  MOVEL' 12345'        ITEMNO
C                  MOVELITEMDS          ITEM
C                  ADD  1               QTY
C                  Z-ADD25.60           COST
C        COST      MULT QTY             XCOST
C                  WRITEDETLIN
C                  ADD  .5              LN
C        LN        CABLT8.5             LOOP
C                  SETON                            LR
```

Figure 12.4 RPG Source for AFP Printing

- Overlay

- Page Definition

- Page Segment

Resource objects contain data and control information that can be used in a print job and that can be shared by different pages and different print data sets. Thus, a form definition or overlay can be applied to each page in a print job. And, once fonts are defined, they can be used on all associated pages until they are replaced or reset. One advantage to resource objects is that they need only be maintained in a single place. When the resource object is updated, then all subsequent output that references it will receive the new object definition. It is a good idea to track all print jobs that use a given resource object to ensure that changes to the object definition do not result in surprises.

12.10   Form Definitions

A form definition defines the position of a page on a form, modifications applied to the form, number of copies of each page, and the modifications that apply to each set of copies. Refer to Figure 12.5

for an example of a form definition. The form definitions in this
example are provided with the AS/400 system in library QSYS.

Name	Across (Inches)	Down (inches)	Presentation	Direction	Bin	Duplex
F1A10110	1/6	1/6	Portrait	Across	1	No
F1A10111	1/6	1/6	Portrait	Across	1	Yes
F1A10112	1/6	1/6	Portrait	Across	1	Tumble
F1A10120	1/6	1/6	Portrait	Across	2	No
F1A10121	1/6	1/6	Portrait	Across	2	Yes
F1A10122	1/6	1/6	Portrait	Across	2	Tumble
F1C10110	1/6	1/6	Landscape	Down	1	No
F10101PA	0	1/2	Portrait	Across	1	No
F10101PD	0	1/2	Portrait	Down	1	No
F10101LA	0	1/2	Landscape	Across	1	No
F10101LD	0	1/2	Landscape	Down	1	No
F1OGL	0	0	Portrait	Across	1	No

Figure 12.5   AS/400 Form Definitions

12.11   Fonts

Fonts are a collection of characters of the same type family, style,
weight, and point size (one point = 1/72 in.). Each character in a
font is identified by a 1-byte or 2-byte code. The structure of fonts
depends on whether the font is for a phonetic writing system
(English), or for a nonphonetic writing system (Kanji).

Example: Courier=Family, Roman=Style, Medium=Weight, 8pt=Size

At least two resources are needed to make up a font: a font
character set and a code page. A third resource, the coded font, is
a special resource type that combines the functionality of the first
two resources to define a font by naming the font character set and
the associated code page. See Figure 12.6 for an example.

Fonts can be fixed-pitch (uniformly spaced) or variable-pitch
(proportionally spaced). The naming convention for uniformly
spaced fonts is AFO0YYYY (the fields are explained in Figure 12.7).
Uniformly spaced fonts are also referred to as *mono-space* fonts.

Type Family	Courier						
Typeface	Roman					Italic	
	Medium	Double wide	Bold	Over strike	Extended	Medium	Double Wide
Type Size	8 pt	8 pt	8 pt			8 pt	8 pt
	9 pt		9 pt		9 pt	9 pt	
	10 pt		10 pt	10 pt	10 pt	10 pt	

Figure 12.6   Example: Courier Font

12.12   Font Character Sets

The *font character set* resource contains the raster patterns for all characters in the font. The resource associates an 8-byte character identifier with each pattern. It provides descriptive information for the entire character set. Each character set contains the characters (letters, digits, punctuation marks, or other symbols) of a single type family, typeface, and size. A character set also specifies the individual character properties (such as bold or italic) and printing attributes (such as space around each character).

Character sets can be stored in three different formats: PMF export format, Bounded-box format, and Unbounded-box format. The AS/400 only supports the Bounded-box format. This format can be used for all combinations of character rotation and text orientation. The S/370 supports all formats. If you have created an Unbounded-box format font on the S/370, it cannot be directly used by the AS/400. If you would like to use it on your AS/400, PMF on the host will allow you to recreate the font in a Bounded box format. This new font can be copied to tape and loaded on the AS/400. Use the CRTFNTRSC command on the AS/400 to convert the file to an AS/400 font resource.

12.13   Code Page

The *code page* resource associates code points with character identifiers. Each character identifier represents a character raster

A = Component	C Character Set G Character group T Code page X Coded font
F = Format or Orientation	Bounded-Box Format 0 Coded Font 0 Character set 1 Character group 1 Code page

	Unbounded-Box Format or PMF Export Format
	1 Character group
	1 Code page
	Coded Font and Print Character
	Character Set Direction Rotation
	    1 Across 0
	    2 Down 0
	    4 Up 0
	    5 Across 90
	    6 Down 90
	    8 Up 90
	    9 Across 180
	    A Down 180
	    C Up 180
	    D Across 270
	    E Down 270
	    G Up 270

O = Original Font	D DCF Release 2 fonts L Library character set (LCS) S 6670 fonts X Reserved for User Y Reserved for User
0 = Reserved Character	
YYYY = Traditional Name	Four characters indicating type family, typeface, and pitch of font
C0S0CB15	Courier Roman Bold 15 pitch 8 points
T1V10037	Code page Canada, United States
X0CR01	Coded Font C0S0CB15 and T1V10037

Figure 12.7   Fonts Naming Conventions

pattern. A *code point* is an 8-bit binary number representing one of the 256 potential characters available in each code page.

12.14   Coded Font

The *coded font* resource associates one or more code pages with the appropriate font character sets. Note that each of the regular, italic, and bold versions of a character set represents a different font. If you require three fonts, each with the bold and regular forms of characters, you will have a total of six fonts.

12.15   Font Global Identifiers (FGID)

Another method of naming a font is by FGID or font id. The FGID identifies the type family and typeface. FGIDs are used in printers that have support for fonts. Examples include the 5219, 3812, 3816, 4028, 4224, 4230, and 4234. A FGID is a numeric value, where each different numeric value identifies a specific typeface. For example, 86 is Prestige Italic, 12 pitch, and 111 is Prestige Bold, 12 pitch.

12.16   Downloadable Fonts

Downloadable fonts are host resident fonts that are downloaded to the printer prior to printing. The following AS/400 printers support downloadable fonts: 3812, 3816, 4028, 3820, 3825, 3827, 3835. A printer may not support all available downloadable fonts. Each font is loaded into printer memory, so enough memory must be available in the printer for the fonts that are required to be loaded for a given document before that document can be output by a specific printer.

12.17   Host Resident vs. Printer Resident Fonts

The AS/400 only supports host resident fonts for the 382X and 383X families of printers. Both host resident fonts and printer resident fonts are supported for 3812, 3816, and 4028. When printing to a printer with resident fonts, and a font id (FGID) that is not resident on the printer is encountered, the system will substitute a printer resident font only if the printer file fidelity parameter is set to *content. If you specify a code font or character set plus code page in your print data stream, the system will download the font to all downloadable printers if the fidelity parameter is set to *content.

12.18   AS/400 Compatibility Fonts

The AS/400 system comes with a number of basic fonts. Only the basic fonts can be assumed to be present on every AS/400 system.

The following font families are provided with the standard AS/400 operating system:

APL
Boldface
Courier
Document
Essay
Format
Gothic
Orator
Prestige
Proprinter Emulation
Roman
Script
Serif
Symbol Set
Text

12.19   AFP Fonts/400 (5738-FNT)

The Advanced Function Printing Fonts/400 product adds additional fonts to the basic support provided with the AS/400. Included in this package are the following fonts:

Sonoran Serif
Sonoran Serif Headliner
Sonoran Sans Serif
Sonoran Sans Serif Headliner
Sonoran Sans Serif Condensed
Sonoran Sans Serif Expanded
Monotype Garamond
Century Schoolbook
Pi and Specials
ITC Souvenir
ITC Avant Garde Gothic
Mathematics and Science
Optical Character Recognition (OCR-A and OCR-B)
DATA1
APL2

Before using these additional fonts, you should determine whether files exploiting them will need to be passed to other systems. Any system receiving/processing a file must support the fonts required for that file. This is a consideration for off-site backup as well as for distributed printing. It is also a consideration when mainframe files are passed to an AS/400 for printing, as well as for AS/400 files passed to a mainframe for subsequent processing. Note that both fonts and other graphics resources such as logos and forms definitions require this type of planning.

12.20   240 and 300 Pel Fonts

Advanced Function Printing Fonts/400 and the compatibility mode fonts are all 240 pel (picture elements an inch) fonts. The pel value is the same as the printer resolution, which is also referred to as DPI (dots per inch). Thus, the 240 pel fonts are compatible with all 240 DPI printers. Other printers with different resolutions require their own fonts. The 4028 is a 300 pel printer requiring its own set of fonts.

If a file is generated for printing on a 240 pel printer, but your backup site only has a 300 pel printer, then you must have both sets of fonts available. Likewise, if a report is distributed into two different areas, one with a 240 pel printer and the other with a 300 pel printer, both sets of fonts are required.

12.21   Page Segments

Page segments are objects containing both composed text and graphics images. Page segments are prepared before formatting and included during printing. One example of a page segment would be a company logo.

12.22   Overlays

Overlays are a collection of predefined data including lines, shading, text, boxes, and logos that can be merged with variable data during printing. An example of the use of an overlay would be for a preprinted form.

The use of overlays can dramatically reduce the amount of processing (and data) required to produce a given report. One example would be an invoice, where only a few hundred characters of text vary and perhaps 98 percent of the output stream data is comprised of lines and other graphics that can be repeated from the form definition. In such cases the use of overlays saves both large amounts of CPU time as well as the bulk of the storage space for output queue elements.

12.23   Page Definitions

Page definitions are resources that format and compose line data into pages. They contain printing controls to specify the following:

- Where data from each input record is to be printed

- Page size (height and width)

- Data fields that can be suppressed

- Page data records containing carriage-control characters

- In-line printing direction

- Number of lines per inch

- List of page segments that may be used

- List of overlays that may be used

- Record definitions

- Constant data to be printed

- List of fonts that may be used

Using multiple page definitions, a single set of data can be output in a variety of different report formats. Without the page definition, no report can be produced. Needless to say, the page definitions for a report are as critical for off-site backup processing as the data in the report and the programs that create the report.

Part

D

OS/400 Online, Interactive, and Distributed

Part D looks at the OS/400 support for online and distributed processing. We emphasize the role of the AS/400 in networks, but also look at the types of mainframe systems that your AS/400 may communicate with. For this purpose, we briefly look at mainframe subsystems including VTAM and CICS. We take an in-depth look at the AS/400 support for distributed processing in a separate chapter.

The VTAM chapter is of particular interest to mainframe staff that are downsizing to an AS/400, or to AS/400 staff who need to define communications with a mainframe system. The VTAM definitions required for AS/400 communications with CICS are discussed in the Communications and VTAM chapters (Chapters 13 and 18). Chapter 17, CICS, discusses both CICS/400 capabilities as well as the roles/functionality of the implementation of CICS for other operating system platforms.

13

Communications

This chapter looks at the communications capabilities of the AS/400. We look at intra-system and inter-system communications. We discuss what APPC and APPN accomplish, and contrast them with mainframe communications capabilities. We discuss how networks of AS/400 systems are defined and managed. Later chapters in this portion of the book discuss PC Support, CICS support, communications with mainframe systems through VTAM, as well as distributed processing in a more general fashion.

The VTAM chapter (Chapter 18) is of particular interest to mainframe staff who are downsizing to an AS/400, or to AS/400 staff who need to define communications with a mainframe system. The VTAM definitions required for AS/400 communications with CICS are also discussed in the VTAM chapter. The CICS chapter (Chapter 17) discusses both CICS/400 capabilities as well as the roles/functionality of CICS for other operating system platforms.

13.1 Intersystem Communications Function (ICF)

The AS/400 provides several methods for jobs to communicate with each other. The *Intersystem Communications Function (ICF)* allows two programs, running in different jobs to communicate with each other. ICF provides a communication vehicle for application programs to exchange information using different protocols and communication architectures between computer systems, be they additional AS/400 systems, mainframe computers, other midsize computers, or desktop systems.

Although designed for communication between systems, ICF also supports *intrasystems communication*. Intrasystems communication allows two programs to communicate while running in the same machine. This is great for testing program to program communication. ICF is often used to debug a program on a single computer that will later be used to communicate between separate computer systems. One advantage of testing programs using ICF on a single system is that no line and controller descriptions are required. Another advantage is that less hardware need be dedicated to development and testing of applications.

ICF allows the application programmer to write a program without regard to the communication protocol. ICF supports the following communication protocols:

- Asynchronous Communication

- Binary Synchronous Communication

- Synchronous Data Link Communication

It also supports the following aspects of Systems Network Architecture (SNA):

- Systems Network Architecture Upline Facility (SNUF)

- Advanced Program-to-Program Communications (APPC)

Refer to Figure 13.1 for an example where Program A communicates with Program B using ICF. This communication is through a special ICF file. The advantage of the ICF file is that the programmer communicates via standard reads and writes to the ICF file rather than via complex communications verbs such as are used by APPC. In our example, Program A and Program B use the same device description. Both programs communicate through *program devices* tied to the same device description. Instead of creating a line description, controller description, and device description, you create a special program device description.

An ICF file is created by the command Create ICF File (CRTICFF). All of the fields and keywords are defined using Data Description Specifications (DDS). DDS is used by the system to define the fields in a data base, display screen formats, printer files as well as communication files.

A single ICF file can communicate with multiple systems or devices. The MAXPGMDEV parameter of the CRTICFF command determines the maximum number of devices that an ICF file can communicate with at any given time.

You create each program device description via the CRTDEVINTR command and alter it via the CHGDEVINTR command. A single program device may be used for several sessions, even where the separate sessions are used for communications with multiple different programs. To tie the program devices to the special device description, an Add ICF Device Entry (ADDICFDEVE) command must be issued specifying the program device name (PGMDEV), remote location name (RMTLOCNAME), and the device description name (DEV) keywords.

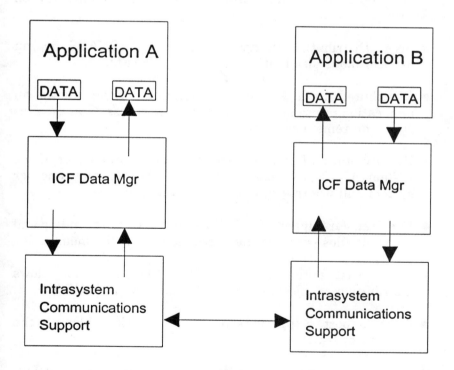

Figure 13.1   Intrasystem Communications Facility

Once testing of applications on a single system is completed, the line, controller and device descriptions must be created on the appropriate production system. Issue a CHGICFDEVE or an ADDICFDEVE to point the program devices to the correct device description.

13.2   APPC/APPN

Included in the AS/400 base operating system (OS/400) is support for both Advanced Program-to-Program Communication (APPC) and Advanced Peer-to-Peer Networking (APPN). APPC is an implementation of IBM SNA LU 6.2 and node 2.1 communication architecture. APPN extends the APPC architecture by providing automatic routing and connection through multiple systems. Also included in the base operating system are the following communication services:

- SNA Distribution Services (SNADS). SNADS is an asynchronous distribution service used for EMAIL.

- Distributed Data Management (DDM). DDM allows an application program or an online user to access database files stored on remote systems.

- Display Station Passthru. This function allows a user of one system (AS/400, System/36 or System/38) to sign on to another system and use that system's data and programs.

- File Transfer Support (FTS). This function allows sending and receiving files with automatic creation of the file member.

- Object Distribution Facility (ODF). This function allows distribution of objects through the network via SNADS.

- Alert Support. Supports reporting of network problems to the network operator.

- Management Services. Provides problem management, performance and accounting management, change management, and configuration management services for the SNA network manager.

In addition to these system services, your application may exploit APPC/APPN for inter-program communication to implement a client/server application or environment. Note that an AS/400 is capable of high-level autonomous network management. AS/400 systems offer better network management functionality than most mainframe environments. This is a result of the robust APPN implementation offered with OS/400. Many mainframe systems still require tedious, manual definition of each network node, and are intolerant of dynamic changes to the network topology. On the other hand, an AS/400 system permits dynamic alteration of the network, and recovers from the failure of network components that might crash a mainframe system.

13.2.1   APPN

The AS/400 APPN implementation is a step beyond the old mainframe node type 2.1 architecture. APPN allows a peer system to participate in a network without the need for a host as a traffic focal point. With APPN, all nodes appear to be logically adjacent, even where no direct physical connection exists. And, APPN networks can be linked such that the network node directory and routing service are available between nodes.

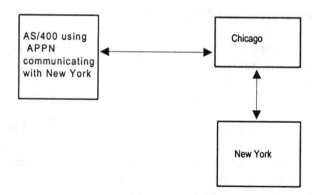

Figure 13.2   APPN Network

The ability to support direct inter-node communications without regard to node adjacency is one of the most powerful extensions of APPN. This means that the details of the network topology are not required to be defined to each intermediate node involved in a transfer. Mainframe VTAM systems often require a full time systems staff member solely to manage the VTAM and NCP definitions. Also, these older communications systems could easily support communications in one direction, but not in the reverse direction, due to the need to precisely define not only the topology of the network, but often the direction of communications. Thus, in Figure 13.2 it is possible for a mainframe system to communicate from Los Angeles to New York through Chicago, but for a communication from New York to Los Angeles to fail because of the network definition inside Chicago. APPN is not subject to such problems, so all possible routings are supported when this diagram represents AS/400 systems.

APPN allows the best path between nodes to be dynamically chosen. This can lead to better performance for APPN, without the need for a dedicated network performance management staff member. It also allows APPN to automatically respond to errors in communications between two nodes, and to reroute around them. This dynamic pathing extends between two networks, because one APPN network can access the nodes inside another network, without requiring that a detailed definition of that network be locally maintained.

13.2.2   Peer-to-Peer File Transfer

The AS/400 frequently offers many different methods to accomplish the same task; file transfer between the AS/400 is not an exception. The following is a list of the different methods in the order of easiest and least flexible to the fastest and most flexible.

- The QY2FTML program supports the sending and receiving of a file member to a remote system. The user ID must exist on the remote system. The large number of parameters can complicate use of this program. Creating a command interface to it can allow easier access and use. See Figure 13.3 for a sample command source interface to QY2FTML.

- The SNDNETF command is the most common method of sending and receiving objects or file member(s) between remote systems. To send multiple objects, the objects are saved in a save file (*SAVF) object which is transmitted to the

```
0001.00  XFER:    CMD       PROMPT('Transfer Physical File Member')
0002.00           PARM      KWD(OPTION) TYPE(*CHAR) LEN(1) RSTD(*YES) +
0003.00                     VALUES(S R) MIN(1) PROMPT('FTS option to +
0004.00                     perform.')
0005.00           PARM      KWD(FROMLIB) TYPE(*NAME) LEN(10) MIN(1) +
0006.00                     PROMPT('From Library')
0007.00           PARM      KWD(FROMFILE) TYPE(*NAME) LEN(10) MIN(1) +
0008.00                     PROMPT('From File')
0009.00           PARM      KWD(FROMMBR) TYPE(*NAME) LEN(10) MIN(1) +
0010.00                     PROMPT('From Member')
0011.00           PARM      KWD(TYPE) TYPE(*CHAR) LEN(6) RSTD(*YES) +
0012.00                     DFT('      ') VALUES('      ') MAX(1) +
0013.00                     CHOICE('Must be blank')
0014.00           PARM      KWD(TOLIB) TYPE(*NAME) LEN(10) PROMPT('To +
0015.00                     Library')
0016.00           PARM      KWD(TOFILE) TYPE(*NAME) LEN(10) PROMPT('To +
0017.00                     File')
0018.00           PARM      KWD(TOMBR) TYPE(*NAME) LEN(10) PROMPT('To +
0019.00                     Member')
0020.00           PARM      KWD(TODATE) TYPE(*CHAR) LEN(6) RSTD(*YES) +
0021.00                     DFT('      ') VALUES('      ') MAX(1) +
0022.00                     CHOICE('Must be blank')
0023.00           PARM      KWD(REPLACE) TYPE(*CHAR) LEN(1) RSTD(*YES) +
0024.00                     DFT(N) VALUES(Y N) PROMPT('Replace Member +
0025.00                     on target sys?')
0026.00           PARM      KWD(RMTLOCNAME) TYPE(*CHAR) LEN(8) +
0027.00                     DFT(RMTSYS) PROMPT('Remote Location Name')
0028.00           PARM      KWD(PASSWORD) TYPE(*CHAR) LEN(10) +
0029.00                     DSPINPUT(*NO) PROMPT('Password on the +
0030.00                     remote system.')
0031.00           PARM      KWD(RTNCODE) TYPE(*CHAR) LEN(1) +
0032.00                     CHOICE('Leave this parameter blank.') +
0033.00                     PROMPT('Return Code')
0034.00           PARM      KWD(MSGID) TYPE(*CHAR) LEN(8) +
0035.00                     CHOICE('Leave this parameter blank.') +
0036.00                     PROMPT('Error Message ID')
-----------------------------------------------------------------------
              Transfer Physical File Member (XFER)

Type choices, press Enter.

FTS option to perform. . . . . .  OPTION
From Library . . . . . . . . . .  FROMLIB      _
From File  . . . . . . . . . . .  FROMFILE     _____
From Member  . . . . . . . . . .  FROMMBR      _____
                                  TYPE         '        '
To Library . . . . . . . . . . .  TOLIB        _____
To File  . . . . . . . . . . . .  TOFILE       _____
To Member  . . . . . . . . . . .  TOMBR        _____
                                  TODATE       '        '
Replace Member on target sys?  .  REPLACE      N
Remote Location Name . . . . . .  RMTLOCNAME   RMTSYS__
Password on the remote system.    PASSWORD     _____
Return Code  . . . . . . . . . .  RTNCODE      _
Error Message ID . . . . . . . .  MSGID        _
```

Figure 13.3   XFER Command for QY2FTML File Transfer

remote system. Objects can be sent to any user ID on the remote system. SNADS must be running for the transmission to take place. If the system storage is greater than 90% full, SNADS will not attempt to transmit the object. Additional storage is required because the system copies the file to a temporary area for transmission. After a successful transmission of the file, the temporary area is deleted.

● An APPC program is the fastest method to transmit a file between two systems. Since this method requires a program to be written on both systems, most customers use one of the two methods listed above. Various OEM products are available that use APPC, large data blocks, as well as data compression for very fast file transfers. Examples of such high-end applications include XCOM and NDM.

To ensure the fastest transmission between systems, use the largest possible frame size for all methods. Be aware that moving large files always takes a lot of elapsed time and can saturate your available communications bandwidth and thus impact all other communications activity for the duration of the file transfer. Large file transfers are often performed in the evening when online system demands on communications are minimized.

13.3   PC Connectivity

The AS/400 supports various ways of attaching PCs. The following are areas of consideration when selecting the hardware/software connectivity options:

● Type of PC

● Amount of memory, type of memory (conventional, expanded, extended)

● Operating system for the PC (DOS, Windows, OS/2)

● Physical connection type (token ring, Ethernet, SDLC, asynchronous, or twinax)

● File transfer and direction (to PC, from PC)

● Control of the PC environment

● Numbers of users

- Printer support (type of printer)

- TSR program (program to stay in memory)

If you have control of the PC environment, PC Support/400 gives you the most flexibility and accesses the full functionality of the AS/400. PC Support provides communication handlers for 5250 terminal emulation support on token ring, Ethernet, SDLC, asynchronous, and local twinax physical connection types for the DOS operating system environment. For the OS/2 operating system, the Communication Manager supports 5250 terminal emulation.

One concern with PC Support/400 is that the base product requires a large amount of conventional memory. Extended PC Support helps alleviate this problem. Another problem is that TSR programs frequently do not run well with PC Support/400. Loading the PC Support/400 router first before any TSR program is loaded usually resolves this problem.

A third problem is the IBM default for the automatic creation of the token ring controller description connection for the PC is INLCNN(*DIAL). This default causes the AS/400 to attempt to establish communication connection when the controller is varied on or when the communication connection has been ended. If the user has rebooted the PC and then tries to restart PC Support, the initial connection may fail because the AS/400 is in a recovery mode. To alleviate the problem of putting the AS/400 system in recovery mode every time PC Support has been ended at the PC, change the controller description keyword INLCNN(*DIAL) to INLCNN(*ANS). To ensure that all new controller descriptions are created correctly, use the model controller support. To use the model controller support, the controller must have been created with the keyword MDLCTL(*YES), and be varied on to the same line that the PCs will be using to communicate with the system.

13.4   PC Support

First let us look at the hardware connection types. If a user is remote to the AS/400, the cheapest solution is to dial in from an asynchronous modem to an asynchronous modem attached to a protocol converter such as the IBM AS/400 ASCII Workstation Controller. The ASCII Workstation Controller provides multiple ports for dial-in or direct connections. Other vendors offer similar protocol converters that attach to communication lines and provide multiple dial-in ports.

PC Support provides a facility for asynchronous support, but because of the memory and setup requirements, many customers are looking for ASCII terminal support such as VT100 or VT102 emulation. VT100 is a Digital Equipment Corporation (DEC) VT series terminal with four function keys. We will discuss VT100 terminal support later in this chapter.

13.4.1   PC Support Connection Example

The following example discusses all of the equipment and software customization that is necessary for a PC to dial into an AS/400 using the ASCII workstation controller. We start by listing the requirements, then look at each one in more detail.

When using the IBM AS/400 ASCII Workstation Controller you will need the following:

● Special cable for modem hooked to the controller

● Special setup for modem on the controller

● Keyboard mapping template (PC Support)

13.4.2   Special Cable for Modem on the Controllers End

The ASCII workstation controller was designed to allow a PC to directly connect to the controller's port without a modem. This means that if a modem is used with the ASCII workstation controller, a special cable (called a null modem cable) is needed at the controller end. See Figure 13.4 for a layout of the pins. The following are the IBM part numbers:

IBM Part Number on Cable: 59X3833
IBM Part Number to Order: 69X7016

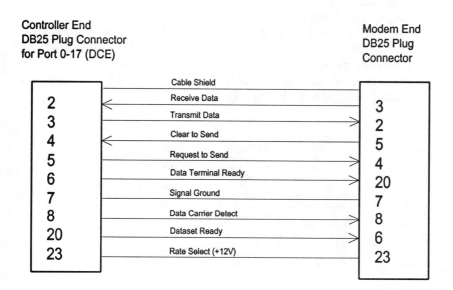

Controller End
DB25 Plug Connector
for Port 0-17 (DCE)

Modem End
DB25 Plug
Connector

2	Cable Shield	
3	Receive Data	3
4	Transmit Data	2
5	Clear to Send	5
6	Request to Send	4
7	Data Terminal Ready	20
8	Signal Ground	7
20	Data Carrier Detect	8
23	Dataset Ready	6
	Rate Select (+12V)	23

Figure 13.4   Special Cable for Modem and PTT Connection

13.4.3   Special Setup for Modems on the Controllers End

When attaching a modem to an ASCII Work Station Controller, if the modem speed is greater than 2400 baud, a special setup may be required for the modem.   See Appendix 3 in the *ASCII Work Station Reference and Example* (SA41-9922) for the various modem setup instructions.   Figure 13.5 contains the modem setup string instructions for a Hayes Smartmodem 9600 or Ultrasmart 9600 or for another totally Hayes compatible modem.

To load these instructions into the modem perform the following steps:

- Attach the modem to the PC using a standard PC serial cable.

- Load a communication program such as Smartcom or ProComm. If everything is connected correctly, the DTR light on the modem should be on once the communications program is initialized.

● Type in "ATZ" (all CAP) and press enter. If "OK" is not
displayed, then type "ATQ0." This enables result codes and
the "OK" should then appear. If you still have problems, check
the cable and the port definition that the communication
program is using. Once you can communicate with the
modem, then key in the command to program for auto-answer
operation (refer to Figure 13.5).

```
COMMAND      FUNCTION
AT&F         Retrieve the factory configuration
ATL2         Medium speaker volume (Default)
ATM1         Speaker on until carrier detected (Default)
AT&J0        RJ-11/RJ-41S/RS-45S Telco Jack (Default)
AT&L0        Dial up operation (Not supported by some modem)
AT&C1        Track presence of data carrier with carrier detect lead
AT&D2        Hang up on on-to-off transition of DTR
AT&S1        DSR operates according to EIA-232C
ATS0=1       Auto answer and answer on first ring
ATS36=3      Present constant speed interface
ATE0         Disable char echo
ATQ1         Disable result codes
AT&W         Store configuration
```

Figure 13.5   For Hayes Smartmodem 9600 or Ultrasmart 9600

For the Smartmodem 9600, remove the front cover of the modem
and move the strap to the Dumb position (modem attached to the
ASCII Work Station Controller end). For most other modern
modems, no physical setup of this type is required.

If you are using PC Support/400, you should use the AS/400 PC
Support menu to create the AS/400 definition for the device instead
of issuing the CRTDEVDSP command. To use PC Support, a user
ID must have already been added to the system directory of the
AS/400.

13.4.4   Creating the Device Definition for PC Support

Type GO PCSTSK to display the PC Support task menu (refer to
Figure 13.6). Option 21 allows you to enroll your users. Option 22
allows you to create/configure the device connection definitions used
for PC Support communications. You need to create a device
definition for every port to which you will be attaching a modem or
a device. Several users can sign-on to different ports, and you

should define as many ports as you anticipate having simultaneous
PC Support users.

```
PCSTSK                    PC Support Tasks

Select one of the following:
  User Tasks
    1. Copy PC Document to database
    .
  Administrator
    20. Work With PC Support administrators
    21. Enroll PC Support users
    22. Configure PC Connections

    30. Change keyboard and conversion table

Selection or command
===> 22_____

F3=Exit  F4=Prompt  F9=Retrieve  F12=Cancel F13=User support
F16=System main menu
```

Figure 13.6 GO PCSTSK, Option 22 Configure PC Connections

```
CFGPCS                    Configure PC Connections

Select one the following connection types:
    .
    .
    5. Asynchronous communication (ASYNC)
    .

Selection or command
===>5_____

F3=Exit  F4=Prompt  F9=Retrieve  F12=Cancel F13=User support
F16=System main menu
```

Figure 13.7 CFGPCS menu. Option 5 Asynchronous Communication

Take option 22 (Configure PC Connections) to select the connection type (refer to Figure 13.7). For token ring and Ethernet connections, the AS/400 will automatically create the controller and device description if the system value AUTOCFG has been set to 1.

```
                      Add PC to ASYNC Connection
 Type choices, press Enter.

    Device description . . PCSUPP____    Name
    Port number . . . . . 00            0-17
    Attachment type  . . . *MODEM       *DIRECT, *MODEM, *PTT
    Attached controller  . CTL02_____   Name, F4 for list
    Text . . . . . . . . . PC Support Modem Connection_____



    F3=Exit  F4=Prompt  F12=Cancel
```

Figure 13.8   Add PC to ASYNC Connection

For the ASCII workstation controller, select option 5 on the Configure PC Connections (CFGPCS) menu to display the ADD PC to ASYNC screen (refer to Figure 13.8).

On the Add PC to ASYNC screen, type:

PCSUPP   Name of the port (examples: PORT0, PORT1 or DIAL0, DIAL2, etc.). In our example, since one connection will be for PC Support and the other will be for VT100 emulation, the port name can simply be chosen to be PCSUPP.

00   Port number 00.

*MODEM   Modem connection.

CTL02   Name of the workstation controller. This example assumes the controller was created before starting this procedure by auto configuration at IPL time or by the CE when it was installed. Use WRKHDWRSC *LWS to determine the controller name.

Text   Description of the connection.

This menu creates a device description with TYPE(5250), LINESPEED(*CALC), WORDLEN(*CALC), PARITY(*CALC), STOPBITS(1). *CALC means that the system will determine the line speed, word length, and parity at connection time.

13.4.5 Add User to PC Support/System Directory

Before a user can use any of the PC Support/400 functions, that user must be added to the system directory. This is the same directory that OfficeVision/400 and SNADS use. If the user has enrolled in local OfficeVision office or was previously added to the directory with a WRKDIR command, then this step is not necessary. Before a user can be added to the directory, a user profile must already exist. To define a user, start with the PCSTSK menu (see Figure 13.9), and select option 21 to display the Enroll PC Support Users screen (see Figure 13.10).

```
PCSTSK            PC Support Tasks


Select one of the following:
 User Tasks
   1. Copy PC Document to database
    .
 Administrator
   20. Work With PC Support administrators
   21. Enroll PC Support users
   22. Configure PC Connections

   30. Change keyboard and conversion table

Selection or command
===> 21_

F3=Exit F4=Prompt F9=Retrieve F12=Cancel F13=User support
F16=System main menu
```

Figure 13.9 PCSTSK Menu, Option 21 Enroll PC Support Users

On the Enroll PC Support Users screen, type:

HUNTER   User Profile name of the user.

JOJO   User ID for user (this could be the User Profile name for an existing entry).

SYS01   SYS01 is the system name for the AS/400 on which
          this user is to be valid.

Text   A description of this user's directory entry.

```
              Enroll PC Support Users

  Type choices, press Enter.

      User profile . . . . . . HUNTER____    Name
      User identifier:
        User ID . . . . . . . JOJO____     Character value
        Address . . . . . . . SOS01___     Character value
      User description . . . . Jojo Hunter on Example One (1)
      AS/400 System_____

  F3=Exit  F12=Cancel
```

Figure 13.10   Add User to System Director

13.4.6   Installing PC Support on the PC

PC Support is menu-installed on the PC for any communication
type (see Figure 13.11). The installation process only loads the
minimum programs needed to start a PC Support session from the
PC to the AS/400. PC Support programs may need to be downloaded to run in the PC. This can be a long and time consuming
process when your connection is dial-up and even for some LAN
connections. Remote users should load all of the programs that PC
Support will need on to their system and customize PC Support to
use the hard disk instead of downloading these programs over the
communication channel. Be sure to copy the language directory for
PC Support when you copy from a local PC.

   If this PC will be running Windows, you may want to install PC
Support from the Windows RUN function of the File menu.
Otherwise you can later customize PC Support to use Windows with
the PC Support configuration program (CFGPCS). The PC Support
router must be started before Windows. Also, if Virtual Print will
be used, it should be started before Windows. Any program that is
started before Windows uses some conventional memory, which

```
┌─────────────────────────────────────────────────────────────────────┐
│                                                                       │
│        PC Support Installation                                        │
│                                                                       │
│  An installation form is provided to record the required information on│
│  and outline the steps needed to complete the installation program.  │
│  For more information, refer to the PC Support/400: DOS Installation and│
│  Administration Guide.                                                │
│                                                                       │
│                                                                       │
│  Select choices, press Enter.                                         │
│                                                                       │
│    Drive to contain PC Support directory . . . . . . [ C]             │
│                                                                       │
│    Drive your personal computer                                       │
│    starts from . . . . . . . . . . . . . . . . . . [ C]               │
│                                                                       │
│                                                                       │
│  ─────────────────────────────────────────────────────────────────── │
│  F3=Exit  F12=Cancel                                                  │
│                                                                       │
└─────────────────────────────────────────────────────────────────────┘
```

Figure 13.11   PC Support Installation, Part 1

may impact Windows or any programs that need a large amount of conventional memory. The Workstation Function should not be started prior to starting Windows. For additional information, see the PC Support and Windows section of this chapter. Refer to Figure 13.12 for automated startup options.

The PC Location Name should be unique to each PC. This is the name of the device that will be communicating with the AS/400. Different users can use a single PC to communicate to the AS/400 but the location name of the PC should not change. Refer to Figure 13.13 for the PC to AS/400 connection screen.

Choose the Line Speed and Communication Port based on the speed of the attached modem and the communication port location (see Figure 13.14).

13.4.7   PC Support and Windows

PC Support can be installed initially from Windows or it can be customized after installation for use under Windows via the PC Support configuration program (CFGPCS.EXE). To customize PC Support, run Windows after PC Support has already been loaded on the PC, load the PC Support Menu (PCSMENU), and select the

```
                PC Support Installation
                  (Startup Options)
                                  Move:
        Select options with the space bar.  Press Enter when finished.

        Start PC Support automatically. . . . .> 1. Yes
                                         2. No

        Reduce messages displayed
        when starting PC Support. . . . . . . .> 1. Yes
                                         2. No

        Initial PC Support menu . . . . . . . . 1. PC Support Menu
                                         2. Organizer menu
                                         3. OfficeVision/400 Menu
                                         4. AS/400 initial menu
                                       > 5. No menu (command prompt)
        PC Support functions to be
        started automatically . . . . . . . . . Virtual Printer
                                         Message Function
                                         Workstation Function

        Enter  Esc=Cancel  F1=Help  F3=Exit  Spacebar
```

Figure 13.12 PC Support Installation, Part 2

Configuration of PC Support option. Once the configuration program is loaded, select General options to display the Microsoft Windows options and select the appropriate function. For any configuration changes to take effect, the PC, PC Support, and Windows must all be restarted.

When PC Support is restarted, the PCSWIN program is loaded to protect the PC Support router from the multitasking activities of the Microsoft Windows programs. When Windows is restarted the PC Support group is created.

PC Support also provides a setup program in Windows (PCSSETUPW). This is a Windows application that sets up the necessary files on the PC to allow PC Support to run with Windows. Additional functions provided by this program are creation of the PC Support group, the installation or removal of the IBM AS/400 network driver, the installation or removal of the IBM AFPDS printer driver, and the installation of RUMBA/400 if the support is available on the AS/400.

```
                PC Support Installation
                (PC to AS/400 Connection)

Select choices, press Enter.

Connection Information
 Press spacebar to select connection type:
   1. Twinaxial
   2. Local Area Network
   3. Synchronous Data Link Control
 > 4. Asynchronous communications

PC Information
 PC location name. . . . . . . . . . . . . [PCSUP01      ]

System Information
 Name of system to connect to. . . . . . . [ SYS01 ]



Enter  Esc=Cancel  F1=Help  F3=Exit  Spacebar
```

Figure 13.13   PC Support Installation, Part 3

13.4.8   PC Support/400 Keyboard Mapping

When using PC Support/400 the default keyboard mapping for a
101-key keyboard is determined as seen in Figure 13.15.

13.5   VT100

VT100 support is the most common terminal emulation support
available on PCs today. Packages such as ProComm, Crosstalk,
Smartcom, and Windows Terminal are just a few of those that
support VT100 emulation. One major issue with using this support
is the requirement of customizing the keyboard mapping to perform
all available AS/400 functions. The AS/400 supports 24 function
keys while a real VT100 has only four function keys. Other
differences in the layout are created because some software
packages have keys that cannot be remapped. When the VT100

```
                Additional Connection Information

Select choices, press Enter.

Connect timer . . . . . . . . . [ 90]    (5 to 255 seconds)

Port number . . . . . . . . . .> 1. COM1
                                 2. COM2
                                 3. COM3
                                 4. COM4

Line speed . . . . . . . . . . . 1. 1200
                                 2. 2400
                                 3. 4800
                               > 4. 9600
                                 5. 19200



Enter  Esc=Cancel  F1=Help  F3=Exit  Spacebar
```

Figure 13.14   PC Support Installation, Part 4

keyboard mapping is configured to look like a real 5250 terminal keyboard, these nonmappable keys cannot be used. Instead, you must decide whether another key will be used for this function or if a multiple key sequence will have to be used. The second issue with VT100 support is that the AS/400 does not support file transfer with this package. A person could write a program on the AS/400 that would automatically perform this function, but at present no one has completed this task with adequate performance.
On CRTDEVDSP (see Figure 13.16), type:

VT100A   Name of the port (example PORT0, PORT1 or DIAL0, DIAL2, etc.). In this example, since one connection will be using PC Support and the other will be using VT100, this port will be named VT100A.

* LCL   For the local ASCII Workstation Controller.

AS/400 Function	PC Keyboard	AS/400 Function	PC Keyboard
ATTN (Attention)	ESC	F1	F1
Backspace	Backspace	F2	F2
Cursor Up	↑	F3	F3
Cursor Down	↓	F4	F4
Cursor Left	←	F5	F5
Cursor Right	→	F6	F6
Cent (¢)	Shift 6	F7	F7
Delete	Delete	F8	F8
Duplicate	Shift Insert	F9	F9
Enter	Enter	F10	F10
Erase EOF	Right Ctrl	F11	F11
Erase Input	Alt End	F12	F12
Error Reset	Left Ctrl	F13	Shift F1
Field +	Pad+	F14	Shift F2
Field -	Pad-	F15	Shift F3
Field Exit	Right Ctrl	F16	Shift F4
End of Line	Alt Pad6	F17	Shift F5
Help	Scroll Lock	F18	Shift F6
Home	Home	F19	Shift F7
Insert	Insert	F20	Shift F8
New Line	Shift Enter	F21	Shift F9
HEX mode	Alt F7	F22	Shift F10
Hot-key Sequence	Alt ESC	F23	Shift F11
Print PC Side	Print Screen	F24	Shift F12
Immediate Reset	Alt Scroll Lock	Print Host Side	Shift Print Screen
Not (¬) Symbol	[	Page Up (Roll Down)	Page Up
Vertical Bar (¦)	Shift backslash (\ )	Page Down (Roll Up)	Page Down
Vertical bar (¦)	]	Clear	Pause
Shift Lock	Alt Caps Lock	System Request	Alt Print Screen
Test Request	Alt Pause		
Cursor Fast Down	Alt ↓	Cursor Fast Left	Alt ←
Cursor Fast Up	Alt ↑	Cursor Fast Right	Alt →

Figure 13.15   5250 Keyboard Mapping Using PC Support

V100   VT100 Device emulation. *CALC is not supported for VT100 device emulation.

```
          Create Device Desc (Display) (CRTDEVDSP)

Type choices, press Enter.

Device description . . . . . VT100A      Name
Device class . . . . . . . . *LCL      *LCL, *RMT, *VRT
Device type . . . . . . . . V100       3101,3151,3161,3162..
Device model . . . . . . . . *ASCII     0, 1, 2, 4, 11, 12, 23..




F3=Exit F4=Prompt F5=Refresh F10=Additional params F12=Cancel
```

Figure 13.16   CRTDEVDSP Part 1

*ASCII   Device model is an ASCII device.

Press Enter to have the definition take effect.

The CRTDEVDSP screen will be redisplayed with additional parameters (see Figure 13.17). Provide this additional data:

05   Port number 05.

*MODEM   Modem connection.

CTL02   Name of the workstation controller. This example assumes the controller was created before starting this procedure. The workstation controller is normally created by auto configuration at IPL time or by the CE when the workstation controller is installed. Use the WRKHDWRSC *LWS command to determine the controller name.

9600   Line speed should be the maximum the Workstation modem supports. If the modem you are using for dial-in is slower, the system will automatically switch to support the lower speed. *CALC requires the first key sequence to consists of "period period carriage return" (. . CR). You do not usually want to

```
   Create Device Desc (Display) (CRTDEVDSP)

Type choices, press Enter.

Device description . . . . .> VT100A     Name
Device class . . . . . . . .> *LCL      *LCL, *RMT, *VRT, *SNPT
Device type . . . . . . . .> V100       3101,3151,3161,3162..
Device model . . . . . . . .> *ASCII     0, 1, 2, 4, 11, 12, 23..
Emulating Twinaxial Device . *TYPE     *TYPE, 3196A2, 3197D2
Port Number . . . . . . . . 01          0-17
Emulating ASCII device . . . *YES       *NO, *YES
Physical attachment . . . . *MODEM      *DIRECT, *PTT, *MODEM..
Online at IPL . . . . . . . *YES       *YES, *NO
Attached controller . . . . CTL02       Name
Keyboard language type . . . *SYSVAL    *SYSVAL, AGB, AGI, BLI...
Inactivity timer . . . . . . *ATTACH    1-30, *ATTACH, *NOMAX...
Line speed . . . . . . . . 9600        *TYPE, *CALC, 150,300 ...
Word length . . . . . . . 7           *TYPE, *CALC, 7, 8
Type of parity . . . . . . . *EVEN      *TYPE, Calc, *EVEN, *ODD...
Stope bits . . . . . . . . 1           *TYPE, 1, 2

                                          More..
F3=Exit F4=Prompt F5=Refresh F10=Additional parameters F12=Cancel
```

Figure 13.17   CRTDEVDSP Part 2

require the user to key in this sequence to get a sign-on screen.

7   Word length. This is the size of a character, which is seven bits when parity is also used.

* EVEN   Type of parity. The parity bit permits many communications errors to be detected.

1   Stop bit.

Press Page Down or Roll Up key.
   On the final CRTDEVDSP screen (this display is not shown as it contains only a single input field), type:

Text   Text for VT100 first device.

13.5.1   VT100 Keyboard Mapping

The keyboard map for the DEC VT100 terminal is provided in Figure 13.18 and Figure 13.19. For ESC sequences, press the ESC key before you press the next key. For CTRL sequences, depress and hold the CTRL key while you press the next key. If you suspend the display via the CTRL/S key, use the CTRL/Q key to resume sending data to the display.

AS/400 Function	PC Key	Map Char	HEX Code	AS/400 Function	PC Key	Map Char	HEX Code
ATTN (Attention)	CTRL/A ESC A ESC a	^A ^[A ^[a	01 1B41 1B61	SYS REQ	ESC S ESC s	^[S ^[s	1B53 1B73
Backspace	Backspace	^H	08	Field Advance	TAB	^I	09
Cursor Up	(Up Arrow)	^[[A	1B5B41	Field Backspace	ESC TAB	^[^I	1B09
Cursor Down	(Down Arrow)	^[[B	1B5B42	Clear	CTRL/L ESC L	^L ^[L	0C 1B4C
Cursor Left	(Left Arrow)	^[[D	1B5B44	Test	CTRL/T ESC T ESC t	^T ^[T ^[t	14 1B54 1B74
Cursor Right	(Right Arrow)	^[[C	1B5B43	HEX	ESC (grave accent)	^[`	1B60
Cursor Select	CTRL/C	^C	03	F1	ESC 1	^[1	1B31
Delete	Delete	⌀	7F	F2	ESC 2	^[2	1B32
Duplicate	CTRL/D	^D	04	F3	ESC 3	^[3	1B33
Enter	CTRL/M Enter	^M	0D	F4	ESC 4	^[4	1B34
Erase EOF	CTRL/E	^E	05	F5	ESC 5	^[5	1B35
Erase Input	ESC i ESC I	^[i ^[I	1B49 1B69	F6	ESC 6	^[6	1B36
Error Reset	CTRL/R ESC R ESC r	^R ^[R ^[r	12 1B52 1B72	F7	ESC 7	^[7	1B37
Field +	ESC P ESC p	^[P ^[p	1B50 1B70	F8	ESC 8	^[8	1B38
Field -	ESC M ESC m	^[M ^[m	1B4D 1B6D	F9	ESC 9	^[9	1B39
Field Exit	(linefeed)	^J	0A	F10	ESC 0	^[0	1B30
Field Mark	CTRL/F	^F	06	F11	ESC -	^[-	1B2D
Help	ESC h ESC ?	^[h ^[?	1B68 1B3F	F12	ESC =	^[=	1B3D
Home	ESC H	^[H	1B48	F13	ESC !	^[!	1B21
Insert	Insert	^[⌀	1B7F	F14	ESC @	^[@	1B40
New Line	ESC (line feed) ESC RTN	^[^J ^[^M	1B0A 1B0D	F15	ESC #	^[#	1B23

Figure 13.18   Keyboard Mapping for DEC VT-100, Part 1

AS/400 Function	PC Key	Map Char	HEX Code	AS/400 Function	PC Key	Map Char	HEX Code
PA1	ESC ESC 1	^[^[1	1B1B31	F16	ESC $	^[$	1B24
PA2	ESC ESC 2	^[^[2	1B1B32	F17	ESC %	^[%	1B25
PA3	ESC ESC 3	^[^[3	1B1B33	F18	ESC ^	^[^	1B5E
Print	CTRL/P	^P	10	F19	ESC &	^[&	1B26
Page Up (Roll Down)	ESC D ESC d	^[D ^[d	1B44 1B64	F20	ESC *	^[*	1B2A
Page Down (Roll Up)	ESC U ESC u	^[U ^[u	1B55 1B75	F21	ESC (	^[(	1B28
Refresh Screen	ESC CTRL/A	^[^A	1B01	F22	ESC)	^[ )	1B29
Display Station Disconnect	ESC CTRL/R	^[^R	1B12	F23	ESC _	^[_	1B5F
Turn Indicators On or OFF	ESC CTRL/W	^[^W	1B17	F24	ESC +	^[+	1B2B

Figure 13.19 Keyboard Mapping for DEC VT-100, Part 2

13.6   AS/400 to AS/400 Using Sub-area Network

In this section we will look at an example of an AS/400 to AS/400 connection. This is a complex example which we will look at in a number of pieces. We begin with the VTAM startup definitions. Refer to Figure 13.20 for the VTAM Startup List and Mode Table. In our example we have the following physical structure:

- AS/400 token ring connected to a 3745.

- AS/400 lease line connected to a 3745 using SDLC.

- Two 3745s, attached to an S/370. A token ring connection, and a SDLC connection.

- Two NCP definitions.

When planning sub-area networks, the following items must be addressed:

- AS/400 and S/370 with different network IDs (NETID). VTAM Nonnative Network Connection XNETALS=YES must be specified in the VTAM Startup List to support different NETIDs. This support is part of VTAM V3R4 or higher. If

```
CONFIG=T5,                                  *
ASYDE=KEEP,                                 *
GWSSCP=YES,                                 *
HOSTPU=ISTSY5,                              *
CDRSCTI=60,                                 *
SSCPID=01,COLD,PROMPT,                          *
HOSTSA=01,                               *
NETID=USEXP201,                          *
SSCPNAME=CDRMSY5,                         *
HOSTPU=SYSHOST                           *
IOINT=600,                               *
SUPP=NOSUP,                              *
TNSTAT,NOCNSL,TIME=60,                      *
NOTRACE,TYPE=VTAM,                          *
CRPLBUF=(320,,29,,64,32),                       *
IOBUF=(468,256,94,,160,234),                     *
LPBUF=(30,,,,8,4),                        *
SFBUF=(102,,,,51,10),                        *
WPBUF=(4042,,,,24,10)
END
```

```
MTLIN    MODETAB
AS400    MODEENT LOAD=AS400,                        *
              FMPROF=X' 13',           *
              TSPROF=X' 07',           *
              PRIPROT=X' B0'           *
              SECPROT=X' B0'           *
              COMPROT=X' 50B1',            *
              TYPE=X' 00',             *
              RUSIZES=X' 0100',            *
              PSERVICE=X' 060200000000000000002F00'
SNASVCMG MODEENT LODMODE=SNASVCMG,                    *
              FMPROF=X' 13',           *
              TSPROF=X' 07'            *
              PRIPROT=X' B0',          *
              SECPROT=X' B0',          *
              COMPROT=X' D0B1',            *
              TYPE=X' 00',             *
              RUSIZES=X' 8585',            *
              PSERVICE=X' 060200000000000000000300'
         MODEEND
```

Figure 13.20   VTAM Startup List and Mode Table

XNETALS=YES is not specified in the VTAM Startup List, then the AS/400 Local Network ID must be changed to match the NETID defined for VTAM.

- AS/400 with different LCLLOCNAME than the VTAM/NCP definition. The AS/400 requires a local location list to resolve the AS/400 LCLLOCNAME with the VTAM/NCP LU name. The use of different AS/400 LCLLOCNAME and VTAM/NCP LU names may cause confusion as the network grows.

● The AS/400 is supported as a Low Entry Node (* LENNODE). The controller that is created must have * LENNODE specified if APPN communication will be used.

The example uses an APPN definition. APPN is not required to use sub-area networking. However, APPN will create the APPC device description dynamically, with APPN (* NO), you must manually create the APPC device description. For simplicity, the device description on both systems will be defined.

XNETALS=YES will not be defined in the VTAM Startup List. This means that the AS/400 that will be initiating the pass-through function must have the same NETID (Local network ID) as is defined in the VTAM Startup List.   The target AS/400 local network ID may be different.   If the target AS/400 will need to initiate a pass-through command, then its local network ID must be the same as the NETID in the VTAM Startup List.   The LU names in the NCP build are not the same as the LCLLOCNAME in the AS/400s.   All parameters are not specified in the examples. Parameters added to support the sub-area network appear in bold.

First we look at the VTAM Startup list to get the NETID and SSCPNAME.   In this example, see the startup specifications NETID=USEXP201 and SSCPNAME=CDRMSY5 (needed for the AS/400 to communicate to the HOST).   System SYS01 issues the pass-through command.   Before making changes, display the network attributes by issuing a DSPNETA command.   Since XNETALS=YES is not defined in the VTAM Startup List, the SYS01 local network ID must be changed to USEXP201 to match the VTAM NETID in the VTAM Startup List.   Refer to Figure 13.21 for DSPNETA output reflecting this change.

CHGNEA LCLNETID(USEXP201)

Next, display the AS/400 Network Attributes for SYS02 using the DSPNETA command (see Figure 13.22). We do not change any of these values because the pass-through function is only available from SYS01 to SYS02 and not from SYS02 to SYS01. Since SYS02 will be the target system, it is not necessary to change the local network ID on SYS02.

```
                    Display Network Attributes
                                  System: SOS01
Current system name . . . . . . . . . . . . . . :   SOS01
  Pending system name . . . . . . . . . . . . :
Local network ID . . . . . . . . . . . . . . . . :   USEXP201
Local control point name . . . . . . . . . . . :   SOS01
Default local location . . . . . . . . . . . . . :   SOS01
Default mode . . . . . . . . . . . . . . . . . . :   BLANK
APPN node type . . . . . . . . . . . . . . . . . :   * NETNODE
Maximum number of intermediate sessions . . . . :   200
Route addition resistance . . . . . . . . . . . :   128
Server network ID/control point name . . . . . . :    * LCLNETID
* ANY
                                      More...

Press Enter to continue.

F3=Exit   F12=Cancel
```

Figure 13.21   SYS01 Network Attributes with LCLNETID Changed

```
                    Display Network Attributes
                                  System: SYS02
Current system name . . . . . . . . . . . . . . :   SYS02
  Pending system name . . . . . . . . . . . . :
Local network ID . . . . . . . . . . . . . . . . :   APPN
Local control point name . . . . . . . . . . . :   SYS02
Default local location . . . . . . . . . . . . . :   SYS02
Default mode . . . . . . . . . . . . . . . . . . :   BLANK
APPN node type . . . . . . . . . . . . . . . . . :   * NETNODE
Maximum number of intermediate sessions . . . . :   200
Route addition resistance . . . . . . . . . . . :   128
Server network ID/control point name . . . . . . :   * LCLNETID * ANY


                                      More...

Press Enter to continue.

F3=Exit   F12=Cancel
```

Figure 13.22   SYS02 AS/400 Network Attributes

```
ZBUILD BUILD BFRS=88,        BUFFER DEFALTS            *
            BRANCH=100,      BRANCH TRACE TABLE         *
            ENABLTO=6,6      MODEM TIMEOUT              *
            LOADLIB=NCPLOAD, DD NAME OF NCP LOAD           *
            LTRACE=8,        MAX NUMBER OF LINE TRACES     *
            MAXSSCP=3,       2 HOSTS 1 NTO              *
            NETID=USEXP201,  NATIVE NETWORK               *
            NEWNAME=NCP1111, NCP LOAD MODULE             *
            NPA=NO,                              *
            ADDSESS=10,                           *
            AUXADDR=22,                           *
            MAXSESS=12,                           *
            NAMTAB=10,                            *
            NUMHSAS=16,      16 HOST SUBAREAS CONCURRENTLY    *
            SUBAREA=16,      SUBAREA NUMBER             *
            TYPGEN=NCP,      NCP GENERATION            *
            TYPESYS=MVS,     OPERATING SYSTEM             *
            USGTIER=3,       USAGE TIERR               *
            VERSION=V5R3     NCP VER 5 REL 3
DRPOOLLU LUDRPOOL NUMTYP2=1500, MAX NUMBER OF SWITCHED LU.2   *
            NUMILU=20   MAX # OF INDEPENDENT LUS
LNTR1 LINE ADDRESS=(1088,FULL)  TIC POS. IN CONTROLLER CHASSIS   *
            OWNER=SSCP1,       SYS5           *
            ADAPTER=TIC2,      TYPE 2 ADAPTER      *
            TRSPEED=16,        16 MEGABITS         *
            PORTADD=01,        USER-ASSIGNER ID NUMBER (0-99)    *
            RCVBUFC=4095,      RECEIVE BUFFER SIZE        *
            MAXTSL=2105,       TRANSMIT SIZE            *
            ANS=CONTINUE,      HOLD CONNECTION IF VTAM DROPS    *
            LOCADD=40037450100,                    *
            UACB=(X$P1AXMX$P1AR)
```
```
SWSYS1    VBUILD                           *
          TYPE=SWNET,        SWITCHED NODE        *
          MAXNO=1
#SYS1   PU    ADDR=01,       (NOT USED)          *
              IDBLK=056,     3174 OR 3274         *
              IDNUM=40415    MATCH DOWNSTREAM DEVICE   *
              ISTATUS=ACTIVE,                 *
              PUTYPE=2,                     *
              USSTAB=USSSNA0,                 *
              SSCPFM=USSSCS,                  *
              MAXOUT=7,      # OF PIUS SET BEFORE A RESP*
              VPACING=7
SYS10415 LU   LOCADDR=0,     1ST LU - INDEPENDENT LU   *
              RESSCB=10,                   *
              MODETAB=MTLEN,                *
              DLOGMOD=AS400
```

Figure 13.23   VTAM/NCP Definition for SYS10415

Let us review the VTAM/NCP Definitions for SYS01 (see Figure 13.23). Our objective is to use LU6.2 for communications.

To include T2.1 Node Support to support the sub-area link, the NCP BUILD must have the following parameters:

- ADDSESS is the number of boundary session control blocks in the unreserved session control block pool for independent LUs, in addition to those reserved by RESSCB on the LU definition.

- AUXADDR is specified to create a control block pool for all peripheral primary LUs. When an independent LU requests a session, the NCP provides VTAM the primary LU address from this pool. Each LU is automatically assigned one address in the NCP generation process. This address represents the secondary LU only. AUXADDR indicates the total number of extra primary LU addresses required by all independent LUs.

- MAXSESS specifies the maximum number of sessions an independent LU may have.

- NAMTAG specifies the number of entries in the Network Names tables. Every network, SSCP and T2.1 node with which the NCP may concurrently have sessions requires an entry.

On the PU statement, specify the following parameters:

- PUTYPE=2 indicates we have a T2.1 node.

- XID=YES must be specified for a T2.1 node. XID specifies whether the physical unit can receive or respond to an XID.

Also, notice on the PU statement that IDBLK and IDNUM are specified for the token ring PU. This means that LCLEXCHID specified on the AS/400 CRTCTLHOST must combine IDBLK and IDNUM. This is how the HOST controls the PU connection by exchanging IDs.

On the LU statement, the following parameters must be specified:

- LOCADDR=0 specifies that the LU is an independent LU.

• RESSCB (NCP and VTAM switched major node only) specifies the number of boundary session control blocks reserved by NCP for an independent LU. Each independent LU session requires a control block, and RESSCB should equal the approximate maximum number of sessions. However, an independent LU can have additional sessions by using control blocks from the unreserved session control block pool, specified by ADDSESS on the BUILD macro for NCP. If the total of RESSCB and available control blocks from the unreserved control block pool are large enough, then an independent LU may establish sessions up to a limit of MAXSESS.

Notice that the label on the LU statement is SYS10415, not SYS01. This means the local location name (LCLLOCNAME) in the AS/400 for SYS01 is SYS10415.

We could change the AS/400 local location name or add SYS10415 to the local APPN configuration list. Adding location names to the APPN configuration list does not impact existing connections. Changing the local location name would require changing the current definitions.

At this point, enough information has been provided to create the host controller on the AS/400. Before we do this, let's first look at the VTAM definition for SYS02. The SYS02 connection to the host is an SDLC line. The LU name is SYSC40D. Since the value of LCLLOCNAME is SYS02, an APPN local configuration list entry of SYSC40D must be added to the APPN local configuration list on the AS/400.

Let us first understand the names on both systems, then create all of the definitions on SYS01 and SYS02. SYS01 is connected through LU SYS10415 and SYS02 via LU SYSC40D. Therefore, for SYS01 to communicate to SYS02, SYS10415 must communicate with SYSC40D. See Figure 13.25 for the SYS01 definition.

The token ring line is used for many other connections such as local PCs and RISC/6000 connections. The key parameter is the token ring line speed. A token ring connection on a given ring must run at the same speed, either 4 or 16 megabits. If one device has a token ring card that can only run at a speed of 4 megabits, then all devices must run at 4 megabits. Most organizations use what is known as a Locally Administered Address (LAA) for each token ring address instead of the hardware token ring address. The locally administered address defines a connection to the ring. A ring could have both addressing configurations, local administered

```
************************** BUILD *******************************
  ZBUILD   BUILD  BFRS=88,            BUFFER DEFAULTS              *
                  LOADLIB=NCPLOAD,    DD NAME OF NCP LOAD MOD      *
                  MODEL=3745,                                     *
                  NETID=USEXP101,     NATIVE NETWORK              *
                  NEWNAME=NCP3333,    NCP LOAD MODULE NAME        *
                  NUMHSAS=16,         15 HOST SUBAREAS CONCURRENTLY *
                  SUBAREA=10,         SUBAREA NUMBER              *
                  TYPGEN=NCP,         NCP GENERATION              *
                  TYPSYS=MVS,         OPERATING SYSTEM            *
                  VERSION=V5R3,       NCP VER 5 REL 3             *
                  ADDSESS=10,                                     *
                  AUXADDR=22                                      *
  ********    SDLC  LINE    *****************************************
  GRPNCP5  GROUP  CLOCKNG=EXT,        EXTERNAL CLOCKED MODEM      *
                  DIAL=NO,            LEASED LINE                *
                  DISCNT=NO,          NO DISCONNECT IF ALL LU' S INACT *
                  DUPLEX=FULL,        FULL DUPLEX COMMUNICATION LINE *
                  ISTATUS=ACTIVE,     INITIAL STATUS ACTIVE       *
                  LNCTL=SDLC,         SDLC LINE TYPE             *
                  MAXDATA=265,        MAX NUMBER OF DATA IN SEGMENT *
                  MAXOUT=7,           MAX NUMBER OF PIU' S        *
                  NPACOLL=YES,                                   *
                  NRZI=NO,            NON-RETURN-TO ZER-INVERTED-MODE *
                  PASSLIM=7,          MAX NUMBER OF CONSECUTIVE PIU' S *
                  PUTYPE=2,           PHYSICAL UNIT TYPE         *
                  SSCPFM=FSS,         REQUIRED                   *
                  TYPE=NCP            NCP LINE GROUP             *
  ************* LINEXP22   LINE TWO EXAMPLE TWO ***************
  LINEXP22  LINE  ADDRESS=(168,FULL),                            *
                  NPACOLL=YES,                                   *
                  SPEED=56000,                                   *
                  OWNER=SSCP1
  SRVEXP2  SERVICE ORDER=(#SYS2C4)
  ********* AS/400  INDEPENDENT LU FOR APPC**********************
  #SYS2C4  PU      ADDR=C4,           HEX 8 BIT LINE ADDR        *
                  PACING=7,                                      *
                  VPACING=7,                                     *
                  ANS=CONTINUE,                                  *
                  XID=YES,                                       *
                  MODETAB=MYLEN,      MODETAB MEMBER            *
                  DLOGMOD=AS400,                                 *
                  USTAB=USSSNA0,                                 *
                  SSCPFM=USSSCS
  SYS2C40D LU      LOCADDR=0,         1ST LU                     *
                  RESSCB=10,                                     *
                  MODETAB=MTLEN,      MODETAB MEMBER            *
                  DLOGMOD=AS400
```

Figure 13.24   VTAM/NCP Definitions for SYS2C40D

addresses for CPU base token ring cards and hardware token ring
addresses for PC connections. In our example, the HOST token
ring address is 40037450100. To create our token ring line
definition, the only parameters required are line name (LIND),
resource name (RSRCNAME), line speed (LINESPEED), and adapter
address (ADPTADR). The line speed is required because the default
token ring speed is 4 and the HOST is on a 16-megabit ring. The
adapter address is specified because LAA is used.

```
CRTLINTRN   LIND(SYS1L1TRN) RSRCNAME(LIN021) LINESPEED(16M)     +
   MAXFRAME(16393) ADPTADR(400094061045)

CRTCTLHOST  CTLD(SYS02CTL) LINKTYPE(*LAN) SWTLINE(SYS1L1TRN)    +
   RMTNETID(USEXP201) RMTCPNAME(CDRMSYS5) SSCPID(050000000001)  +
   LCLEXCHID(05640415) ADPTADR(400037450100) CPSSN(*NO)         +
   NODETYPE(*LENNODE) TEXT(Controller for Subarea Network to SYS2)

CRTDEVAPPC DEVD(SYS2C40D) RMTLOCNAME(SYS2C40D) LCLLOCNAME(SYS10415) +
   RMTNETID(USEXP101) CTL(SYS02CTL) MODE(AS400)

CRTMODD  MODD(AS400) MAXSSN(8) MAXCNV(8) LCLCTLSSN(4) PREESTSSN(0)
```

Figure 13.25   AS/400 Definition for SYS10415

Let us review the AS/400 host controller definition:

- RMTNETID - USEXP201 is the name of the remote network ID on which the adjacent control point resides. This value came from NETID parameter in the VTAM Startup List.

- RMTCPNAME - CDRMSYS5 is the name of the remote control point. This value came from the SSCPNAME parameter in the VTAM Startup List.

- SSCPID - 050000000001 is used to identify the host controller when a connection is established and the host system sends an activate physical unit (ACTPU) request. The system service control point identifier is a twelve-character hexadecimal value; the first two characters are hex 05. The ending characters 01 came from the SSCPID parameter in the VTAM Startup List.

- LCLEXCHID - 05640415 is an eight-digit hexadecimal value used to identify the local system to the remote system. The first three digits came from the IDBLK parameter and the next five from the IDNUM parameter of the PU macro in the NCP definition.

- ADPTADR - 400037450100 is the HOST LAN remote adapter address (LAA). This value comes from the LOCADD parameter in the NCP token ring line definition for SYS10415.

- CPSSN - *NO states that the controller does not support control point-to-control point sessions.

- NODETYPE - * LENNODE is the type of node that this controller represents. * LENNODE is a low-entry networking node in an APPN network. This is required for sub-area networking support.

- APPN - * YES defines the APPN functional capability of the HOST controller. Since * YES is the default value, this keyword was not specified.

The creation of the device description is not required in an APPN network. APPN (* YES) creates the device description on both systems at the time the pass-through command is initiated. We will discuss the mode definition when we cover the pass-through functions.

Now let us review the APPN configuration list definition. APPN uses this list to find the routing to systems, lines and controllers when communications are initiated. Use the WRKCFGL command to configure a local alias name for SYS01. If the * APPNLCL type list does not exist, create it with QAPPNLCL as the object name (see Figure 13.26). Type a 2 next to the configuration list, type * APPNLCL to change the list, and press Enter. Add the new local location name, text, and press Enter.

After adding the local location name to the * APPNLCL configuration list, we must add an entry for the remote location name to the * APPNRMT configuration list (see Figure 13.27). If the * APPNRMT type list does not exist, create an * APPNRMT list with QAPPNRMT as the object name. Type a 2 next to the configuration list, type * APPNRMT to change the list, and press Enter. Then add the following values:

- SYS2C40D - Remote location name. This is the name of the LU attached to SYS02.

- APPN - Remote Network ID. This is the network ID of SYS02.

- SYS10415 - Local location name. This is the name of the LU attached to SYS01.

```
         Change Configuration List              SYS01

Configuration list . . :  QAPPNLCL
Configuration list type :  *APPNLCL
Text . . . . . . . . :  Local APPN Configuration List


Type changes, press Enter.

-----APPN Local Locations-----   -----APPN Local Locations----

Local                    Local
Location Text                 Location Text
SYS10415 AS/400 SYSTEM ONE



                                   More...
F3=Exit  F12=Cancel  F17=Top  F18=Bottom
```

Figure 13.26   SYS01 APPN Local Location List

- CDRMSY5 - Remote control point name. This is the value on the SSCPNAME parameter in the VTAM Startup List.

- USEXP201 - Control point network ID. This is the value on the NETID parameter in the VTAM Startup List.

Default values are used for the Location Password and Secure Location fields. Once all the fields have been entered, press Enter.
Now let us review the AS/400 definition for SYS02. The SYS02 connection is a V.35 SDLC line from the 3745 to the AS/400. The physical connection is a point-to-point connection. The site uses 3270 emulation and an RJE session to the host and does not want to impact these definitions with a new definition for an APPC connection. There would then need to be two controllers, one for 3270 emulation and RJE and the other for the APPC session. In order to configure two or more controllers on a line, the CNN keyword must be *MP. The 3270 emulation and RJE definition will not be included in this example. Also, note that 3270 emulation, RJE and APPC sessions can run under the same HOST controller. Let us review the keywords for the line definition:

```
                Change Configuration List           SYS01

Configuration list . . :  QAPPNRMT
Configuration list type :  *APPNRMT
Text . . . . . . . . . :

Type changes, press Enter.

-----------------------APPN Remote Locations-------------------

        Remote          Remote    Control
Remote  Network  Local  Control  Point    Location       Secur
Location ID      Location Point   Net ID   Password       Loc
SYS2C40D APPN    SYS10415 CDRMSY5 USEXP201 _____       *NO
_____  *NETATR *NETATR _____ *NETATR _____       *NO
_____  *NETATR *NETATR _____ *NETATR _____       *NO

                                         More...
F3=Exit  F11=Display session info  F12=Cancel  F17=Top F18=Bottom
```

Figure 13.27   SOS01 Remote Location List

```
CRTLINSDLC   LIND(LINEEXP2) RSRCNAME(LIN081) ROLE(*SEC)
    INTERFACE(*V35) CNN(*MP) EXCHID(056000C3) NRZI(*NO) MAXCTL(2)
    CLOCK(*MODEM) LINESPEED(56000), TEXT( LINE FOR EXAMPLE TWO)

CRTCTLHOST   NAME(SYS01CTL) LINKTYPE(*SDLC) SWITCHED(*NO)          +
    LINE(LINEEXP2) RMTNETID(USEXP201) RMTCPNAME(CDRSYS5) STNADR(C4) +
    APPN(*YES) CPSSN(*NO) NODETYPE(*LENNODE) AUTODLTDEV(*NO)        +
    TEXT(Controller for pass thru using subarea network)

*** APPC device description can be automatically created by system ****

CRTDEVAPPC   DEVD(SYS10415) RMTLOCNAME(SYS10415) LCLLOCNAME(SYS2C40D) +
    RMTNETID(USEXP201) CTL(SYS01CTL) MODE(AS400) APPN(*YES)
*****************************************************************

CRTMODD      MODD(AS400) MAXSSN(8) MAXCNV(8) LCLCTLSSN(4) PREESTSSN(0)

CRTDEVDSP    DEVD(EXPDSP01) DEVCLS(*VRT) TYPE(5251) MODEL(11)        +
    CTL(QPACTL01) TEXT(Example display one for pass thru)
```

Figure 13.28   AS/400 SYS2C40D Definition

- NRZI - *NO. Nonreturn-to-zero inverted transmission coding method. This value must be the same as the line definition in the HOST. If you review the NCP definition for SYS2C40D, you will find this value specified as part of the GROUP macro.

- MAXCTL - 2. This line will support only two controllers. The default value is 40.

- INTERFACE - *V35. This is the physical interface between the AS/400 and the modem.

- ROLE - * SEC. This states that the AS/400 assumes a secondary role when communicating with the HOST.

- EXCHID - 056000C3. This is the exchange identifier that the AS/400 SYS02 sends to the HOST. The first three digits must be 056. On the HOST, XID=YES must be on the PU definition for this connection.

- CLOCK - *MODEM. The clock or speed of the transmission is controlled by the modem.

- LINESPEED - 56000. The speed of the connection. This is an informational field and does not affect the actual speed between modems.

- CNN - *MP. This allows more than one controller to be attached to the line.

A review of the controller definition follows:

- RMTNETID - USEXP201 is the name of the remote network ID in which the adjacent control point resides. This value comes from the NETID parameter in the VTAM Startup List.

- RMTCPNAME - CDRMSYS5 is the name of the remote control point. This value comes from the SSCPNAME parameter in the VTAM Startup List.

- STNADR - C4 is the SDLC station address. This is a 2-digit hexadecimal value. This value comes from the ADDR parameter of the PU macro in the NCP definition of SYS2C40D.

- CPSSN - *NO states that the controller does not support control point-to-control point sessions.

- NODETYPE - * LENNODE is the type of node that this controller represents. * LENNODE is a low-entry networking node in an APPN network. This is required for sub-area networking support.

- APPN - * YES specifies the APPN functional capability of the HOST controller. Since * YES is the default value, this keyword was not specified.

The creation of the device description is not required in an APPN network. Most of the fields in the device description will be added to the APPN configuration list.

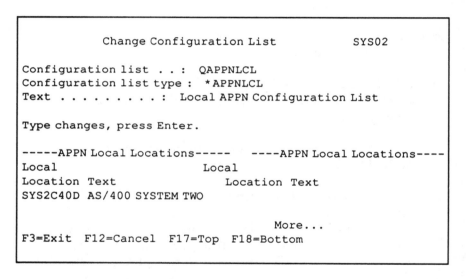

Figure 13.29 SYS02 APPN Local Location List

The mode description describes the session characteristics and the number of sessions used to negotiate the allowable values between the local and remote location. When the pass-through command is issued, the mode name is passed through the S/370 to other AS/400s. Therefore, there must be a *modetab* defined on the HOST with the same name as the mode name on the AS/400. The mode description has the following values:

```
              Change Configuration List              SYS02

Configuration list . . :  QAPPNRMT
Configuration list type :  *APPNRMT
Text . . . . . . . . :


Type changes, press Enter.


-----------------------APPN Remote Locations--------------------
          Remote           Remote   Control
Remote    Network  Local   Control  Point    Location      Secur
Location  ID       Location Point   Net ID   Password      Loc
SYS10415  APPN     SYS2C40D CDRMSY5 USEXP201 _____   * NO
_____  *NETATR  *NETATR  _____ *NETATR  _____   * NO
_____  *NETATR  *NETATR  _____ *NETATR  _____   * NO
_____  *NETATR  *NETATR  _____ *NETATR  _____   * NO
                                     More
F3=Exit  F11=Display session infor  F12=Cancel  F17=Top F18=Bottom
```

Figure 13.30 SOS02 APPN Remote Location List

- MODD - AS400. This name must match the name in the MODETAB definition on the HOST. The mode name cannot be blank (*BLANK). There should be at least two MODEENT macros on the HOST, one for SNASVCMG and other for the pass-through command from the AS/400. See Figure 13.20 for the MODETAB example.

- MAXSSN - 8 is the maximum number of sessions that can be active at once for this mode. Eight is also the default value.

- MAXCNV - 8 is the maximum number of conversations that can be active at one time with the remote system that is allowed by this mode. Eight is also the default value.

- LCLCTLSSN - 4 is the minimum number of locally controlled sessions that need to be established and owned by the source programs on this system for this mode. Four is also the default value.

- PREESTSSN - 0 is the number of concurrent sessions that are to be established when the mode is started. Zero is also the default value.

When the AS/400 and HOST definitions are complete, the line and controller description should show active when a *vary on* is performed. The device description will not exist until the first STRPASTHR command has been issued. If you created the device description first, then these devices will be in a *vary on pending* state.

Now for the last phase of the example. The STRPASTHR command should be issued as follows:

```
STRPASTHR RMTLOCNAME(SYS2C40D)
MODE(AS400) LCLLOCNAME(SYS10415)
RMTNETID(USEXP0201)
```

- RMTLOCNAME - SYS2C40D is the name on the LU statement for SYS02 in the NCP definition on the HOST.

- VRTCTL/VRTDEV - *NONE is the name of the virtual controller or device on the target AS/400. This parameter requests automatic creation of the device description on the target system. The user profile invoked on the target will be the owner of the description. It is better to predefine the controller and devices on the target system and specify the controller or device name on the STRPASTHR command.

- MODE - AS400 is the name of the mode statement that will control communication between the source and target system.

- LCLLOCNAME - SYS10415 is the name on the LU statement for SYS01 in the NCP definition on the HOST.

- RMTNETID - USEXP201 is the name on the NETID parameter of the VTAM Startup List.

14

TCP/IP

14.1   TCP/IP Connectivity

Transmission Control Protocol/Internet Protocol (*TCP/IP*) has become the de facto standard communication between non-IBM hosts, especially within the UNIX world. TCP/IP is a set of vendor-independent communications protocols that support peer-to-peer connectivity functions for both local and wide area networks. TCP provides host-to-host transmission and IP provides data routing from source to destination. TCP/IP was originally developed to link military, government, research, and university networks. These networks are collectively referred to as the Internet. The terms client/server are also used for nodes within a TCP/IP network. A *server* system makes specialized services available to other computers on the network referred to as *client* systems. The actual software clients can be any program that communicates with or uses the services of TCP/IP.

Networks are linked together by sharing a common node called a *gateway*. A gateway can be either an IP router or a bridge. The purpose of the gateway is to route packets (IP datagrams) between the networks that it connects.

The network connection of each node on an inter-network is assigned a unique address. This *internet address* differs from a physical hardware address because it can be assigned or reassigned according to standard conventions. The address is a 32-bit integer. The address is expressed in the form www.xxx.yyy.zzz, where each field is the decimal representation of one byte (8 bits - 0 to 255) address. Example: X'9C790601' is expressed as 156.121.6.1.

Within your own network, you can assign addresses according to your preference. However, to connect to the Internet, your internet addresses must be assigned by Government Systems, Inc.

14.2   Understanding the Internet Address

Internet addresses have two parts: a network ID and a host ID on the network (4-byte address). The first range of addresses is reserved for class A networks. These are very large networks. The first byte of a class A network address can have a value from 0 to 127. The remaining three bytes are the Host ID. Therefore, class A networks can use host IDs that range from 0.0.1 to 255.255.254. Because only 128 class A networks can be defined, they are reserved for the government or for the very few largest companies.

The second range of addresses is reserved for class B networks. These are medium-sized networks which have a two-byte address. The first byte of a class B network address can have a value from 128 to 191. The second byte can be 0 to 255. The remaining two bytes are the Host ID. Class B networks can use host IDs that range from 0.1 to 255.254. Quite a few class B networks have been defined, and it is common for large companies to use them.

The third range of addresses is reserved for class C networks. These are relatively small networks made up of less than 255 hosts. The first byte of a class C network address can contain a value from 192 to 223. The second and third bytes can be 0 to 255. The remaining byte is the Host ID. Therefore, class C networks can use host IDs that range from .1 to .254.

On each network, a Host ID consisting of all 1 bits is reserved as a broadcast address. For example, the broadcast address on a class B network is 156.121.255.255 where 156.121 is the network ID and 255.255 is the broadcast address. Traffic sent to the broadcast address is delivered to each node defined within the local network.

14.3   Domain Name

A domain name identifies your system within a hierarchy of groups of systems and can be used by remote servers to associate an internet address with the domain name of your system. This provides an easier way to identify systems in the network instead of using an internet address. Domain names consist of labels that are separated by periods (ABC.DEF.EFG). A shortened version of a domain name is a host name (ABC).

A domain name or a host name is a text string having 2 to 255 characters. Domain names consist of one or more labels separated by periods. Each label can contain up to 63 characters. The first and last character of the host name must be an alphanumeric character. The AS/400 only uses the first 24 characters of a host name to resolve a system name to an internet address.

14.4 AS/400 TCP/IP

The AS/400 supports the following applications under TCP/IP:

- The TELNET Client protocol allows the client to access and use the resources of a remote system (server) as if the work station were locally connected to the remote system. The AS/400 supports both client and server connections. AS/400 client/server supports 5250, 3270, VT100 and ASCII line mode terminal emulation. When the AS/400 is using VT100 client support, cursor movement, delete key, and CTRL key functions are different from a real VT100 terminal. When using Telnet between two AS/400s, be sure to adjust the inactivity timeout value for Telnet (CHGTCPA command) to avoid premature disconnection.

- The File Transfer Protocol (FTP) is a function that allows the client to send or receive copies of files to or from remote systems across a TCP/IP network. In addition, FTP provides functions for renaming, appending, and deleting files. FTP does not support any other AS/400 object distribution. One way around this limitation is to save the object to a savefile, copy the savefile to a database file, and transmit the file to the target system, which then copies the database file just received to a savefile and restores the objects.

- The Simple Mail Transfer Protocol (SMTP) function allows you to send or receive electronic mail. The AS/400 uses SNADS coupled with SMTP to provide the distribution services.

SNADS is part of the OS/400 operating system. Without OfficeVision (the AS/400 Word Processing and Mail system), the SMTP receive function is not practical.

14.5 TCP/IP Example Configuration

In this section, the sample TCP/IP configuration cover the AS/400 side of a AS/400 to RISC/6000 TCP/IP connection. The names and addresses are as follows:

- AS/400 SYS01 TCP/IP Host Name is SYS1

- AS/400 SYS01 TCP/IP Domain Name is SYS1.NET.COM

- RISC/6000 TCP/IP Host Name is SYS5

- RISC/6000 TCP/IP Domain Name is SYS5.NET.COM

- AS/400 SYS01 TCP/IP Internet Address is 156.121.6.1

- RISC/6000 TCP/IP Internet Address is 156.121.6.5

- Network Server Internet Address is 192.99.120.9

- Another System Node Internet Address 156.121.6.9

Once the TCP/IP support has been loaded on the AS/400, the configuration of TCP/IP can be done through the CFGTCP command. Key CFGTCP on the command line and press Enter. The menu shown in Figure 14.1 should appear.

We must first create the host table. The host table contains the internet address and the host and domain names. The host name is used to select the internet address. The system can also use a server (another system) for finding an internet address.

Take option 1 (Work with TCP/IP host table entries), to add the host name and internet address from the CFGTCP menu.

Add the internet address and the domain name. Also add the internet address and the host name (short version of the domain name). You can enter up to five versions of the domain name with the same internet address.

```
                  Configure TCP/IP
                                System: SYS01
Select one of the following:

  1. Work with TCP/IP host table entries
  2. Work with TCP/IP links
  3. Work with TCP/IP route entries
  4. Change local domain name
  5. Work with names for SMTP
  6. Work with TCP/IP remote system information

 10. Change remote name server
 11. Change TCP/IP attributes
 12. Work with TCP/IP port entries
 13. Change SMTP distribution retries
 14. Change TCP/IP tuning values

 25. Convert host table

Selection or command
===> 1

F3=Exit  F4=Prompt  F9=Retrieve  F12=Cancel
```

Figure 14.1 CFGTCP Menu, Option 1 - Host Table Entry

After you exit the Work with TCP/IP Host Table Entry screen, you will get a screen asking you if you want to convert the host table to internal format. Your respond is Y.

Next lets look at the relationship of the internet address to the line description in the AS/400. Option 2 (Work with TCP/IP Links) on the CFGTCP menu provides this function. Take Option 2.

On the Work with TCP/IP Links screen, type 1 and the line description name and press Enter. The line description should have already been created before this step.

On the Add TCP/IP Link screen, type the internet address and press Enter. (Refer to Figure 14.3.) The automatic start option default is * YES. This means that when the QTCP subsystem is started, the TCP/IP Link is also started automatically. A * NO on this option means that you will start the link later using the STRTCPLNK command or option 9 on the Work with TCP/IP Link. The default was used for the rest of the fields.

```
               Work with TCP/IP Host Table Entries
                                      System: SYS01
    Type options, press Enter.
      1=Add  2=Change  4=Remove  5=Display

          Internet         Host
    Opt   Address          Name
          156.121.6.1      SYS1
          156.121.6.1      SYS1.NET.COM
          156.121.6.5      SYS5
          156.121.6.5      SYS5.NET.COM



                                       Bottom
    F3=Exit F5=Refresh F12=Cancel F15=Print list  F17=Position to
```

Figure 14.2 ADD TCP/IP HOST TABLE ENTRY

```
                  Work with TCP/IP Links
                             System:  SYS01
    Type options, press Enter.
     1=Add  2=Change  4=Remove  5=Display  9=Start  10=End

          Line         Internet        Link
    Opt   Description  Address         Type
    1     SYS1L1TRN



    F3=Exit F5=Refresh F12=Cancel F15=Print list F17=Top F18=Bottom
```

Figure 14.3   ADD TCP/IP LINK (ADDTCPLNK)

For each communication line that will be using TCP/IP, an entry must be added with the Add TCP/IP Link (ADDTCPLNK) command or the 1 option on the Work with TCP/IP Links menu. In our example, SYS1LTRN is the only communication line in SYS01 that will be using TCP/IP. (Refer to Figure 14.4.)

```
                  Work with TCP/IP Links
                                System:  SYS01
Type options, press Enter.
 1=Add  2=Change  4=Remove  5=Display  9=Start  10=End

        Line        Internet       Link
Opt   Description    Address        Type
      SYS1L1TRN    156.121.6.1     *TRLAN




F3=Exit  F5=Refresh  F12=Cancel  F15=Print list  F17=Top  F18=Bottom
```

Figure 14.4   ADD TCP/IP LINK (ADDTCPLNK)

Next we must build the routing list for the AS/400 for all TCP/IP requests to another system. Each link should be added to the route table. On the CFGTCP menu, option 3 is the Work with TCP/IP route entries. Type 3 and press Enter on the CFGTCP menu to display this screen.

Let us review the various fields that must be entered on the Add TCP/IP Route Entry screen.

● Network. This is the network ID potion of the internet address. In our example, this consists of the first two bytes of the internet address. You should also define *DEFAULT as a network ID. The *DEFAULT network allows the system to send datagrams to internet addresses that are not defined in the routing table. Without this parameter, your system ignores datagrams destined for networks not defined by routing entries.

● First hop. This is the internet address of the first system in the route from your system to the destination system. A value of *HOME means that no intermediate routing is required to reach the destination system. That is, your system and the destination system are directly connected. If the first hop value is an internet address, it must be an internet address of a host that can be reached using *HOME as a route entry for the first hop. Therefore, destinations that do not have a network ID of 156.63 will be routed through 156.121.6.9.

- Maximum datagram size. This is the maximum size (in bytes) of IP datagrams sent on a route. If you specify *CALC, the size is calculated for you based on values found in the AS/400 line description. You should specify a value that is the smallest of the maximum values for each system supported during the routing of the datagrams. This includes bridges and other IP routers. In our example this value will 576.

- Subnet mask. This is a bit mask that defines which part of the internet address forms the subnetwork field of the internet address. A subnet mask of 0.0.255.0 defines a class B subnetwork consisting of all the bits in the third byte of the internet address. In our example, we do not have a subnetwork. Therefore, we use *NONE in the example.

- Subnet value. This is combined with the network address and the subnetwork mask to define a unique subnetwork. Each byte of the subnetwork value must be a binary subset of the corresponding byte of the subnetwork mask. For example, a class B network ID of 156.121, a class B subnetwork mask of 0.0.255.0, and a class B subnetwork value of 0.0.6.0 define 156.121.6 as the subnetwork. In our example, this value will also be *NONE.

On the Work with TCP/IP Route entries: Type option 1 to add, *DEFAULT for the Network field, and press Enter. You will see the screen shown in Figure 14.5.

On the Add TCP/IP Route Entry (ADDTCPRTE) screen, type the following information:

- Network - 156.121

- Line description - SYS1L1TRN

- First Hop - 156.121.6.1

- Maximum datagram size - 576

- Subnet mask - *NONE

- Subnet value - *NONE

```
                    Work with TCP/IP Route Entries
                              System: SYS01
       Type options, press Enter.
        1=Add   2=Change   4=Remove   5=Display

                     Line              Maximum
       Opt Network       Description First Hop      Datagram Size

        1  *DEFAULT




       F3=Exit      F5=Refresh F11=Display subnet information F12=Cancel
       F15=Print list F17=Top     F18=Bottom
```

Figure 14.5   TCP/IP Route Entry

Add a second entry with:

● Network - 156.121

● Line description - SYS1L1TRN

● First Hop - *HOME

● Maximum datagram size - 576

● Subnet mask - *NONE

● Subnet value - *NONE

14.5.1   Configuring the Local Domain Name

Within TCP/IP, the local domain name is the primary name of your
system. This name is used by SMTP to identify any mail you send.
To change the local domain name, select option 4 on the CFGTCP

```
                Work with TCP/IP Route Entries
                              System: SYS01
Type options, press Enter.
 1=Add  2=Change  4=Remove  5=Display

              Line                 Maximum
Opt  Network      Description  First Hop      Datagram Size

    *DEFAULT      SYS1L1TRN   156.121.6.1         576
     156.121      SYS1L1TRN   *HOME          576




F3=Exit     F5=Refresh  F11=Display subnet information  F12=Cancel|
F15=Print list F17=Top      F18=Bottom
```

Figure 14.6   TCP/IP Route Entry

menu. Enter the names of the Local host and the local domain.
The local domain name is the rest of the domain name, excluding
the host name. See Figure 14.7 for an example of this screen.

```
                Change Local Domain Name
                              System:  SYS01
Type choices, press Enter.

 Local domain name . . . .  NET.COM



 Local host name . . . . .  SYS1


F3=Exit  F12=Cancel
```

Figure 14.7   Change Local Domain Name

Note: The Work with TCP/IP remote system information is used
for an X.25 link. In our example, we are not using an X.25 link.

14.5.2   Configuring a Remote Name Server

If you configure TCP/IP on your AS/400 system to use a remote name server, your system sends a request to the remote name server each time it wishes to know the internet address associated with a name. When a host name is specified without a domain, the AS/400 system appends the local domain name to the host name before sending the request. If the remote name server does not respond or does not find an internet address for a name, your AS/400 system looks at its own local host table to resolve the internet address. The use of a remote name server adds significant overhead to internet processing. (Note: An AS/400 system cannot be a remote name server.)

Select option 10. Then, change the specification of the remote name server on the CFGTCP menu, and press Enter. Refer to Figure 14.8 for an example.

```
                    Change Remote Name Server
                               System: SOS01
     Type choices, press Enter.

       Server address . . . . . .  192.88.195.10    Internet address
       Server port . . . . . . .  53               0-65534
       Server protocol . . . . .  *UDP              *UDP, *TCP
       Retries . . . . . . . . .  3                1-99
       Time interval . . . . . .  30               1-99 (seconds)



     F3=Exit   F12=Cancel
```

Figure 14.8   Change Remote Server

In our example, 192.99.120.9 is the remote name server internet address. The default values will be taken for all other parameters.

Chapter

15

Distributed Processing

This chapter looks at *Distributed Processing* in general and specifically for OS/400 systems. Distributed Processing is a term used to describe any process that is performed across multiple platforms or nodes. Classical programming solutions involve only a single system. When multiple steps are required for a classical application, they are usually performed serially on that single system. In modern distributed applications, the various pieces of an application are performed by different systems, wherever they are handled most efficiently or the best business solution can be provided. The pieces of a distributed application may be performed at the same time by different computing systems.

The structure of LANs, WANs, and the coupling of MVS, VM, VSE, RS6000, PC DOS/OS2 systems with AS/400s will be discussed in some detail in this chapter. Emphasis is placed on the system management issues created by distributed processing. Extensive use is made of graphics to illustrate the system structures discussed.

15.1 Data Processing Model

To discuss distributed systems, we must first understand classical or basic data processing. Let us define a few terms then look at distributed processing. We will talk about user directed applications, and the structure of a typical application.

A *user directed application* is a process that receives input or direction from a user, and that produces output that is received by the user. All online applications fall into this category, as well as most modern batch processing that is initiated by a user.

An online application can be viewed as made up of a number of layers. Information flows through the layers, and is manipulated or processed within each layer. Figure 15.1 illustrates the layers we will discuss.

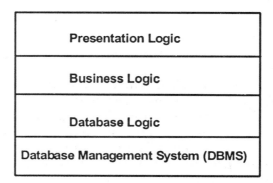

Figure 15.1 Application Layers

In our diagram we see that we have four layers. Each layer usually communicates with the adjacent layer(s) using a formal Application Programming Interface (API). The use of an API ensures that the details of a given layer may be changed without impacting the content of associated layers. As we shall we, the CICS BMS facility, the SQL language, and COBOL command level are each examples of APIs.

The *Presentation Layer* interfaces with the outside world. It takes data given to it, and formats it for the output device. In a classic online application, communication was via dumb terminals, so the presentation layer formatting was usually geared towards 3270 or 5250 displays. A *dumb* terminal is any terminal device without local intelligence, such as the AS/400s 5250 display. For CICS, the BMS facility usually performs the functions of the presentation layer.

Modern applications frequently use programmable workstations as their output device, and the presentation layer functionality is potentially more feature-rich and, accordingly, more complex. Of course, many modern applications treat programmable workstations as dumb terminals by using IRMA 3270 emulation hardware or the equivalent.

The *Business Logic* layer performs application logic. This usually is a mixture of simple number crunching and string manipulation for typical COBOL applications. For a CICS transaction, this code is written by the application programmer and generally does not involve large amounts of CICS processing.

The business logic component of an application is usually the most portable part of the application. COBOL is frequently used as the programming language, and COBOL is portable to a variety of operating systems and platforms. It is not unusual to develop the business logic on one platform (usually a programmable workstation), but execute it productively on a different platform.

The *Database Logic* layer implements the API used by the application to retrieve and update records. The actual database could be a SAM file, a VSAM file, a DL1 database, or even a real relational database. For CICS, the database logic API is accessed in command level via an EXEC CICS or an EXEC SQL command. For a relational database, the SQL language is the usual API.

It is key that a formal application programming interface (API) be used to access the database logic layer. Doing so facilitates rearchitecting or splitting out this logic. Thus, the formal CICS command level database logic interfaces allow database logic to be executed within a separate CICS system, or even by a non-CICS platform.

The *Database Management System* (DBMS) layer performs the actual database logic and I/O processing. This is frequently separate from the online system. For CICS and SQL, the DBMS function is performed in the separate SQL partition. Only the DBMS layer is aware of the details of how information is stored for a modern database.

15.2 Distributed Systems

The term *distributed processing* refers to splitting the logic of an application across two or more programs, which in turn may be split across several processors. The key is to usually split up functionality at a layer boundary. Thus, we can handle the presentation layer in one system, and the remaining layers in another system for a distributed application.

When multiple processors are involved, they may be of the same type of hardware or of different hardware types. The processors may run the same or different operating systems. The application should not have to be aware of any processor dependent rules for the formatting of data, character sets, or the passing of parameters.

Splitting an application across several CICS systems connected via MRO or ISC is an example of distributed processing. Different portions of a distributed CICS application may be done by different CICS systems, and freely moved between CICS systems without redesigning the application.

Another modern example of distributed processing is a PC Local Area Network (LAN). The location of files seen by a PC connected to a LAN is transparent to the PC application. Files may be freely moved from the local PC to the LAN server, with no application changes.

Most SQL/DS applications employ distributed processing since the database logic is performed by a different partition than the rest of the logic. The flexibility of the SQL/DS API allows transparent access to any SQL database from any application.

Distributed processing is a very general term. The terms *cooperative processing* and *client/server processing* describe specific types of distributed processing environments. Thus, while a PC LAN is an example of a distributed system, it is also an example of client/server processing. Let us look at these other terms.

15.3 Cooperative Processing

Cooperative processing is a form of distributed processing. This term is often used for a distributed system where the user interface is separated from the main logic of an online application. This is one of the easiest forms of distributed processing to understand or to write, and one of the oldest. Products such as Easel are available to easily separate the user interface from a CICS application. The user interface is moved to a PC while the main programming logic remains on the mainframe CICS.

Note that although the user interface moved, it did not necessarily exploit the capabilities of the PC display. Many mainframe applications are run using PCs as the user interface, where the PC looks just like a dumb terminal. Although cooperative processing may involve layers other than the presentation layer, the classical examples occur at this level.

A formal API may be used to implement cooperative processing. The CICS basic mapping support (BMS) interface is an example of an IBM mainframe interface that facilitates development of cooperative processing applications. XWINDOWS is an example of a cooperative processing protocol used in the UNIX environment.

Cooperative processing is an old example of distributed processing. Most modern distributed systems split out more than simply the user interface portion of an application. An application employing cooperative processing may also employ *client/server processing* to expand on the basic cooperative processing functionality. Let us look at this term next.

15.4   Client/Server Processing

Client/server processing applies to applications whose processing is split across multiple computer systems. A formal API is used to invoke each process distributed to another system. The requesting system is called the *client*. The system owning the requested process is called the *server*. A client/server application may be split at any point including file management, the user interface, and even within portions of the general processing logic.

What distinguishes client/server from cooperative processing? All client/server systems are a form of cooperative processing. But, client/server systems exploit the unique characteristics of their hardware. Thus, a PWS client may implement a presentation layer that fully exploits the GUI capabilities of the PWS.

AS/400 systems lend themselves to the development of client/server applications. Applications split across systems via CICS MRO are a classic example of client/server processing. The CICS file control mechanism acts as a formal API that allows files to be present upon the same computer system as the application that accesses them, or upon a totally separate system. The CICS application need not be cognizant of where a file is located. Similarly, one can split CICS transactions into multiple programs which are spread across several systems.

CICS allows us to distribute the components of our client/server application across several systems, even between different operating systems. With the advent of CICS support on other hardware architectures, CICS client/server computing can involve AS/400 systems, VSE/VM/MVS mainframe systems, OS2 personal computer systems, and even RS/6000 systems.

15.4.1   Distributed Presentation

One of the simplest forms of a client/server environment is provided by *Distributed Presentation*. Distributed Presentation is a form of distributed processing where the presentation layer is split between the client and server systems. The client owns only a portion of the presentation layer. The server owns a portion of the presentation function layer plus the whole business logic layer and the whole data management layer.

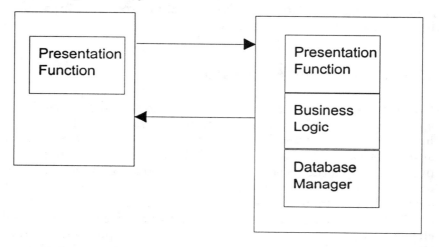

Figure 15.2   Distributed Presentation

In general, the client portion of the presentation layer is that portion with knowledge of the unique hardware characteristics of the display. The server portion is concerned with the logical content of the display, but not the exact implementation of the display. Refer to Figure 15.2 for an illustration of the distributed presentation environment.

Examples of a distributed presentation structure are found in X-Windows, Easel, Infront, and the OS2 Presentation Manager. Easel and Infront are front-end display management products that facilitate the migration of mainframe legacy applications to a PWS environment. X-Windows is a UNIX client/server environment based upon low-cost limited-function displays connected to a larger multiple-user server system. OS2 Presentation Manager uses the distributed presentation model in its communications between application and the Presentation Manager.

AS/400 applications frequently use distributed presentation with PCs. Doing so provides for high-end graphical displays not facilitated by the primitive AS/400 5250 dumb terminals. The use of PC Support/400 facilitates the development of client/server applications where the graphical display and some processing is performed by PCs and the remainder of the application functionality is provided by the AS/400.

15.4.2 LANs

A *Local Area Network* (*LAN*) is an example of client/server processing. Figure 15.3 illustrates this. Each of the client PCs has programming that filters disk I/O requests. Any requests for a disk (or disks) not resident upon the local PC are passed to the server for processing. A well-defined API that is part of the PC operating system implements this function.

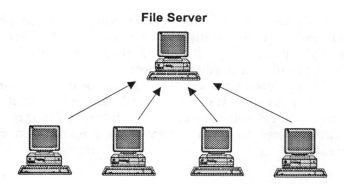

Figure 15.3   LAN as Client/Server

The server receives file I/O requests from clients, and performs them on behalf of the clients against its disk storage. The LAN server contains logic to arbitrate access to the same file, and implements locking mechanisms to prevent two applications from writing to the same area. The server is often a fast PC, which with adequate buffers will often provide data access times that are very close to that of locally resident data.

We have concentrated on the use of a LAN to share data. A LAN also provides a mechanism to share expensive hardware. Thus, we find LANs that provide shared access to large hard disks (including

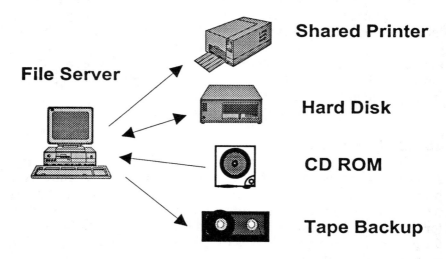

Figure 15.4   LAN Facilitates Hardware Sharing

reliable RAID redundant array DASD systems), laser printers, CD/ROM readers, tape backup systems, and WORM (Write Once Read Mostly) optical drives. Refer to Figure 15.4 for an example of a LAN being used as a hardware server.

The AS/400 is often used as a LAN server or as a component of a LAN system. As such, it can offer hardware server functionality through access to AS/400 owned DASD, printer, and tape resources. It also can be used to provide server-based application support across a LAN.

15.4.3   Token Ring

A *Token Ring* is a type of LAN where the different nodes sit on a ring. Messages and data circulate around the ring, and can be processed by any node. Token ring is the most common means of attaching local AS/400 systems. Refer to Figure 15.5 for an example of a token ring LAN with three AS/400 systems.

The AS/400 supports token ring connectivity via an optional adapter card for entry-level models and as a standard feature on many larger models. The token ring permits multiple AS/400's to be interconnected and provides low-cost access to mainframe systems, as well as LAN connectivity for AS/400 systems. Token-

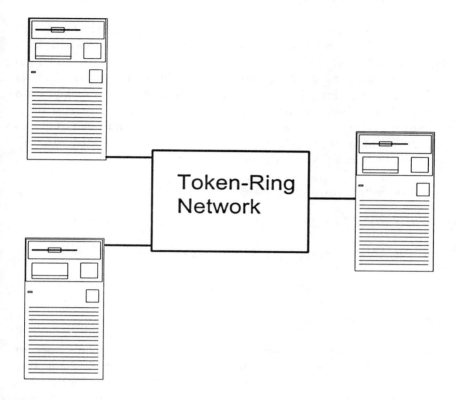

Figure 15.5   Token Ring LAN Example

ring connections are an inexpensive, high-performance pathway for
AS/400-based distributed applications development.

15.5   CICS OS2

The availability of CICS/OS2 means that applications may now be
distributed between your host CICS system and PCs running
CICS/OS2. In this mode *function shipping* and *transaction routing*
may be used to either offload a portion of an application or the
whole application to a workstation. We will also look at *Distributed
Program Link* and *Distributed Transaction Processing* between a
host CICS and workstations.

15.5.1   CICS Intersystem Communications

CICS/VS may communicate with CICS running on other physical systems. The *InterSystem Communications* facility (called *ISC*) allows a transaction request to be routed from the system on which it is requested to another system on which the transaction is implemented. Thus, ISC allows a transaction to be invoked by a terminal attached to one system's CICS, but actually run on a separate system. This separate system may be another CICS/400 or a different type of CICS system. The following can all communicate with CICS/VS via ISC:

- CICS/400 running on an AS/400 system

- CICS/MVS or CICS/ESA running on an MVS system

- CICS/VM running on a VM system

- CICS/VSE running on a VSE/ESA system

- CICS/OS2 running on a PC

Transaction routing is employed to get improved performance, or to run a transaction from a terminal attached to a CICS system that does not implement the transaction. Transaction routing can offer performance improvements when the network delay required to ship a transaction request is less than the time saved by running the request remotely. Two examples of the second type of transaction routing are accessing a VM/ESA DB2 transaction from a CICS/400 system, or running a VSE/ESA DB2 database transaction from CICS/OS2 routed through an AS/400. Figure 15.6 illustrates the routing of a transaction request from an AS/400 system to an MVS DB2 system.

Another alternative to routing a whole transaction to access a resource on a remote facility is to route only the request for the required function to the remote system. This is called *Function Shipping*. We will look at this next.

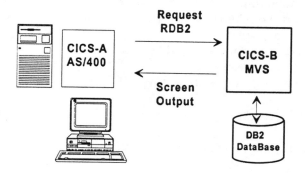

Figure 15.6   Transaction Routing from AS/400 to MVS

15.5.2 CICS/OS2 Function Shipping

Function shipping allows a request to access a CICS controlled resource to be automatically routed to another CICS system where it is processed. Thus, a CICS transaction running on CICS-A can access files owned by CICS-B. (See Figure 15.7.) Just as you might employ function shipping to distribute portions of an application across several AS/400 systems, you can use ISC to split the work between your AS/400, a VSE/ESA system, and one or more PCs running CICS/OS2.

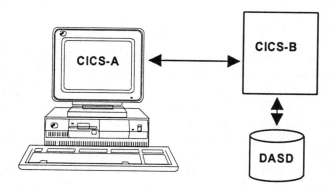

Figure 15.7   CICS/OS2 and CICS/VSE Communications

The performance of a CICS application employing function shipping is dependant upon a number of factors. Let us briefly list the components of the response time of a distributed request:

- Transmission time to send request

- Time waiting in queue on target CICS

- Request processing time

- Transmission time to return result

Certainly the transmission time is unique to distributed processing. It is also a straight "add-on" cost for the transaction, since time spent doing data transmission is not overlapped with other processing of the requesting application. The time in queue on the target CICS is usually small, but can become significant if the target CICS is busy. In this case, the request cannot be processed until the current application can be interrupted, and any higher-priority CICS tasks are first serviced. The time to process the request may be less or more than it would be in a nondistributed environment. If the target system is much faster than the requesting system, it is possible for the request processing time to compensate for the transmission time. In fact, an actual performance improvement may be seen, but rarely.

15.5.3 CICS Distributed Program Link

CICS allows an application to issue an EXEC CICS LINK command to pass a request for processing by a separate CICS/400, CICS/OS2, CICS/ESA, or CICS/VSE system. This support is called *Distributed Program Link (DPL)*. DPL ships the CICS COMAREA from the requesting OS2 system to the remote processing CICS. DPL in effect allows a CICS/OS2 program to employ LU6.2-based distributed processing without the need for LU6.2 programming.

DPL is a powerful means of providing AS/400 and workstation access to AS/400 SQL tables, mainframe resident SQL/DS databases, or large VSAM files. It is also a way to utilize older macro-level CICS programs that are unable to be ported to CICS/OS2. However, like transaction routing and function shipping, DPL can introduce performance problems.

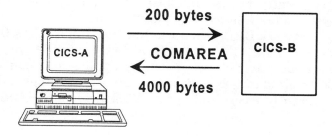

Figure 15.8   CICS/OS2 DPL Example

The CICS COMAREA is often the source of DPL performance problems.   The CICS COMAREA can range in size up to 32KB. Data transmission of a large COMAREA can account for the bulk of the response time of a distributed application.   CICS trims trailing hex zeroes (low values) from the COMAREA.   For this reason, you should left justify any data sent within the COMAREA. If you send a 200-byte request, but expect to receive a 4000-byte response, the time to send the request is minimized if the 200 bytes are left justified within the 4000-byte COMAREA.

Figure 15.8 illustrates the data transfers used by DPL.

15.5.4   Distributed Transaction Processing

Distributed Transaction Processing (DTP) allows a transaction on one system to initiate then communicate with a transaction on another system.   DTP may be used by CICS/400 to initiate a transaction on CICS/OS2, then to exchange information with the workstation transaction.   DTP is an alternative to DPL when data owned by a remote CICS system is to be accessed from another system.   Application programs employing DTP may use CICS commands to control an APPC conversation.

15.6   SQL/DS DRDA

AS/400 online and batch database programs may access a database on a VSE system or VM system connected via the network.   Also, VSE/ESA SQL/DS 3.4 offers *Distributed Relational Database Access* support (called *DRDA*). This means that VSE/ESA applications may transparently access database information distributed on AS/400 systems (as well as multiple VSE images.)

SQL/DS acts as a DRDA server to Remote Unit of Work (RUOW) applications. Thus, SQL/DS 3.4 allows VSE/ESA to offer a client/server environment where client applications can request access to remote data. For example, any AS/400 application can now transparently access and update VSE resident SQL/DS tables.

PC Support/400

This chapter looks at the PC Support facilities of the OS/400 system. *PC Support/400* is a set of programs that allows PC users to access and store information in AS/400 folders as though it were PC resident, transfer data between the PC and the AS/400, emulate an AS/400 workstation with your PC, and access PC printers as though they were attached to the AS/400 as well as AS/400 printers as though they were PC attached. In addition, PC Support/400 offers easy to use menus for many of the common commands of both the PC and the AS/400. This chapter discusses each of these areas. PC Support operates on PCs running both the DOS and the OS/2 operating systems. We will use the term *PC Support* in this chapter to apply to PC Support/400.

16.1 File Storage and Sharing

PC Support allows you to treat your AS/400 as a file server for your PC. As such, you can store and access files on the AS/400, and you can also access other PC Support users files that have been stored on the AS/400. All file access is done through file folders. A *file folder* is an OS/400 term for a facility where files may be grouped together.

You may choose to keep most of your data on the AS/400, or on your PC, and you may easily move data between the two. Which option you choose depends upon where the data will be most frequently used, as well as on your choice of backup vehicles. One advantage of storing data on the AS/400 is that many different PCs may access that data. Another advantage to AS/400 storage is that your AS/400 backup procedures are usually more elaborate and better controlled than PC backup procedures.

16.1.1 File Folders and PC Drives

The AS/400 organizes files into *folders*. Your PC groups files by disk letters, and then within directories. Normally, PC disk letters are associated with individual disk drive devices. Thus, your floppy disk has a drive letter (usually A:), and your hard drive has a disk letter (usually C:). However, you may also associate PC drive letters with *virtual disk drives*. These are simulated disk devices, or devices not part of your system. Thus, you can use drive letters to access network disks and the PC Support simulated PC disks. With PC Support, you select an AS/400 folder and associate it with an available PC drive letter. You may associate several file folders with a single drive letter. You may associate multiple AS/400 file folders with multiple PC drive letters, and you can change which folders are currently accessible while using the system.

Select the *Use Folders on Host System* entry from the PC Support menu to interactively associate file folders with a drive letter. Or, you may use the FSPC command to manually assign file folders to a drive letter. The folder names are mapped into simulated PC directories on the designated drive letter. If folder LETTERS is within folder MYDATA on drive J, the simulated address and directory name will be J:\MYDATA\LETTERS.

You may choose to map all of the folders on a single system into one PC drive letter. Thus, FSPC K: //SYSPROD will assign disk letter K to all folders available on the system named SYSPROD. Any available PC tool may be used to display the directory tree simulated for this drive letter. In fact, all PC commands that operate upon disk letters and directories will function with folders. You can copy all members of a folder with a single command. Thus, COPY J:\MYDATA\LETTERS*.* A: will copy all members of the folder LETTERS within the FOLDER MYDATA to the floppy drive A. The standard XCOPY PC command is also available to copy whole groups of subdirectories.

Use the command FSPC STATUS to display a summary status of all drive letters. You can also see this summary information by selecting the *Use Folders on Host System* menu item. The menu displays all used and available drive letters. For drive letters currently in use, the folder selection is displayed. When a system level assignment was specified, the display lists (All Folders) to indicate the selection; otherwise the specific folders are displayed.

16.1.2 Releasing Drive Letters

You can release drive letters associated with AS/400 file folders. You should do this when you are done with a drive to prevent accidental access or deletion of information you do not intend to use, and to make the drive letter available for reuse. Select the *Use Folders on Host System* menu entry and specify RELEASE from the list of options. If you choose option 2, then all drive letters will be released.

If you choose option 1, then you may select which drive letters are to be released. A list of all current drives is displayed for you to pick from. You may also decide to release drives manually via the FSPC RELEASE command. Thus, FSPC RELEASE K will release the folder(s) associated with the K drive letter, while the command FSPC RELEASE * will release all folders from all drive letters.

16.1.3 Shared Folders and File Check-out

Several different PCs can each be running PC Support, accessing the same file folder, and the same AS/400 files within that folder. If several users make copies of a file, update that file, and return it to the AS/400, some data loss can occur. Because AS/400 programs can access and update the contents of file folders which are in use by PCs, other types of conflicts can also arise. For example, an AS/400 program may be run that reads a file only half built by a PC, and thus only processes half of the information. PC support provides a file check-out and check-in mechanism to coordinate access to files and prevent this type of data loss and data confusion. This mechanism is only available when extended PC support is provided and this feature was selected when your PC was set up.

16.2 File Transfer Functions

PC Support offers functions that allow data to be transferred from the PC to the AS/400 as well as from the AS/400 to the PC. You can easily access records within an AS/400 database, extract the fields needed for a spreadsheet application on the PC, and ship the data to the PC. This avoids the need to rekey data, with the loss of time and the risk of errors. You can also input data on your PC and transfer it to the AS/400 for subsequent processing. This allows the use of your PCs as data entry stations, and thus eliminates the need to have both PCs and regular AS/400 terminals for most users.

Before you can transfer data, you must first create a transfer request that defines where the data is currently located and specifies the portion of the data to be transferred, the sort sequence of the data, and where the data is to be placed on the target system. Most meaningful AS/400 object types are supported for transfer. PC Support will transfer data from both physical and logical databases on the AS/400, but can only receive data into a physical database. A sample file named QCUSTCDT is provided in the library QIWS for you to use to practice transfers from the AS/400 to your PC.

Data is transferred from and to members of AS/400 files. You can transfer an existing AS/400 member to a PC. When you transfer data from the PC it can be placed into a new member of a new or existing file, or it can replace an existing member of a file.

16.2.1 Transfer from AS/400 to PC

The process to follow for transfers to and from the AS/400 is similar. We will look at the AS/400 to PC transfer first, then the PC to AS/400 process in the next section. To set up a transfer request, perform the following steps,

- Enter the PC support main menu and select *Transfer Data*.

- Press F10 and select Create to define a new transfer request.

- Press the Enter key to display prompts for the data to enter.

- Provide the requested data (System Name, FROM, SELECT, WHERE, ORDER BY, and Output Device).

The System name is specified to identify the source AS/400 system for the request. Your PC can be attached to multiple AS/400 systems, and you need to specify from which AS/400 you will be transferring data. Your default system is automatically provided and will be used if not altered.

FROM specifies which files you wish to transfer. Code the file as library-name/file-name(member-name,record-format-name). Only the file-name portion of this is required, as the AS/400 will search for the rest of the information for you. Remember that the file-name is restricted to 10 characters in length. When the library-name is not provided, then *USRLIBR will be searched. You can also press F4 to see a list of all available libraries. If you have selected a library, then you can press F4 to see a list of files in that library. You can specify multiple file names by separating the names with commas. The member-name is also optional. If it is omitted, then the transfer will use the first member of the specified file. The record-format-name field is only needed if the file selected has multiple record formats. If you are not sure of the record-format-name, you can press F4 after providing the member name to display a list of available record formats. For our sample file, you would specify QIWS/QCUSTCDT to identify library QIWS and file QCUSTCDT.

The SELECT prompt identifies which fields in which record format you wish to include in the transfer. The default value is asterisk (*), which means that all fields are to be included in the transfer. If you only need certain information from the records, then specify the names of the fields, separated by commas in the order you wish the data to be provided. You can specify either detail or summary data fields. Detail fields are taken from every record in the file. Summary fields are derived from the detail field values. The summary data supported includes the average, maximum value seen, minimum value seen, the sum of the values seen, and a count of fields. The summary facility is a powerful tool that can allow you to transfer much less data as well as eliminate some simple programming.

The WHERE prompt is optional. It is specified to perform tests upon fields to determine whether or not the record containing them is to be processed. If the WHERE information is not provided, then all records will be transferred, or processed for summarization. The WHERE prompt supports complex specifications which will not be discussed in detail here. Refer to the PC Support/400: Users Guide for details.

The ORDER BY prompt is optional. If it is omitted, then the data is transferred in no special sequence. It is important to understand that you can assume nothing about this order -- the same transfer run twice in a row could produce different record sequences if ORDER BY is not provided. To specify an output record sequence, simply list the names of the fields to sort separated by commas. You may only specify the names of the fields from the SELECT prompt, you cannot sort on fields not included in the transfer.

The Output Device prompt identifies how the data is to be used on the personal computer. Specify Display (1) to simply display the selected data on your screen. Specify Printer (2) to print the selected data. In this case you will need to identify the printer to be used for output. Specify Disk (3) if the data is to be stored in a PC file. In this case you will need to identify the disk letter as well as the path and target file name. When data is transferred to a PC file, you can have the transfer description saved in a separate PC file. This description file is required if you later wish to transfer the data from the PC back to the AS/400.

16.2.2 Transfer from PC to AS/400

Let us now look at the transfer of PC data to the AS/400. The steps are similar to those we looked at in the prior section. We will discuss the steps of this process, noting differences that depend on whether we are returning data to the AS/400 previously retrieved via PC/Support, or instead simply transferring data originating on the PC to the AS/400. To set up a transfer request from your PC to the AS/400 perform the following steps on the PC:

- Enter the PC support main menu and select *Transfer Data*.

- Press F10 and select Create to define a new transfer request.

- Press the Enter key to display prompts for the data to enter. Note that to this point the steps are identical to those of the prior section.

- Provide the requested data (System Name, TO, FROM, Use PC File Description, Description File Name, Create AS/400 Objects, AS/400 File Type, and Field Reference File name).

The System name is specified to identify the target system for the request. Your PC can be attached to multiple AS/400 systems, and you need to specify to which AS/400 you will be transferring data. Your default system is automatically provided and will be used if not altered.

Code TO to identify the target AS/400 library, file, and member as library-name/file-name(member-name,record-format-name). Only the file-name portion of this is required, as the AS/400 will search for the rest of the information for you. Remember that the file-name is restricted to 10 characters in length. When the library-name is not provided then *LIBL will be used as the default target library. You can press F4 to see a list of all available libraries (those present in *USRLIBL). If you have selected a library, then you can press F4 to see a list of files in that library. If you have not specified a library, you can key *USRLIBL/ and press F4 to see a list of the files in all libraries in the list. The member-name is optional. If it is omitted then the transfer will use the first member of the specified file. If you specify the name of a member that does not exist, it will be created. If you specify the name of an existing member, it will be totally replaced by the data transferred from the PC. You may press F4 after specifying a file to see a list of available member names. The record-format-name field is needed only if the file selected has multiple record formats. If you are not sure of the record-format-name, you can press F4 after providing the member name to display a list of available record formats. If you create a member during a transfer, then the default record format of QDFTFMT will be used, if none is specified.

The FROM prompt specifies the PC file you will be transferring to the AS/400. You may provide any valid PC file name, including the drive letter, directory path, file name and extension. If you are returning a file previously transferred from the AS/400, select the Use PC File Description option. If the member name is the same as was used to download the PC, you need not specify the File Description file name as PC/Support will use a default of "name.FDF" where "name" is the original data file name and FDF is the extension automatically supplied to the description file.

The Create AS/400 Objects prompt allows you to specify if the member named in the TO prompt is new. If you select Yes (option 2), then you will be prompted for additional data. The AS/400 File Type prompt is used to specify the type of file you wish to create. Usually this will be Data (option 2). The Field Reference File name prompt is provided to allow you to identify the file containing the field descriptions for a new file you are creating. The Authority prompt is used to specify if other users are permitted to access the new file you are creating (option 1 allows other users read/write access). The File Text prompt is used to provide a description for a new file. This is optional, but encouraged. The Member Text prompt is used to provide a description for a new member being created.

16.2.3 Saving Transfer Requests

It would be cumbersome to supply the information for an often repeated transfer request. PC/Support allows you to Save, Recall, and Execute transfer requests once the information has been provided. You should save a transfer request if you plan on using it multiple times. After providing the specification, press F10 and select Save and supply the following data.

- Name of Request. The name of the PC file in which the request is to be saved. Note this is different from the name of the data file you are transferring with the request.

- Replace Old File. Specify the action to be taken if the transfer definition file already exists. Select No if this is a new transfer definition, and Yes if you are intentionally replacing an old transfer definition file.

- Description. You can provide an optional description of the transfer definition file. The description can be up to 40 characters long. You are encouraged to always describe your request definition files.

Once you have saved a transfer request, you can retrieve it via F10 and Recall, followed by the name of the request file. If you do not remember the name you used, you may press F4 for a list of available transfer request files. Once the transfer request file name is provided or selected from the list, the transfer request details will be displayed. You can proceed to modify it, save it, or run it. To modify a request, simply make the desired changes and save it as originally was done, remembering to specify that the transfer request file may be replaced. To run a transfer request you have displayed, press F5. Or, use F10 and select run from the list of actions and specify the transfer request file to execute.

16.3   PC View of PC Support

This is a brief discussion of the view of PC Support from the PC user's standpoint. For a more detailed treatment of this subject, refer to the IBM manual *PC Support/400: DOS User's Guide*. This manual covers PC Support for both DOS and Windows users.

When not actually running PC Support, your PC behaves as it normally does. That is, the standard PC command line interface is available, and used to start PC Support and to perform other tasks. Usually, you issue the STARTPCS command to initiate PC Support (unless your environment has defined another command to do so). When PC Support is started this way, a menu is displayed providing access to the various PC Support functions. Depending upon how PC Support was installed on your system, either the PC Support Organizer menu or the standard PC Support menu will be displayed. You may access the PC Support menu from the Organizer menu by selecting option 4 (PC Support).

16.3.1   Ending PC Support

Once PC support has been started, your displays will look like, and behave like, those on any AS/400 terminal until PC Support is ended. Note that you should NEVER end PC Support by rebooting your PC. That is, do not use Ctrl-Alt-Del to exit PC Support. Doing so can result in communications errors, or perhaps even the loss of some data. You should also not power off your PC in the evening while PC Support is still active. This also can cause problems. Instead, choose the sign off option to exit the PC support menus, then power off or reboot your machine if that is desired.

Once PC Support has been ended, you may wish to remove its components from your PC memory in order to make memory available for other programs. If running the Organizer, first select option 90 to exit the Organizer. Press the F3 key to exit the PC Support menu. When you use F3 to exit PC Support, you are returned to the PC command line. You may then issue commands to remove PC Support components from memory. The RMVPCS command will display a special menu used to interactively select which PC Support components are to be removed from memory. You may also choose to manually remove parts of PC Support by using the RMVPCS command in a batch mode with operands specifying what components are to be removed.

16.4   Windows and PC Support

PC Support functions within the Windows operating environment. This may be very desirable for users who need to run PC Support as well as other PC programs. Because PC Support has very large storage requirements, you often do not have enough memory to run PC Support and other programs with DOS.   However, with Windows you can isolate PC Support in a virtual DOS session, while you run other DOS programs. In this case, your usual DOS applications do not see most of the memory occupied by PC Support and appear to have more memory available than they otherwise would have.

CICS Connectivity

This chapter looks at CICS/400 as well as OS/400 connectivity with other CICS transaction processing systems. CICS is a transaction processing environment supported on mainframes, midsize systems, and even the desktop. In a transaction processing environment, a number of online users share access to a smaller number of applications and data files. Because the data files are shared, the changes made by one online user are seen by all. We will look at various environments that CICS is supported in, and briefly discuss the merits of each in a distributed system.

CICS applications are easily distributed. In a distributed environment, applications may reside on a different system than the data, and perhaps a different system than the one the online user terminals are physically connected to. Distributed processing is discussed in detail in Chapter 15. Here we briefly look at some distributed CICS specific issues.

17.1 CICS/400 at a Glance

The AS/400 supports a fully functional CICS that may function standalone, or in conjunction with other CICS systems. In addition, special functionality is provided for the AS/400 system that employs PC Support/400. The mainframe compatible COBOL and CICS support of the AS/400 makes it a particularity interesting choice for rightsizing existing mainframe applications.

CICS/400 is built on top of the existing AS/400 architecture to ensure that AS/400 programmers and users do not require retraining in order to use CICS. At the same time, the functionality of the AS/400 is extended to include CICS facilities and features. In some cases, this is done by emulating mainframe functions. Let us quickly look at emulated features, then move on to native function added to the AS/400 base by CICS.

17.1.1 CICS/400 Emulated Function

CICS/400 implements some CICS functionality that is unique to the mainframe environment by emulation. Thus, the portion of Basic Mapping Support (BMS) which allows 3270 compatible screens to be described at a high level is emulated for AS/400 users. And, the CICS/VSAM file interface is emulated using the AS/400 integrated file system.

17.1.2 CICS Added Function

Additional function added to the AS/400 system by CICS/400 includes:

- Temporary storage facility

- CICS error condition handling

- CICS intersystem communications

- Basic Mapping Support (BMS)

17.1.3 CICS Limitations

Although the CICS/400 implementation is quite robust, some limitations with respect to other CICS implementations are present. The limitations for CICS/400 V2.3 include:

- Only command level COBOL support (no macro level, no PL/I).

- Terminals are restricted to 24 by 80 and 27 by 132.

- Data access emulates VSAM files but not BDAM nor DL/I.

- COBOL COMP fields must be changed to binary, pointers are 16-bytes long, and the special register length changed.

- Multiple-phase commit is not currently supported.

17.2 CICS OS2

The availability of CICS/400 and CICS/OS2 means that applications may now be distributed between your AS/400 host and PCs running CICS/OS2. In this mode *function shipping* or *transaction routing* may be used to either offload a portion of an application or the whole application to a workstation. In *function shipping*, a single function of an application may be performed by a different CICS than the rest of the application. In *transaction routing*, the whole transaction may be performed by a different CICS than the one owning the terminal and receiving the initial request. We will also look at *Distributed Program Link* and *Distributed Transaction Processing* between the AS/400 and workstations.

17.2.1 Intersystem Communications

CICS/400 may communicate with CICS running on other physical systems. The *InterSystem Communications* facility (called *ISC*) allows a transaction request to be routed from the system on which it is requested to another system on which the transaction is implemented. Thus, ISC allows a transaction to be invoked by a terminal attached to one system's CICS, but actually run on a separate system. This separate system may be another CICS/400 system or a different type of CICS system such as CICS/VSE. The following can all communicate with CICS/400 via ISC:

- CICS/400 running on another AS/400 system

- CICS/MVS or CICS/ESA running on an MVS system

- CICS/VM running on a VM system

- CICS/VSE running on a VSE/ESA system

- CICS/OS2 running on a PC

- CICS/6000 running on an RS/6000

- Other CICS systems are being developed as this is written

Transaction routing is employed to get improved performance, or to run a transaction from a terminal attached to a CICS system that does not implement the transaction. Transaction routing can offer performance improvements when the network delay required to ship a transaction request is less than the time saved by running the request remotely. Two examples of the second type of transaction routing are accessing a DB2 transaction from a CICS/400 system, or running an AS/400 database transaction from CICS/OS2. Figure 17.1 illustrates the routing of a transaction request from a VSE/ESA system to an AS/400 system.

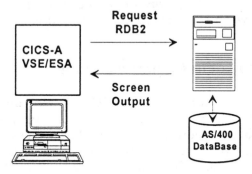

Figure 17.1 Intersystem Communications — VSE to AS/400

Another alternative to routing a whole transaction to access a resource on a remote facility is to route only the request for the required function to the remote system, while running the rest of the transaction on the originating system. This is called *Function Shipping*. We will look at this next.

17.2.2   CICS/OS2 Function Shipping

Function shipping allows a request to access any CICS controlled resource to be automatically routed to another CICS system where the resource is present and the request is processed. Thus, a CICS transaction running on CICS-A can access files owned by CICS-B. (See Figure 17.2.) Just as you might employ function shipping to distribute portions of an application across several AS/400 systems, you can use ISC to split the work between your AS/400 system and one or more PCs running CICS/OS2.

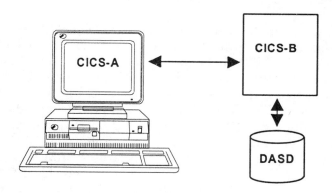

Figure 17.2 CICS/OS2 and CICS/VSE Communications

The performance of a CICS application employing function shipping is dependent upon a number of factors. Let us briefly list the components of the response time of a distributed request:

● Transmission time to send request

● Time waiting in queue on target CICS

● Request processing time

● Transmission time to return result

Certainly the transmission time is unique to distributed processing. It is also a straight "add-on" cost for the transaction, since time spent doing data transmission is not overlapped with other processing of the requesting application. The time in queue on the target CICS is usually small, but can become significant if the target CICS is busy. In this case, the request cannot be processed until the currently executing application can be interrupted, and any higher priority CICS tasks are first serviced. The time to process the request may be less or more than it would be in a nondistributed environment. If the target system is much faster than the requesting system, it is possible for the request processing time to compensate for the transmission time. In fact, an actual performance improvement may be seen, but rarely.

17.2.3 CICS Distributed Program Link

CICS allows an application to issue an EXEC CICS LINK command to pass a request for processing by a separate CICS/400, CICS/OS2, CICS/ESA, or CICS/VSE system. This support is called *Distributed Program Link (DPL)*. DPL ships the CICS COMAREA from the requesting OS2 system to the remote processing CICS. DPL in effect allows a CICS/OS2 program to employ LU6.2-based distributed processing without the need for LU6.2 programming.

DPL is a powerful means of providing AS/400 workstation access to VSE/ESA SQL/DS databases, or to large VSAM files on MVS systems. It is also a way to utilize older macro level CICS programs that are unable to be ported to CICS/OS2. However, like transaction routing, and function shipping, DPL can introduce performance problems.

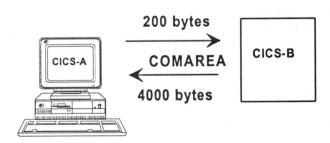

Figure 17.3 CICS/OS2 DPL Example

The CICS COMAREA is often the source of DPL performance problems. The CICS COMAREA can range in size up to 32KB. Data transmission of a large COMAREA can account for the bulk of the response time of a distributed application. CICS trims trailing hex zeroes (low values) from the COMAREA. For this reason, you should left justify any data sent within the COMAREA. If you send a 200-byte request, but expect to receive a 4000-byte response, the time to send the request is minimized if the 200 bytes are left justified within the 4000-byte COMAREA. Figure 17.3 illustrates the data transfers used by DPL.

17.2.4 Distributed Transaction Processing

Distributed Transaction Processing (*DTP*) allows a transaction on one system to initiate then communicate with a transaction on another system. CICS/400 fully supports DTP. DTP may be used by CICS/400 to initiate a transaction on CICS/OS2, then to exchange information with the workstation transaction. CICS/400 may also use DTP to access VSE and MVS mainframe resident databases. DTP is an alternative to DPL when data owned by a remote CICS system is to be accessed from another system. Application programs employing DTP may use CICS commands to control an APPC conversation.

Chapter

18

VTAM

This chapter discusses VTAM. VTAM is the principal mainframe communications protocol. We include an overview of VTAM structure. Information is provided on VTAM supported hardware, LAN interfacing, and of the functions of the host and the NCP, because these are often poorly understood areas when AS/400s are connected to mainframe systems.

VTAM is an acronym for *Virtual Telecommunications Access Method*. VTAM is the primary MVS, VM, and VSE remote device access method. As such, VTAM implements *System Network Architecture* (*SNA*) for mainframes. Thus, when your AS/400 is communicating with a mainframe, it is talking to VTAM, and through VTAM to your target application.

This chapter assumes some basic familiarity with VTAM terminology. For the new AS/400 user, we will look at the structure of VTAM, how you describe your network to VTAM, and how the NCP is generated, all from the viewpoint of an AS/400 user who desires to communicate with a system running VTAM. The IBM manual *IBM VSE/Enterprise Systems Architecture: Networking Support* (SC33-6508) is an excellent source of information on VTAM basics plus a simple guide for defining the network to a VSE system.

The IBM manual *VTAM Network Implementation Guide* (SC31-6404) is a good source of configuration information. This manual contains a chapter titled "Tuning VTAM for Your Environment" that is a good source of basic VTAM tuning guidelines.

18.1 VTAM at a Glance

VTAM operates at several software and hardware levels. We will look briefly at these levels, and at what impact each level has upon communications performance. We will look at the VTAM subsystem, the user application, and the operating system software components.

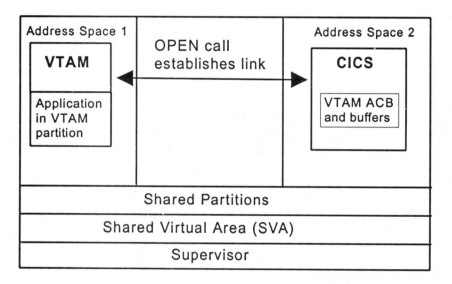

Figure 18.1 VTAM Overview

VTAM runs as a job in the mainframe. For VSE/ESA, VTAM runs in a VSE partition as illustrated in Figure 18.1. It consumes CPU time, uses large amounts of virtual storage, and performs many I/Os in the VTAM partition. This portion of VTAM is the one most users think of as being the real "VTAM." The VTAM partition serves as an interface between your application and the hardware for which VTAM manages the communications.

VTAM is accessed from an application. Generally, each application occupies its own partition. The application establishes a connection to VTAM by issuing an OPEN. It then makes requests of VTAM. These requests are performed partially in the VTAM partition and partially in the application partition. Resources are required in both partitions. CICS is an example of a VTAM application that occupies its own partition.

VTAM processing also involves code that runs as part of the operating system. This code allows VTAM early access to I/O status information, provides communications services across partitions, and ensures that VTAM cleanup is performed as applications terminate.

18.2   VTAM Network Structure Terminology

VTAM manages communications within a network of nodes. Nodes are made up of computer systems, control units, and devices. VTAM has its own terminology for the different types of node. In this section we will familiarize ourselves with some of this VTAM terminology.

A *Network Addressable Unit (NAU)* is a single addressable node in a VTAM network. Each node is an NAU. Each NAU has a network address used to access it.

A *Session* is a connection between two NAUs. A session is uniquely identified by the addresses of its two NAUs. NAUs are the elements of the VTAM network, and sessions are the connections between such elements. The next three definitions are for the different types of NAUs.

A *System Services Control Point (SSCP)* is a central location point within a VTAM network where the network under that point is defined and where network messages may be directed for operator action. A network may have one or more SSCPs. When several VSE systems are interconnected via VTAM, each VSE is a separate SSCP. The domain of an SSCP is the set of physical units (PUs), logical units (LUs), and links defined under that SSCP.

An SSCP offers services to other nodes within the network. These services can take the form of programs running as VTAM applications, or could be simply to provide access to other SSCPs.

A *Physical Unit (PU)* manages the resources of a node. The PU is directed by an owning SSCP. An SSCP creates a session to manage the resources attached to the PU node.

A *Logical Unit (LU)* is a port through which a user accesses the network. Each LU can support at least two sessions, one session to an SSCP and the second to another LU. An LU is either a *Primary LU (PLU)* or a *Secondary LU (SLU)*. The PLU is the LU requesting a session via a bind. The SLU is the LU that participated in a session after being requested. A single LU can be the PLU for one session, while it is an SLU for another session.

18.3 VTAM Device Support

VTAM is able to manage a variety of different devices. In this section, we briefly look at the hardware resources supported by VTAM. Since VTAM is a communications package, we generally think of VTAM as supporting hardware used to connect two systems but VTAM also supports a number of nonintelligent devices.

Terminals supported by VTAM include both local and remote devices. One advantage of using VTAM for local terminals is that only a single address is defined to the system for local SNA terminal controllers. Non-SNA controllers treat each terminal as a separate device and require that each terminal be uniquely added to VSE at IPL time.

Terminals defined to VTAM include both "dumb" devices such as 3270s and also terminals with local intelligence such as modern LU6.2 devices. PCs attached to local terminal controllers via IRMA cards or other 3270 emulation cards appear the same to VTAM as any dumb terminal. As DFT devices, most such emulation cards also provide for PU2.0 connectivity of PCs. PCs can also be attached using SNA cards that look like SNA controllers and permit full LU6.2 functionality. Token-ring attachment of PC LANs is also supported by VTAM.

VTAM supports *Channel-To-Channel-Adapters* (*CTCAs*). A CTCA is the best way to communicate information between two mainframe systems. Although the systems must be physically close and a CTCA is not inexpensive, it is the only channel speed way to pass large amounts of data between mainframe systems.

VTAM remote device support involves communication control units. VTAM supports devices such as the 3745 that have their own control programs (NCP) that VTAM may load. You define how the bandwidth available to a communication controller is to be divided between your various communications links.

18.3.1 NCP Generation

VTAM requires a *Network Control Program* (called an *NCP*) to be run within 3725 and 3745 control units. The NCP handles communications between the host processor and SNA devices. (See Figure 18.2.) The NCP definition is comprised of a description of

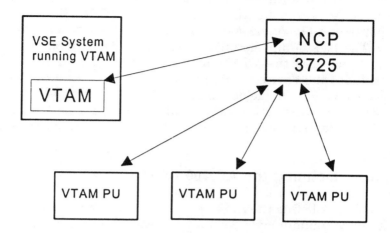

Figure 18.2   VTAM NCP in Relation to VTAM

the links, physical devices, and logical devices to be interfaced. The NCP definition is processed by the System Support Program (SSP) on the VSE/ESA host system, and the actual NCP is built as a phase (usually in the PRD2.CONFIG sublibrary) or as a sequential file. The phase or file contains the control program image for the 3725 or 3745 control unit. This phase is downloaded to the control unit by VTAM. If you use the phase option to load the NCP, then you must have enough available space in the program area of the VTAM partition for the largest NCP phase. You can save this VTAM partition storage by using only the sequential file load method. Several NCPs may be defined, each with its own name.

The remainder of this section describes the NCP definition in more detail. The description of the link contains a variety of information. Each link has a unique name. It indicates whether the link is on a leased or switched line. The address of the link on the control unit is also defined. The data mode tells NCP to communicate in half-duplex (HDX) or full-duplex (FDX) mode. The SPEED definition identifies the transmission rate of the link.

The physical unit definition describes a physical device attached to a link. The subsystem group definition identifies the device as a display/printer system or as an intelligent system. The physical unit type defines the device number and model information. The SDLC station address is the hexadecimal byte value associated with this device and must be unique within a link. The identification block and identification number are IDs that are used to tag message traffic by the NCP. You provide SDLC token ring parameters to describe devices attached via a token ring LAN.

The logical unit definition describes the path through which a user accesses the VTAM network. The logical unit specification includes the device name, the local address, and the VTAM/CICS parameters. The device name is a generic name of a given set of device characteristics. The local address is a port number for a 3270 terminal, or a label assigned within an intelligent system.

18.4 Defining the AS/400 to NCP

You must define the AS/400 as part of your NCP generation if you wish to communicate between the AS/400 and a VTAM controlled node. Each AS/400 controller is defined as a separate physical unit (PU) to VTAM. Let us look at the key parameters for defining an AS/400 for an SDLC line.

- PUTYPE the physical unit type is 2.

- ADDR the station address you specified in your CRTLINSDLC or CRTCTLHOST specifications.

- ISTATUS specifies whether or not the physical unit is assumed ACTIVE or INACTIVE when this NCP's VTAM becomes active.

- MAXDATA specifies the amount of data that the AS/400 can receive. This value MUST match the MAXFRAME value specified on your AS/400 system. The default (assumed) value is 521 bytes which is a 512-byte buffer with a 9-byte header. You may specify values of 265, 521, 1033, 1466, 1994, and 2057. Remember that whatever size you specify to VTAM/NCP must match your AS/400 MAXFRAME specification.

- MAXOUT specifies the number of frames that NCP sends to the AS/400 before waiting for a response. Specify seven for best performance.

- IDBLK and IDNUM. Specify IDBLK as 56 (required for the AS/400). Specify IDNUM the same as the EXCHID parameter you entered with the CRTLINSDLC command.

- SSCPFM specifies USSSCS for support of AS/400 character coded messages.

Note that the SSCPID value is given in hexadecimal notation on the AS/400, but is specified as decimal on the mainframe system. Also, the mainframe MAXDATA value must match the AS/400 MAXFRAME value. These values are each opportunities for problems that can be fun to diagnose.

18.5 Accessing the AS/400 from CICS/VS

Customer Information Control System for Virtual Storage (CICS/VS) is used on a host mainframe system that communicates with AS/400 systems. The SNA Upline Facility (SNUF) is the enabling software on the AS/400 for distributed processing with mainframe systems. The mainframe may be running either IMS/VS (MVS only) or CICS/VSE (MVS and VSE). SNUF provides for both batch and online communications with the host system. SNUF provides the following facilities:

- AS/400 programs can initiate tasks on the host system.

- Host systems can initiate programs on the AS/400.

- SNUF can share a single SNA communication line with other AS/400-based SNA programs.

- SNUF applications can communicate records with data lengths of up to 32,767 bytes.

- SNUF applications can be written using any of the AS/400 high-level languages in conjunction with data description specifications (DDS).

- SNUF 3270 support allows the AS/400 to communicate with host applications through 3270 data streams.

SNUF supports a variety of communications line types including SDLC, X.25, token ring, and Ethernet. You define the line to SNUF using the Create Line Description commands. For example, you use CRTLINSDLC to define SDLC lines and you use CRTLINTRN to define token-ring connections. You define the controller to SNUF using the CRTCTLHOST command. And, you define the device to SNUF using the CRTDEVSNUF command.

To diagnose problems with SNUF, you will wish to display your definitions so that you can review them. Use the DSPLIND, DSPCTLD, and DSPDEVD commands to display your current definitions. SNUF is fully documented in the IBM manual *AS/400 Communications: SNUF Programmer Guide.*

18.6 LAN Considerations

Many mainframe and midsize customers are attaching Local Area Networks (LANs) of PCs to their systems. LANs can represent a significant percentage of your total network load, and must be considered when performing resource allocation. The first rule is a simple one; a LAN is not a single device. A LAN is actually as many devices as PCs attached to the Local Area Network, and perhaps even more. If you treat a LAN as so many local devices, you will take a step in the right direction. However, LANs do not behave exactly the same as many "standard" VTAM local connections and have their own set of tuning tips and techniques.

Figure 18.3 illustrates a small LAN of five nodes attached via a server to a 3174 owned by one system. The LAN is accessible to a second system attached via a CTCA. Activity on any one LAN node will impact the other LAN nodes as well, and may even affect the host systems. For example, a file transfer running from a System A application to any node could cripple the performance of the other four LAN nodes, plus impact all other System A to System B communications. Even something as simple as the submission of a large job or the transmission of a printout to a LAN node could have the same effect as the file transfer.

LFBUF thrashing is one area where special considerations apply. Thrashing is prevented by increasing the *baseno* value, or by adjusting the *xpanno* value to include an extra page of buffers. You should not count on the *xpanno* parameter for controlling thrashing for a token ring LAN. If your network contains many (40 or more) local PU 2 devices, then your only option to prevent LFBUF

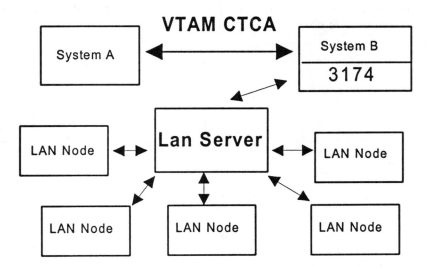

Figure 18.3   LAN Connections

thrashing is to increase the *baseno* value. This problem commonly occurs for 3174 token ring gateway configurations.

File transfer operations also affect resource allocation for LAN attached devices. We frequently estimate message traffic based on the applications being used, the average user "think" time, and similar factors. A single file transfer can generate more message traffic than several days of typical application usage! A file transfer can also employ message sizes that were not anticipated when your buffer size specification was made. If file transfers are a part of your LAN use, you should perform measurements during a typical file transfer to choose better buffer size, *baseno*, and *xpanno* values.

When file transfer operations occur frequently, then sporadic cases of long response time can be seen. These are caused by buffer exhaustion, line capacity over utilization, LAN server congestion, etc. If a single function (such as a file transfer) uses most of the available buffers, than all other users will wait, and **very** long delays can be seen. If a file transfer uses a large percentage of the available line bandwidth, then all other network activity will be seen to slow down. When a file transfer swamps the LAN server, then large sporadic delays will be common. Alleviating one of these bottlenecks will often have little effect as another area of contention surfaces when the first is corrected. In this case, leave the first performance fix in place, and continue tuning until improved performance is observed.

E

OS/400 System Management

Part E looks at OS/400 System Management tasks including security issues, the save/restore process, designing recoverable applications, tuning, and database management.

Separate chapters (Chapters 19 and 20) are provided on system security and application/system recoverability. We look at both the technical aspects of recoverability as well as the logistical issues that a company must address in order to have a viable disaster recovery plan.

A Tuning chapter (Chapter 21) is provided to cover basic OS/400 performance management and tuning issues. We also briefly look at the available tuning and capacity planning tools. The System Storage Management chapter (Chapter 22) describes your responsibilities for managing and cleaning up the system datasets including logs and journals.

Chapter

19

Security

This chapter looks at security issues of OS/400 systems. Our discussion reviews the object-oriented security system unique to the AS/400 architecture, and also discusses methods you can employ to strengthen this security system, as well as how to manage it. Our discussion is somewhat abbreviated. However, a number of suggestions are made to assist you in managing a secure system. Refer to the IBM manual *AS/400: Security Reference* for a more technical discussion of system security parameters.

19.1 Security and Object Architecture

The AS/400 is one of the very few modern computer systems that is able to be fully secured at both the user level and the data level. The object-oriented architecture is the reason for the ability to secure data. When the AS/400 was designed, security was directly incorporated into the structure of objects. To understand what this means, let's look at how other security systems work.

Many computer systems (including mainframe systems such as MVS, VM, and VSE) associate security with the name of a data item. This means that if a secured data item is copied to another name, it can then be accessed as though the original security did not exist. Mainframe systems also work with user IDs. By pretending to be a user other than yourself, you can access secured data and obfuscate any audit trail mechanism.

The AS/400 security system works with objects, not with names. Each object includes *security authorization information* as part of the object header. When an object is copied, this information follows the copy. It is not possible to bypass security on the AS/400 by obtaining a copy of a secured object. On the AS/400, every user profile, every program, every command, every user interface, and every piece of data is a separate object, each with its own set of security information to protect itself from unauthorized usage.

19.1.1 Object Verification

AS/400 security is built in to each object. As such, it is performed as part of the normal validity checking done each time an object is accessed or altered. The AS/400 hardware verifies objects each time they are processed by validating the data type and function to be performed as well as the user's authorization to perform the function on the current object. Security encompasses both processing/data integrity and processing/data authorization.

Data integrity checks prohibit you from attempting to CALL a piece of data as well as prohibit adding to a piece of non-numeric data. The object design automatically handles arithmetic between mixed types of data by converting data as needed. Note that most other computer systems do not incorporate such checks, and that random (but usually very bad) results occur when data is executed or invalid/mixed numeric operations are performed. Thus, data integrity checks simplify the process of developing programs and verifying program correctness.

Automatic type conversion is only possible on a system such as the AS/400. This is a result of the need to allocate storage for a copy of data in a temporary data type. The object manager allocates and tracks workspace as needed. In fact, the machine-level interface does arithmetic operations using internal datatypes and is often managing several copies of a data item, in several different formats. This permits programs to access data without concern about the user-defined data format or the actual machine format or about storage requirement differences.

Authorization checks ensure that the program attempting to access or alter an object has compatible access privileges. The privileges of a program can be inherited from an online user or be implicit to the program itself. The first method ensures that a user does not utilize a program they are not entitled to, and the second approach can be used to allow an unprivilaged user guarded access to a powerful system utility.

The combination of data integrity checks, datatype conversion, and access authorization checks ensures that AS/400 commands and programs are robust but unable to be misused.

19.1.2 Object Granularity

One common issue for securing data access in conventional computer systems is the granularity of the security system and the granularity of the data. Computer systems that secure data by the name of a file are unable to secure specific types of records or fields within a record without additional special logic. In contrast, the AS/400 allows any level of data granularity to have its own unique security attributes.

From the physical view of data you have Fields, Records, and Files. Each of these is an object with its own security. Thus, one user may be able to see but not alter the employee salary information field yet still be able to alter the employee vacation field information. Another user may be unable to see selected fields, while the file administrator might be able to see and alter any field as well as grant/alter access rights to users.

From the logical viewpoint you have Logical Fields, Records, Members of Files, Files, Libraries, Library Lists, Reference Tables, and Dictionaries. Each of these is a separate object that can also have its own set of security attributes. Although the AS/400 offers this extreme level of granularity, the security administrator need not worry about specifying each object separately unless this is desired. *Inheritance* is as aspect of the object-oriented architecture that permits objects to take on attributes of associated or component objects.

19.2 User Profiles

Each user has an associated user profile which lists the access authorization privileges of that user. The *user profile* is an object. Every object within the AS/400 system is owned by some user profile. The *owning user profile* is that of the user who created the object or was granted ownership to the object once it was created.

This owner may grant selected authorities to other user profiles. Such delegation may be either temporary or permanent.

All processes execute under the control of a specific user profile. All functions performed by such a process are validated using the user profile attributes, ensuring that the referenced objects are authorized to this user. These checks occur for each reference, not just at logon or allocation time. This ensures that trojan horse applications cannot get far, even if they are brought into a system.

The user profile also defines user-specific information used to customize the behavior of the system for each user. For example, the language to be used for messages is specified in the user profile. This is a powerful *user-friendly* facility of the AS/400. You are encouraged to define user profiles for each of your system's users. And, in a secure environment, you MUST do this, as the system will not automatically define user profiles when the security level is 20 or higher.

Because a user profile contains a large amount of information, it would be a burden to have to specify all of the information for each new user. The AS/400 provides for *group profiles* as a tool to reduce the effort of defining new users, and to reduce errors that could impact security or usability. Users belonging to a group inherit defaults for their user profile values from the group profile. Groups should be used to consolidate security definitions for all members of a department or workgroup. They also should be used to define common customization values for individuals with the same preferences.

19.2.1 Batch Jobs

Batch jobs are run by the system as directed in their *Job Description* definition. Each batch job is like a user, and runs under a user profile. This profile must allow access to any libraries, files, and programs referenced by the job. The job description profile also provides the name to be associated with the job's output.

19.3 Security Level

The AS/400 supports four different security levels. Each level enables a different type of environment. You determine the *security level* by setting the system value QSECURITY to the level number. The levels are:

- 10 — No security is enforced. The system is shipped with QSECURITY set to 10. You should immediately define your users and change to another value.

- 20 — User sign-on security. A valid user ID and password is required to sign-on to the system. All signed on users are given access to all objects. This level is discouraged except for development environments as it is no better than classical mainframe security.

- 30 — Object security. A valid user ID and password is required for sign-on. All object access is authorized via the user profile. Minimum suggested security level for a production environment.

- 40 — Object plus Integrity security. Same as level 30 plus additional integrity checks. Encouraged for some production environments.

The AS/400 system arrives with level 10 specified. You should immediately switch to level 20 to ensure that the system is not compromised. You may change the value by issuing the WRKSYSVAL *SEC command (same as selecting option 1 from menu SETUP). Note that any change does not take effect until the next IPL.

19.4 Security System Values

In this section we look at system values related to security. All of the supported values are not discussed, only those of general utility or for which specific recommendations are made are covered here. Refer to the IBM manual *AS/400: Security Reference* for a complete discussion of system security values. The ones we will look at include:

- QAUDLVL determines the system audit level

- QCRTAUT create authority

- QDSPSGNINF controls sign-on information display

- QINACTITV is the inactive job time-out interval

- QINACTMSGQ determines the action taken for inactive jobs

- QLMTSECOFR restricts special authority sign-ons

- QMAXSIGN restricts the number of failed sign-on attempts

- QMAXSGNACN specifies the action for QMAXSIGN exceeded

- QPWDEXPITV password expiration interval

- QPWDMINLEN password minimum length

- QPWDRQDDIF requires different passwords

- QPWDPOSDIF verifies amount of password difference

- QRMTSIGN controls remote sign-on

19.4.1 QAUDLVL

QAUDLVL determines which events are logged to the QAUDJRN security journal. The security journal is a valuable tool in detecting attempts to penetrate your system. Multiple values may be specified for QAUDLVL. A value of * NONE disables all logging and should not be used except in a test environment.

For security level 30, you should specify * AUTFAIL to force logging of all security failures. For security level 40, you should also specify * PGMFAIL to enable logging of integrity failures. The specification of other QAUDLVL values depends upon how your system is used.

* SAVRST causes all restore operations to be logged. Its use is encouraged in a secure environment and for general system management. * SECURITY causes all security attribute changes to be logged and should be specified in any highly secure environment to detect penetration of secured user profiles and to facilitate

system management/problem determination. *CREATE causes logging of object creation and is usually desired in a test environment as well as in some production environments. *DELETE causes logging of all object deletion and has the same applicability as *CREATE. *OBJMGT causes all object move and renames to be logged and is only generally used in a test environment. Note that the security journal can become large in active systems when too much logging has been enabled. This can consume large amounts of space and seriously impact performance.

19.4.2 QCRTAUT

QCRTAUT specifies the public authority for newly created objects. *CHANGE is the suggested value and allows the public to change newly created objects. *USE or *EXCLUDE confer better security but result in problems due to the design of OS/400. For example, if QCRTAUT is set to *USE or *EXCLUDE then public authority is not adequate to allow signing on to new devices.

19.4.3 QDSPSGNINF

QDSPSGNINF is set to 1 to display sign-on information or 0 to suppress this display. The display includes the date/time of last sign-on as well as the number of days until the current password expires and the number of invalid sign-on attempts. A value of 1 is highly encouraged to prevent users from letting their IDs expire without warning. This value also can assist in detecting attempts to penetrate each user ID. Note that QDSPSGNINF is the system default value and that the display of individual user information may be controlled within each user profile.

19.4.4 QINACTITV and QINACTMSGQ

The QINACTITV value is specified in minutes and is the amount of time a job may remain inactive before an action is taken. The action performed is determined by the setting of the QINACTMSGQ value and ranges from ending the job to logging the inactivity to a message queue. A user terminal is considered inactive if it is waiting for user action at a menu or waiting for message input.

The use of this option is encouraged as users frequently leave terminals unattended. Access to a terminal that has been signed-on by a highly authorized user is the same as access to a system without security. Although users may complain, values of a half hour or less are usually desirable for this option to be effective. Of course, if access to your terminals is prevented through physical means then use of the QINACTITV value may not be required.

The QINACTMSGQ value determines what action is taken. A value of * DSCJOB causes the job to be disconnected, thus requiring a sign-on to regain access to the job. A value of * ENDJOB causes the job to be terminated. These two values take drastic actions and are only useful in controlled environments. Note that * DSCJOB is treated the same as * ENDJOB for PC Support/400 jobs.

The third possible value is the name of a message queue. Message CPI1126 is sent to the specified message queue when the time out interval specified by QINACTITV has been reached. The message queue must already exist, and is automatically cleared at each IPL. Note that a user or a program can monitor the message queue and take user ID dependent actions for various time outs. This allows you to disconnect users at specified times of the day without impacting other users.

19.4.5 QLMTSECOFR

Specify QLMTSECOFR to restrict signing on a user with * ALLOBJ or * SERVICE authority to any workstation. Specify a value of 1 to restrict such users to workstations that have been specifically authorized. This value is strongly encouraged for all but the simplest environments. Restricting highly authorized users to a few terminals enhances system security by allowing physical terminal access restriction to be used in conjunction with user ID/password secrecy to reduce the chance of security penetration.

19.4.6 QMAXSIGN and QMAXSGNACN

QMAXSIGN controls failed sign-on attempts. A value of * NOMAX may be specified to permit unlimited failed sign-on attempts. This value is strongly discouraged as it allows an intruder unlimited attempts to penetrate your system.

Any numeric value is the number of failed sign-on attempts that are allowed. Once this count is exceeded, a message is sent to the QSYSOPR message queue as well as the QSYSMSG queue if it is present in library QSYS. A suggested value is 3, and any value larger than 5 is generally considered to negate security while a value of 1 is usually too restrictive.

QMAXSGNACN determines the action taken once the QMAXSIGN value has been exceeded.

- 1 disables the device.

- 2 disables the user profile.

- 3 disables both the device and the user profile.

A value of 2 or 3 is suggested. When physical access to terminals is restricted, then a value of 3 is strongly encouraged. In any case, the QSYSOPR message queue should be periodically inspected for failed sign-on attempts.

19.4.7   QPWDEXPITV and Other Password Controls

The QPWDEXPITV value is used to specify the amount of time a password remains valid. Specify *NOMAX to permit passwords to remain unchanged indefinitely. This is discouraged as it increases the chance that a password could be compromised by an ex-employee or through the accidental viewing of a password.

Specify a numeric value from 1 through 366 as the number of days that a password will remain valid. Once this number of days has elapsed, the user will be required to change the password at the next sign-on. The suggested value is about 20 to 30 days. A value of about a month is infrequent enough to not impose a burden upon your users, but also ensures that a password does not remain compromised for long if it does become known. Small values in the range of 1 to 15 are discouraged as they tend to cause users to make up poor-quality passwords.

The QPWDMINLEN value specifies the minimum length of a password. You are encouraged to specify a value of 5 or larger to prevent users from specifying initials or a spouse's first name or common acronyms as their password. The maximum value that can be specified is 10 which is the maximum length of a password. The QPWDMAXLEN value specifies the maximum length of a password. Although the AS/400 permits passwords to have up to ten characters, some systems that you may connect to your AS/400 restrict password information to eight characters. If you wish to communicate your user profile password to such a foreign system for an automatic logon, you may wish to set QPWDMAXLEN to 8. That is the only suggested use for this value.

The QPWDRQDDIF value is set to 0 to disable password difference validation. You are encouraged to specify a value of 1 to require that each new password be different from the prior 32 passwords. This prevents use of passwords such as the name of the month or the repetition of a small series of passwords such as the names of children or a list of birthdays.

QPWDPOSDIF is used to ensure that passwords differ in each position. When specified as 0, users may specify passwords such as pat1 and pat2 and pat3 and pat4. These pass the checking enabled by QPWDRQDDIF, but are alike, and often easy to guess. You are encouraged to specify QPWDPOSDIF 1 in a secure environment to prevent use of passwords with a character in the same position as the prior password. This option may not be desired in a casual environment as it has been found to annoy users who accidently repeat a character. A password validation program may be a better option in any case, as it can be used to verify that no two consecutive characters occupy the same position which is less annoying and thus, a better check.

The QPWDVLDPGM value specifies the name of a user password validation program. Note that this program is only called after a new password passes all other built-in checks. The validation program can accept or reject a supplied password. Suggested uses of a password validation program are to refine the QPWDPOSDIF checking to only invalidate passwords with two or more characters the same as a prior password, or to reject passwords found in a list of known common *bad* passwords, or to prohibit changing passwords more than one time a day.

You should not write passwords to a disk file in a QPWDVLDPGM program as doing so compromises system security. Note that the IBM-supplied program DSPPWD uses a password validation program to save passwords in a disk file. This is discouraged as such information is not encrypted and could be used to access all passwords for all users.

IBM documents an example password validation program called PWDVALID. The example is written in CL and verifies that passwords are not changed more than one time a day. This is a good starting point for your own validation program. You should also consider verifying that two consecutive positions are not identical between the old and new passwords. Note that any validation program should be placed in the QSYS library. Doing so ensures that it is restored as part of recovery of your system from a disk failure.

19.4.8   QRMTSIGN

The QRMTSIGN value determines how the system handles remote sign-on requests. Values include:

- *REJECT to disallow all remote sign-on attempts. Suggested if you do not want pass-through or PC Support/400 access. Note that this option makes remote system maintenance essentially impossible.

- *FRCSIGNON forces remote access through normal sign-on. Suggested when unrestricted remote access is desired. Suggested for environments requiring remote system maintenance.

- *SAMEPRF allows automatic sign-on when the user profile name matches. This option is acceptable for some distributed AS/400 environments, but its use should be carefully considered to avoid creating a security loophole.

You may also specify a remote sign-on authorization program that runs at the start of every pass-through session. This option provides the best security and is encouraged for most distributed systems.

Recoverability

In many businesses, the computer is required for day-to-day operation of the business. In fact, frequently there are applications on the system that are critical most of the time, others that are critical at various times of the year, and still others that are not critical. Before developing a backup plan, first you must identify into which category each of your applications falls. Any mission-critical applications must be covered by your plan, the intermediate ones may optionally be covered, while the least critical applications may be omitted from a plan.

A good backup strategy is concerned about recoverability time. If all of your computer data is backed up on a regular basis but you have not determined which applications should be installed first, the amount of time it would take to restore the data, rebuild access paths (indexes), perform data resynchronization; then your backup is worthless, because you lack a viable *backup plan*. A backup plan is both the data necessary to restore your system, as well as the tools, training and strategy to use them to do so in a timely fashion.

20.1   Important References

This chapter covers many of the issues involved in creating a backup plan. You are also encouraged to look at the IBM manual: *Advanced Backup and Recovery Guide* (SC41-8079). Some of the operational issues of recoverability are covered in the book *AS/400: A Practical Guide to Programming and Operations*.

20.2   AS/400 Recovery Facilities Considerations

In this section we list the AS/400 system components/facilities
provided that are used in a backup plan. In subsequent sections we
take each of these and look at them in more detail. The following
facilities of the AS/400 operating system aid in recoverability:

- DASD Attention SRC

- Licensed Internal Code Completion

- Delayed Termination

- AS/400 UPS Support

- User ASPs

- Checksum Protection

- Mirroring Protection

- Device Parity Protection (RAID)

- Journal and Commitment Control

- Save and Restore Commands

The *Advanced Backup and Recovery Guide Version 2* (SC41-8079)
covers each of the above areas in great detail.

20.3   DASD Attention SRC

If the DASD subsystem detects an error that is outside of the disk
enclosure, the system will post a SRC 11 A6XX 0266 error. The
purpose of this is to allow the system to stay up during nonfatal
DASD failures such as *drive not ready*, thus preventing potentially
destructive or long duration re-IPL and access path rebuild. The
system will stack up all DASD I/O requests for the failing drive
until the situation has been corrected. For DE failures, you would

still need to have checksum, mirroring, or RAID DASD in order to prevent a nonrecoverable system interruption.

20.4 Licensed Internal Code Completion

The OS/400 operating system includes a function to allow the system to complete inflight MI Instructions before an abnormal system end. This ensures that fewer system and user objects are marked as unusable upon a system failure. The system also dumps a copy of main storage to disk to aid in system diagnosis.

20.5 Delayed Termination

When your system is terminated, it is desirable to complete all current transactions. As a minimum, it is necessary to ensure that the state of your data is consistent. In order to ensure this, a delay of termination until DASD updates are completed is usually required. Support was placed in the AS/400 system for storage management delayed termination of 10 seconds. Flags are set for:

- Hardware System Reference Code (SRC)

- SM shutdown (UPS exhausted)

When the delay flag is on:

- Main storage is saved to disk

- No opening of access paths is allowed

- Current access path operations are allowed to finish

20.6 AS/400 UPS Support

Uninterruptible Power Supply (UPS) systems provide auxiliary power during a failure of normal building power. The AS/400 supports two types of UPS. These are *complete* and *limited* UPS. All of the new systems have a battery power unit to support *limited*

UPS function for the CPU. The purpose of this UPS is to provide an orderly shutdown to reduce recovery time when power is restored. If the power interruption is less than the time the UPS supports, then the system does not see any down time.

20.6.1   Complete UPS Support

Complete UPS support supplies power to the CPU (central processing unit), all disk units, the console, all racks, and optionally other workstations. This allows the system to continue processing until utility power is restored, or through a normal power down of the system via the PWRDWNSYS command.

20.6.2   Limited UPS Support

Limited UPS support supplies power to the CPU, Disk unit 1 (System Load Source Device), and all storage device controllers. This allows the system to retain the contents of main storage at the point of power failure. Under limited UPS support the system writes the contents of main storage to the dump area on Disk Unit 1, then uses that copy to initialize storage for the next IPL when power is restored.

20.6.3   UPS System Values

In this section we look at the system parameter values that control and effect the UPS process.

- QUPMSGQ. Uninterruptible Power Supply Message Queue. Determines which message queue any power supply messages are sent to. The system will always send a message to QSYSOPR, so QUPMSGQ can be used to specify an additional queue.

- UPSDLYTIM. Uninterruptible Power Supply Delay Time. Specify *BASIC if the uninterruptible power supply provides limited support. Code 0 if the system is to immediately save main storage and then power down (this value is not normally used). Specify nnn as a delay time until automatic system shutdown after a power failure. This value should be less than the duration of your battery's charge, and larger than the time it normally takes the system to save main storage. Specify *NOMAX to tell the system that you do not want this function to save main storage and then power down. Only use *NOMAX when you are controlling the uninterruptible power supply conditions with a program.

- QPWRRSTIPL. Power Restore IPL Option Following a Power Down. This value controls what happens if the system is ended when utility power is off and the power is later restored. Specify 1 if the system is auto IPL after power is restored. Code a 0 if manual start is preferred.

20.6.4   Setting QUPSDLYTIM

The QUPSDLYTIM value specifies the time in seconds to save system Main Storage and Power Down. The amount of time required depends upon the amount of system main storage that is present. Suggested values are:

- 16M or less = 5 minutes

- Each additional 16M = 1 minute

Calculation Example: 32M System

Battery rating	15
Save and Powerdown	-6
	9
Buffer	-2
	7
Convert to seconds	x 60
QUPSDLYTIM	420

20.7   Using a Program to Handle UPS

Although the AS/400 includes default logic for the handling of power fail conditions, it may be desirable to control the power shutdown process in order to meet special needs of your environment. OS/400 provides for user handling of UPS via the following procedure:

- Specify a value other than QSYSOPR for QUPSMSGQ and *nomax for QUPSDLYTIM.

- Program must allocate the message queue specified in QUPSMSGQ.

- User Program handles messages sent to interactive users, ends batch jobs, dynamically changes UPS values, monitors for power restore, and performs an orderly PWRDWNSYS.

20.8   User ASPs

An Auxiliary Storage Pool (ASP) is a group of DASD units defined from all units available on the system. ASPs are used to isolate data to reduce the amount of data lost when a single drive fails, and also to reserve DASD resources for a specific use. User ASPs have been around since the early days of the S/38. Initially their use was limited to journals, journal receivers, or save files. Now if an object is not a composite object such a spool file or job queue, it can exist in a user ASP.

20.9   Disk Drive Failure

In a current environment, if there is a single disk drive failure on an unprotected unit, then a hard system failure will occur. The required recovery procedure is a full system restore. A full restore could take days before the system would be available to the users. To alleviate the effects of a disk failure, User ASPs, Checksum Protection, Mirroring Protection, and Disk Parity Protection were added to the systems.

20.10   User ASP Enhancements

The AS/400 supports up to 15 user Auxiliary Storage Pools (ASPs). ASPs 2-16 can contain one of the following,

- Journals, Journal Receivers, and Save Files

- Libraries

Libraries using an ASP (CRTLIB with the ASP parameter) provide better recoverability options than specifying the ASP parameter on CRTJRN, CRTJRNRCV, and CRTSAVF commands. Libraries on a user ASP can contain most objects except:

- Configuration Descriptions

- Communications Definitions

- Authorization List

- Folders

- Documents

- Output Queue

- SQL Collections

20.10.1   User ASP Restrictions

Although ASPs are a powerful feature, their use incurs certain costs and some restrictions. Let us briefly list the issues created by ASPs:

- Recovery is not automatic.

- May require more disk devices.

- System will NOT continue with a failing unit in ANY ASP (except if failing unit has an active mirrored unit).

- IPL will NOT be successful with a failing unit in ANY ASP (except if failing unit has an active mirrored unit).

- Objects in User ASP can overflow to the System ASP, but System ASP will not overflow to a user ASP.

- No Database Network can cross an ASP boundary.
  No access paths from files in different ASPs.
  No shared access paths from different ASPs.
  No SQL Collections in User ASPs (SQL uses views of files in QSYS).

- Can NOT move objects across ASPs. Currently the system changes the object library pointer when the MOVOBJ command is issued. However, no actual object movement occurs. When moving objects between ASPs, the object must be recreated on that ASP.

20.10.2   Planning the ASP Configuration

Be sure to leave enough DASD for the System ASP. If you run out of space for OS/400, the system will crash. Also, remember that if a user ASP fills up, it will overflow its data to the System ASP, which could fill up the System ASP, and thus crash the entire system. ASPs can be used to reserve space for a specific application use, but you must ensure that enough space remains for the system to continue to operate.

If an ASP will only be used for journaling, the journals and the receivers should be in the same ASP unless you are using dual journal receivers. In the case of dual journal receivers, the journal should be in the same library as the files to be journaled.

20.11   CHECKSUM

Checksums can be used to automatically reconstruct data lost due to the failure of a single disk device. The advantage of this function is that it minimizes recovery time, avoids full restore if the function is on the System ASP, and reduces the number of damaged objects.

The disadvantage to checksums is that this function has a 10% hit on the CPU as well as a small CPU memory increase requirement. Checksum protection uses approximately 40,000 bytes of main storage for each storage unit in a checksum set. All but the smallest systems can easily afford the storage requirement. However, any saturated system can be crippled by the requirement for 10% of the CPU.

20.11.1 How CHECKSUM Works

Disk units are automatically grouped into a Checksum Set. A minimum of three devices and a maximum of eight devices are gathered into each Checksum Set. All devices in a Checksum Set must be identical. Refer to Figure 20.1 for an example.

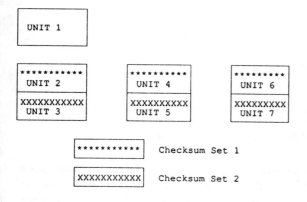

Figure 20.1 Checksum Sets

Space equal to one unit is stored in the Checksum data stripe. Checksum data is calculated for all permanent writes. The system only checksums permanent objects. At checksum startup the percent of unprotected storage for each disk is set by the user. If a single disk unit in the set is lost, the contents can be reconstructed. If more than one disk drive in a set fails, then checksum cannot recover the data. Also, checksum cannot recover data if the affected disk sectors are in memory and the system abnormally ends without saving main storage.

Each disk is divided into multiple data stripes. The checksum stripe will be a different stripe for each disk in the checksum set.

For simplicity, lets think of the checksum as the exclusive ORing of all the bits on all disk drives in a set (except the checksum drive) to create the checksum stripe data. If any one disk drive fails, the system can recreate the lost data using the checksum stripe and the remaining data. If two drives are lost, nothing can be done.

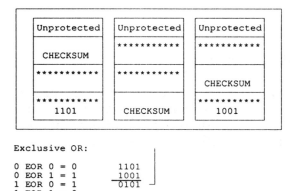

Exclusive OR:

```
0 EOR 0 = 0          1101
0 EOR 1 = 1          1001
1 EOR 0 = 1          0101
1 EOR 1 = 0
```

Figure 20.2   Checksum Operation

20.12   Planning Checksum Protection

It is important to understand the difference between unprotected and protected storage. Unprotected storage contains system machine data (licensed internal code and dump space) and temporary objects. If the reserved unprotected storage is too small, then temporary objects will flow into the protected storage area which will cause a serious performance impact. If the protected storage area becomes full, then the system will halt with a machine check.
    Use the WRKSYSSTS, WRKACTJOB, and WRKJOB commands to determine the amount of storage that is needed.

20.13   Mirroring Protection

Mirroring provides the best protection for DASD related failure. However, mirroring is also the most costly form of protection. The system writes all data onto two drives concurrently. The disk drives must be identical. If one disk drive fails in a mirroring pair, the system suspends mirroring protection on that mirroring pair and continues to run using only the surviving drive. The failing disk drive can be repaired later and returned to the system. The customer can then resume mirroring on that pair. The system will copy the data from the running drive to the repaired drive while continuing to run existing jobs in the system. The following are the different levels of hardware protection used to manage DASD:

- Bus Level Protection may allow the system to run when a bus fails. However, if bus 0 fails, the system will fail. Also, note if the bus that fails is not bus 0, the system will continue to run, but workstations, printers and communication lines attached to that bus will not be usable until repairs are done and the system restarted. Concurrent maintenance with system operation is not possible for a bus failure. Bus failures are very rare.

- IOP Level Protection allows the system to continue to run if a single IOP failure occurs in a mirrored pair. If the cable to an IOP fails, the system will continue to run. Concurrent maintenance of the disk drive is available with IOP level protection.

- Controller Level Protection allows the system to continue to run if a single controller failure occurs in a mirrored pair. Concurrent maintenance of the disk drive or controller is available with controller level protection. If the IOP must be reset, then concurrent maintenance is not available.

- Disk Level Protection allows the system to continue to run if a single disk drive failure occurs in a mirrored pair. For the 9406, concurrent maintenance is possible for certain types of disk unit failures.

20.13.1   BUS Levels of Protection

The first type of protection is to have separate busses, with a controller and DASD on each bus. (Refer to Figure 20.3 for a diagram of bus level protection.)

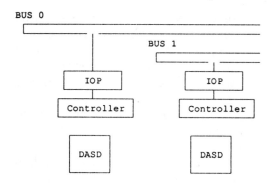

Figure 20.3 Bus Level Protection

Bus level protection has the following characteristics:

- Two DASD devices of a mirrored pair each have their own bus.

- If one of the DASD units, a controller, and IOPs, or a bus fails (and the bus is not Bus 0), the system will continue to run.

- This is the best protection possible. No single I/O related piece of hardware can result in a failure of the system. This option costs the most, but may be required for the most mission-critical applications where lack of availability can suspend business operations and cost both current and future business. It may also be required where computerized records are required for continued operation or for legal reasons.

The second level of protection involves a single bus, but with a separate IOP and a separate controller for each DASD. (Refer to Figure 20.4 for an example.) For small systems, this may be the best available option, as multiple busses are not supported for all models of AS/400. Duplicate small systems are a best case recoverability option for such environments that we will not discuss at length.

The characteristics of IOP level protection are:

- The two DASD devices of a mirrored pair are connected to different IOPs but are on the same bus.

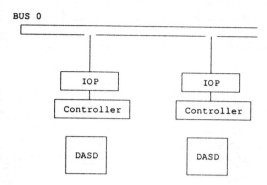

Figure 20.4   IOP Level Protection

● If one of the DASD units, a controller, or an IOP fails, the system will continue to run.

● If the bus fails, the system will crash. Bus failures are rare, and many applications can accept the small risk associated with this type of structure.

In the third level of protection we simply use multiple DASD control units, all on the same IOP, on the same bus (see Figure 20.5 for an example.)

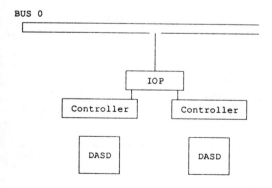

Figure 20.5 Controller Level Protection

- The two DASD devices of a mirrored pair are connected to different controllers, but are under the same IOP and bus.

- If either DASD device or DASD controller fails, the system will continue to run.

- If the IOP or bus fails, the system will crash. Because IOP and bus failures are rare, this may be acceptable for other than the most mission-critical applications. Because mirrored DASD are used, the data is still secure. A hardware failure will result in loss of availability of the critical application, but not of the data written since the last backup was taken.

In device level protection we separate data across multiple DASD units, all on the same control unit, IOP, and bus (see Figure 20.6.)

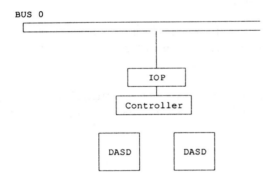

Figure 20.6 Device Level Protection

- The two DASD devices of a mirrored pair are in separate boxes, but they are under the same controller, IOP, and bus.

- If either DASD actuator fails, the system will continue to run.

- If the controller, IOP, or bus fails, the system will crash. This is the basic essential level of recoverability. Because mirrored DASD are used, the data is still secure. A hardware failure will result in loss of availability of the critical application, but not of the data written since the last backup was taken.

20.13.2   Planning for Mirroring

When considering mirrored protection, you will need to take the following steps:

- Decide which ASP or ASPs to protect with mirrored protection. If a disk fails in a nonmirrored ASP, the system may not continue to run if the nonmirrored ASP is not using device parity protection. A disk unit failure in an ASP with checksum protection will cause the system to be down until the failure is repaired and checksum recovery is completed.

- Determine disk storage capacity. A mirrored ASP requires twice as much auxiliary storage as an ASP that is not mirrored. You must have an even number of the same disk units.

- Determine the level of protection you want for each mirrored ASP. Base your decision upon how critical the data is, as well as the time to recover in the event of a total failure.

- Determine the extra hardware needed for mirrored protection. Include any hardware you will need for performance reasons. Use the Calculate Mirrored Capacity function of STRSST and the WRKHDWRSC TYPE (* STG) command to assist in this determination. Mirrored protection uses 30KB of main storage from the machine pool for general purposes, plus 4KB from the machine pool for each mirrored pair. During synchronization, mirrored protection uses an additional 68KB for each mirrored pair that is being synchronized (the largest pool).

- Order the hardware.

- Plan the installation of the additional hardware.

- Install the new hardware.

20.14   Device Parity Protection (RAID)

What is RAID? *RAID* is short for *Redundant Array of Inexpensive Disks*. In the mid-1980s, the University of California at Berkeley performed a study using small inexpensive disk drives grouped into arrays. The Berkeley paper hypothesizes that a collection of low-end devices (small, low $/MB, low capacity, relatively low reliability and performance) could provide improved performance relative to high-end devices (high reliability, $/MB, capacity, and performance) by aggregating the data rates of several devices in an array. This could be done while achieving or exceeding data availability characteristics of high-end DASD through redundancy in the array. Overall cost per megabyte was envisioned as being improved through the use of inexpensive devices.

Note: The inexpensive parameter in the RAID acronym has recently been changed by the Berkeley author team to independent in acknowledgement of the need for highly reliable devices to meet the needs of the customer environment. Thus, where the Berkeley project originally targeted low cost DASD units, low cost is no longer an assured part of a RAID setup.

The Berkeley analysis considered only the device hardware itself, data placement or striping techniques, and parity implementation techniques. Little to no consideration was given in the Berkeley paper to buffering, caching, or cache extended functions to address any of the inherent constraints in array design.

The Berkeley paper defined five availability strategies:

- RAID-1 is mirroring. A primary and secondary copy of data is kept on separate disk drives within the subsystem enclosure.

- RAID-2 and RAID 3 synchronize spindles and access arms to make the individual disk drives in this array appear to the host as though they were one single, large disk drive. Data is "striped" to all disk drives in parallel. RAID-2 uses multiple parity drives while RAID-3 uses a single dedicated parity drive for array protection.

- RAID-4 uses a single dedicated parity disk drive to store the checksum information to provide protection for the array. The disk drives are not synchronized, allowing individual drives improved performance. However, because the dedicated parity drive must be updated for all writes to any of the other drives in the array, it quickly becomes a performance bottleneck.

- RAID-5 is very similar to RAID-4. The difference is that a distributed parity scheme is used for protection. This means that the equivalent capacity of one disk drive is distributed among the disk drives in the array. This creates stripes of reserved space used to contain the checksum information necessary for protection. By using a distributed parity scheme, the workload is balanced and performance is enhanced. Like RAID-4, the checksum information must be updated whenever a write operation occurs. This results in two reads and two writes for every host-generated write operation. This is called the "write penalty" and is something every RAID-5 implementation must contend with. The AS/400 uses a slight modification of RAID-5 implementation.

AS/400 device parity protection protects data from being lost because of a disk unit media failure. When a disk media failure occurs on a storage unit with device parity protection, the controller reconstructs the data from other units in the 9337 disk subsystem.

Device parity protection is built into the 9337 disk unit Models 1XX, and 2XX serials. The models with device parity protection use a data redundancy technique similar to checksum protection. These models can have four to seven storage units plus one write assist storage unit. The parity information is spread across the first four units to improve performance. When a storage unit fails the system continue to run with a performance decrease. Performance returns to normal after the failing unit is repaired and the device completes data recovery. The advantage of mirroring is that there is a copy of the data on a duplicate disk drive, so when one drive fails, there is very little impact on performance.

If multiple storage units fail in a 9337 disk subsystem with device parity protection, the system becomes unusable. You will have to restore the data to the ASP that contains the 9337 disk subsystem. Device parity protection does not protect against system outages that can result from failures in other disk-related hardware like a disk controller, a disk IOP, or a system bus.

20.15   Application Recovery

In order to effectively discuss how an application can recover from a failure, let us look first at the types of Application failures:

- Abnormal Termination.   ENDJOB   * IMMED, ENDSBS
  * IMMED, System Request Menu Option 2, System Request

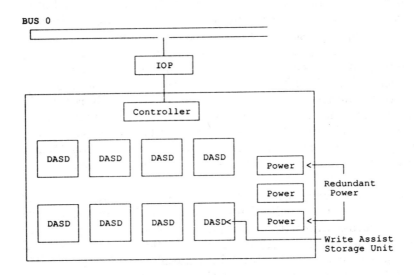

Figure 20.7   Device Parity Protection

Menu Option 90, Terminal failure, and program errors. A properly designed application will terminate without any data loss.

- Main Storage Loss. Power failure or RE-IPL before shutdown. Data loss is possible.

- Data Loss in Disk Drive. Hardware failure and Abnormal termination. Data loss is probable.

- Programmer, Operator, or User Errors. Data loss is possible.

The risk in any type of failure is that data is not written to disk or is only partially written to disk. There are two types of writes that a system can perform:

- Synchronous Writes. The program issues a write to the object, control is not returned back to the program until the system has completely written the data on DASD. The program then can issue the next instruction.

● Asynchronous Writes. The program issues a write to the object, control is returned back to the program before the data is actually written to disk. The program can then continue with the next instruction. The AS/400 virtual storage management controls when to write to the DASD.

20.15.1 Abnormal Termination

Most application programs update multiple files. If the program terminated before updating all files, then the data between the files are not synchronized. In most cases, this problem must be fixed manually. The only way to ensure that all files updates are synchronized is to use commitment control.

20.15.2 Main Storage Loss

Let's look at why memory failures can causes the problem of lost data on disk. When a program on the AS/400 issues a write command to write data to a database file and the force write ratio value (FRCRATIO) is the default value of *NONE (the system determines when that data is forced to DASD storage), then control is passed back to the program before the data is written to the DASD unit. The program can issue a force data to DASD command which will cause the program to wait until the records have been written to DASD, thus impacting the performance of the program. A busy system will normally cause the changed pages of the database to be written to DASD on a frequent basis. When the system becomes less active, however, then some records will remain in main memory for a longer period of time before being written to DASD.

The system will also force all changed records to DASD when the last job that had a file open has ended. If a system failure occurs before the data changes are written to disk, then these changes may be lost. Another method to ensure that changes to a database are written to disk is to change the force write ratio of a file to 1. This has a performance impact on the system.

The best way to ensure that changes that are made to the file are reflected on the DASD is to use journaling. The system will resynchronize the journals and the physical file at IPL time.

20.15.3 Programmer, Operator, and User Errors

Programmer, operator, and user errors are errors that occur such as running a program in the wrong sequence that updates records or a program that fails after a partial update due to a programming error.

If the files are journaled, the changes could be backed out of the file by user id, program name, or date. If the files are not journaled, the files would have had to have been saved before the changes, in order to restore the files to their original state.

20.15.4 Journal Management Components

● Journal - *JRN identifies journaled files, current journal receivers, and all journal receivers on the system associated with this journal.

● Journal Receiver - *JRNRCV captures record activity for a journaled file (Journal Entries).

20.15.5 Functions of Journal Management

● Recovers damaged data file members

● Decreases time required to save files

● Decreases time required for recovering damaged access paths

● Provides audit trails

● Provides activity reporting

● Aids in debugging

Journal management provides the following features:

● Before and after record images in sequence of occurrence.

- Open, Close, Add, and Delete member records in sequence of occurrence.

- Physical file based, not job or program based. There are no programming changes necessary when journaling files.

- Journaling is not ended at IPL or end of job.

- Files are automatically synchronized with the receiver at IPL.

The major decisions to be made are:

- Which files to journal?

- Which files to group in each journal?

- How many journals?

- How many journal receivers?

- Dual journal receivers per journal?

- Are before images needed?

- User ASP?

To get the best performance when using journaling, the journaling receivers should be in a separate ASP. During batch update processing of the file, if the program is using a transaction log, then journaling could be turned off. The file should be saved before the update, so if an error occurs during the update, the file could be restored and the update rerun.

20.15.6   Example of Journal Data Flow

In Figure 20.8, there are two programs, PGMX and PGMY. PGMX updates FILE A and FILE B. PGMY updates FILE B and FILE C. FILE A and FILE B are journaled. FILE C is not journaled. When program PGMX issues a write to FILE A or FILE B, the system intercepts the write command, logs before images if that option is turned on, logs the change data, and returns to the program. When program PGMY writes to FILE B, the system performs the same functions as it did for PGMX. When program PGMY writes to FILE C, no journal records are created. Since journaling is at the file level and not the program level, the source code in both programs is the same.

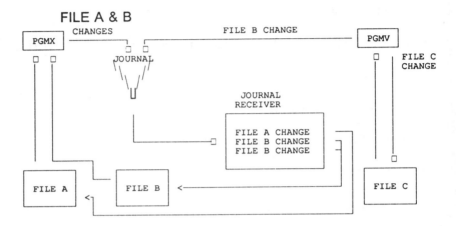

Figure 20.8 Journaling Data Flow

The system also supports access path journaling. The main reason to do access path journaling is to reduce IPL and file open time after an abnormal system end. If for some reason the access path was damaged, the system could rebuild the access path very quickly using access path journaling. Access path journaling requires a significant amount of auxiliary storage. The system writes out the access path change at the same time that it writes the record change entry.

Requirements to do access path journaling:

- Physical files over which the access path is built must be journaled.

- All physical files must be journaled to the same journal as the access path.

- Each access path that is journaled must be specified by naming a specific file.

• Maintenance attributes must be *IMMED or *DLY.

20.15.7 Journaling Command

To start journaling, the following commands will need to be used:

• CRTJRNRCV - Create journal receivers. When the journal receiver reaches its specified threshold (size), a program could automatically create a new journal receiver and attach it to the journal. The user program would wait for the threshold message on the journal message queue.

• CRTJRN - Create journals. Specifies the journal receiver and the message queue (the default message queue is QSYSOPR).

• STRJRNPF - Start file journaling. Specifies the physical file and the journal.

• STRJRNAP - Start Access path journaling (optional).

• SAVOBJ or SAVLIB - Save the files that are being journaled.

Some additional journal commands that can be used in recovery:

• APYJRNCHG - Apply journal changes command. It allows the user to apply a specified number of journal entries to a file based on date and time, job name, user id, and job number or last save date.

• RMVJRNCHG - Remove journal changes command. It allows the user to remove a specified number of journal entries to a file based on date and time, job name, user id, and job number or last save date.

• WRKJRN - Work with journal command. It allows you to perform forward or backward recovery of the physical file, display journal status, recover a damaged journal, and recover damaged journal receivers.

• CHGJRN - Change journal command. It changes the journal receivers, the message queue, or the text associated with the specified journal. Use this command to have the system create a new journal receiver and attach it to the journal.

● CMPJRNIMG - Compare Journal Images command. It allows the user to compare and note differences in the before and after images of record level changes for a specific file when IMAGES(*BOTH) was specified for the Start Journal Physical File (STRJRNPF) command. It also allows access to images of a specific relative record if IMAGES(*AFTER) was specified on the Start Journal Physical File (STRJRNPF) command.

20.15.8   Commitment Control

Commitment control is an extension of the basic AS/400 journal function. Refer to Figure 20.9 for the commitment cycle.

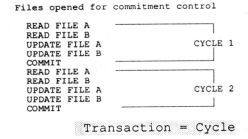

Figure 20.9   Commitment Cycle

Commitment control provides the following facilities:

● Defines transaction boundaries.

● Insures all changes within a transaction are completed for all files affected.

● Provides automatic backout of incomplete transactions.

● Allows backout by user.

● Provides for application restart.

- Provides "all or nothing" capability for a transaction.

- Locks all records until a transaction is completed (COMMIT).

- Rolls back uncommitted changes automatically when a program ends.

- Initiates rollback on demand from system or user programs.

To use commitment control, the following conditions must be met:

- All database files under commitment control must be journaled.

- All committed files must be journaled to the same journal.

- * BOTH images must have been specified on the STRJRNPF command.

- The job must issue STRCMTCTL and ENDCMTCLT commands.

- The program must issue a COMMIT operation instruction.

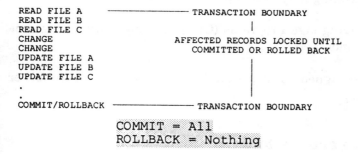

```
READ FILE A       ──────────── TRANSACTION BOUNDARY
READ FILE B
READ FILE C                         |
CHANGE                       AFFECTED RECORDS LOCKED UNTIL
CHANGE                         COMMITTED OR ROLLED BACK
UPDATE FILE A
UPDATE FILE B
UPDATE FILE C                       |
.
.                                   |
COMMIT/ROLLBACK   ──────────── TRANSACTION BOUNDARY

            COMMIT = All
            ROLLBACK = Nothing
```

Figure 20.10   ALL or Nothing

20.15.9   Notify Object Parameter

A notify object is a message queue, data area, or database file that contains information identifying the last successful transaction (commit ID). The notify object is specified on the STRCMTCTL command. The commit ID associates the commitment operation with a specific set of database changes. This commit ID is also added to the journal. The commit ID for the current transaction is placed in the notify object if the system ends abnormally, if the job ends abnormally, or if uncommitted changes exist when a routing step ends normally. This information can be used to find a point to start an application again.

The commit ID can be specified on the following statements:

● CL - COMMIT command

● RPG - COMMIT operation code

● PL/I - PLICOMMIT subroutine

The commit ID or notify object function is not supported on the COBOL COMMIT verb or the SQL COMMIT statement. The following are the commitment control considerations:

● After failure, determining restart points for jobs may require extensive analysis.

● Record locking may create difficulties.

● Control Language Programs (CLP) and application programs must be modified.

● Poorly designed transaction boundaries may cause other problems.

20.16 Save and Restore Considerations

As recovery requirements become more critical, the amount of data to backup and the frequency that it must be saved will increase. To help reduce the amount of time spent performing the save process, let's look at a few factors that affect save time performance:

● The number and size of objects saved can have an impact on save performance. When a save command is executed, the system must preprocess each and every object to be saved. Part of this processing is to build a directory that contains information about each object. Once this directory (or table) is completed, it is written to the tape or save file, followed by the objects themselves. The directory allows the user to display a list of objects saved on tape or save file, as well as to easily restore individual objects.

● In most cases, a save of many small objects will take more time than the save of fewer large objects that are equal in total size. For example, 1000 1K objects can take longer to save than ten (10) 100K objects.

● Save performance can also be affected depending on whether or not the system is in a restricted state or a nonrestricted state. A system *restricted state* occurs when all subsystems except the controlling subsystem are ended and the controlling subsystem will only allow one job to run. The system is considered to be in a *nonrestricted* state if any subsystem other than the controlling subsystem is active or if multiple jobs can run in the controlling subsystem.

● Placing the system in a restricted state is required for various functions including SAVSYS, SAVLIB (*NONSYS), as well as the SAVSTG function.

● When saving large amounts of data, the type and number of save commands used can affect performance or the save operation. For example, when saving multiple libraries via a single SAVLIB command, the system will begin by processing each object in the first library. Once processed, all objects in the first library will be written to the save media. While the objects are being written to the save media, the system will also begin processing the next library. This overlap of processing allows for a more efficient save. If each library was saved with a separate command, then overlapped processing would not be possible.

● If the system operator or the user performing the save has the special authority of *SAVSYS specified in their user profile, then security checking of the object to be saved is bypassed. Without *SAVSYS authority, each object must be checked to make sure that the user is authorized to save the object. This security checking is quite expensive.

● The AS/400 offers two types of data compression, HDC (Hardware Data Compression) and SDC (Software Data Compression). Software data compression normally takes longer and requires more CPU to perform.

Model Unique Licensed Internal Code
LICENSED INTERNAL CODE
CONFIGURATION OBJECTS (I/O)
DISTRIBUTION OBJECTS
USER PROFILES and SECURITY OBJECTS
QSYS (OS/400)
LICENSED PROGRAM PRODUCTS LIBRARIES
QGPL and QUSRSYS
USER DATA
OFFICE FOLDERS AND DOCUMENTS

Figure 20.11   Objects that Makes Up the AS/400

20.16.1   Objects That Make Up the AS/400

A number of different objects makeup the AS/400 system (see Figure 20.11.) These are described below:

MODEL-UNIQUE LICENSED INTERNAL CODE - (MULIC) is considered a piece of the CPU hardware and is not the same thing as Licensed Internal Code (LIC). Each model type of the AS/400 has a unique MULIC. MULIC is shipped on a separate tape with its own serialized number as the AS/400. MULIC is not saved by any save command, and cannot be distributed with software.

LICENSED INTERNAL CODE (LIC) - also referred to as the vertical and horizontal microcode for the AS/400 is the machine dependent instruction code. It is the first file on an OS/400 tape.

CONFIGURATION OBJECTS

● Line descriptions definition

- Controller description definition

- Device description definition

- Class of Service definition

- Mode descriptions definition

DISTRIBUTION OBJECTS are used internally for object and office distribution purposes.

- DRQ - Distribution Recipient Queue. This queue contains incoming object distribution entries, incoming document distribution entries, outgoing document distribution entries, and error distribution entries. This queue is created when a user is added to the directory.

- DTO - Distribution Tracking Object is used to control office distribution. It is created when a note or document is sent.

- DUO - Document Unit Object is an internal document that combines the document and the distribution details.

USER PROFILES AND SECURITY OBJECTS

- IBM and user-created profiles

- Authority holders objects

- Authorization list objects

LICENSED PROGRAM PRODUCTS LIBRARIES (LPPs)

- RPG, OfficeVision, PC Support, etc.

- Start with the letter Q.

- Optional parts of the LPPs

- May use QSYS, QUSRSYS, and/or QGPL

QGPL

- IBM and user-supplied objects

- PTF index (before Version 1 Release 3)

QUSRSYS

- IBM journals and receivers

- Office enrollments and user calendars

- IBM output queues, message queues, translate tables

USER DATA is any object that a user has created and placed in either an IBM-supplied library or a library the user has created.

OFFICE FOLDERS AND DOCUMENTS

- Contains object type *QDOC (document)

- Contains Object type *FLR (folder)

- *QDOC and *FLR can only be stored in library QDOC

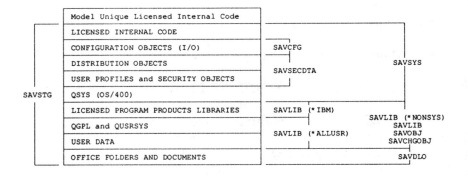

Figure 20.12 What Save Commands to Use?

20.16.2   SAVE Command

Figure 20.12 summarizes the save commands. Remember that the Model Unique Licensed Internal Code is not saved by any AS/400 command.

- SAVSTG - Save Storage is a OS/400 function available starting with Version 1 Release 2.0. The SAVSTG command produces a tape that is a sector-by-sector copy of all permanent data stored on the disk drives, including the Licensed Internal Code. If the system has mirroring protection enable, then only one active unit from each mirrored pair is saved. SAVSTG is an image copy of all permanent data that resides on the AS/400 configured disk drives. Therefore, it should only be restored on an identically configured system. SAVSTG requires the system to be in a restricted state.

- SAVSYS - Save System saves the Licensed Internal Code (LIC), the system library QSYS (OS/400), configuration objects, distribution objects, user profiles and security objects and all permanent and temporarily applied microcode, OS/400 PTFs and the PTF index located in QGPL. After Version 1 Release 1.1 the PTF index can only be saved with the SAVSYS command. Prior to Version 1 Release 2.0, SAVLIB of QGPL could only save the PTF index. SAVSYS does not save IBM Licensed Program Products (RPG OfficeVision, PC Support, etc.) optional parts of OS/400, office documents or folders, QGPL, QUSRSYS or user libraries. SAVSYS requires the system to be in a restricted state.

- SAVCFG - Save Configuration command saves all configuration and System Resource Management (SRM) objects without requiring a system to be in a restricted state.

- SAVSECDTA - Save Security Data command saves distribution objects, user profiles and security objects without requiring the system to be in a restricted state.

- SAVLIB (*NONSYS) - Save Library Non-System. This command saves all libraries except QSYS, QDOC, and the Licensed Internal Code on the system in alphabetic order. Note: The system must be in a restricted state.

- **SAVLIB** - Save Library command will save from 1 to 50 libraries that could be IBM Licensed Program Products libraries, library QGPL and QUSRSYS, and any user-created libraries. This command does *not* require the system to be in a restricted state.

- **SAVOBJ** - Save Object command will save an individual object or multiple objects. This command can save objects in the IBM Licensed Program Products libraries, objects in library QGPL and QUSRSYS, and any user-created objects in any user-created libraries. This command does *not* require the system to be in a restricted state.

- **SAVCHGOBJ** - Save Change Object will save objects that have been changed since the last SAVLIB or based on a date and time. SAVCHGOBJ should not be used to save IBM Licensed Program Products libraries. This command does *not* require the system to be in a restricted state.

- **SAVDLO** - Save Document Library Object saves specified documents or folders located in library QDOC or all Document Unit Objects (DUOs) in library QUSRSYS. A DUO is an unfilled document in library QUSRSYS which has an entry on a user's mail log. SAVDLO does not save office user data such as calendars, document details, etc. These are saved when library QUSRSYS is saved. SAVDLO DLO(*ALL) does not require a restricted system as of Version 1 Release 3. When running the command in a nonrestricted system, check the joblog for documents or folders bypassed and not saved because they are "in use." This command should not be run during peak usage periods.

- **SAVLICPGM** - Save Licensed Program is not specifically intended for backup and recovery purposes. Rather, it is intended for use with software distribution. When using the SAVLICPGM command, be sure to note the PTF level of OS/400 (QSYS). It is recommended to issue the SAVSYS command prior to issuing the SAVLICPGM command to ensure that the PTF level of OS/400 remains compatible with the PTF level of the saved Licensed Program Products.

- SAVE - Save is a S/36EE save command used to save disk files. Such files can only be restored to an AS/400.

- SAVS36F - Save S/36 File is an S/36EE save command which saves disk files. Files can be restored to an S/36 or AS/400.

- SAVELIBR - Save Library is an S/36EE save command which saves an entire library. The saved library can only be restored to an AS/400.

- SAVS36LIBM - Save S/36 Library Member is an S/36EE save command used to save source or procedure members. Saved members can be restored to an S/36 or AS/400.

SAVLIB/SAVOBJ/SAVCHGOBJ ACCPTH (* YES) is used to save the access path. By saving the access path, on restore, the system does not have to rebuild the access path. This can save a significant amount of time. The average access path rebuild time is 10,000/minute. If an AS/400 model D45 has a 2 million record file with two logical views, rebuilding the access path would take six hours and forty minutes.

Rules for saving access paths:

- Access paths must specify either MAINT (* IMMED) or MAINT (* DLY).

- Access paths are saved with physical files.

- Access paths should be in the same library as physical files. If an access path is not in the same library, restore sequence problems may occur.

SAVLIB/SAVOBJ/SAVCHGOBJ SAVFDTA (* YES) is the default for saving the save file data when saving an object or library. The default value changed from *NO to *YES in Version 1 Release 3.

SAVLIB/SAVOBJ/SAVCHGOBJ/SAVDLO SAVACT (* SYSDFN | * LIB) is the Save While Active function. This function was added to the system to reduced the save window. The Save While Active function allows most objects being updated to be processed by the save process. All object description changes and clearing of the physical file are not allowed until after the checkpoint process phase. The Save While Active function will not save any objects with an outstanding exclusive allow read (* EXCLRD) or exclusive lock (* EXCL).

If an application makes changes to objects, recoverability of the objects is much simpler if the application is ended before the save command is performed and then restarted after checkpoint processing has completed. This can dramatically reduce the save command elapsed time.

If the application is not stopped, and commitment control is not used, then saved database objects may have synchronization problems upon restoration. Example: A program has updated two of three files when the save checkpoint has been established for all three files. Upon restoration, the saved objects would be out of synchronization. If the files have to be restored from the save while active tape, the files would have to be synchronized by a manual or programmed process.

SAVACT (* NO | * LIB | * SYSDFN)

- * NO - Save While Active will not be used.

- * LIB - Save While Active will time stamp ALL objects in each library with the save value.

- * SYSDFN - Save While Active function will group objects into sets. The system determines the number of snap shots. This is better performing than using *LIB. This function should not be used with applications making updates to the objects being saved unless the application has been ended during checkpoint processing or unless all application-dependent objects reside within a single library and all application-dependent objects are database files that are journaled.

SAVACTWAIT (0 - 99999 | * NOMAX)

- 0 - 99999 is the number of seconds the system will wait for a lock on an object to perform the checkpoint processing or to wait for an object to reach a commitment boundary.

- *NOMAX - There is no maximum time to wait for a lock on an object or to wait for an object commitment boundary.

SAVACTMSGQ (* NONE | * WRKSTN | Message-Queue-Name) Notification message that all checkpoint processing is complete for the last checkpoint object group in the library.

- *NONE - No notification message is sent. This is the default value.

- *WRKSTN - The notification message is sent to the workstation message queue. This option is only valid for interactive jobs. The job receives an escape message CPF378A and the save request ends if this option is specified for a batch job.

- Message-Queue-Name - The system sends the notification message upon initialization checkpoint phase completion.

20.16.3   Verifying Backup Design

QUSRTOOL contains programs that can help verify what objects are being saved and when.

- CHKSAV - Check Save tool determines whether any libraries have any members or objects that have changed since the last save.

- PRTLIBANL - Print Library Analysis tool will analyze all objects by library (single or all libraries) and summarize by days, what objects have been changed, saved or not saved. This summarization helps to easily identify any exposure.

- CHKSAVSTS - Check Save/Restore Status checks a joblog that includes save/restore commands and prints a listing with the completion messages and the diagnostic messages for that save. It basically summarizes the joblog used during a save/restore process.

- PRTSAVSTS - Print Save/Restore Status tool is intended to be used following a save of multiple libraries. PRTSAVSTS creates a printed output that contains a description of one or more library names, save dates, save commands, and the volumes the libraries were saved to. This list should then be stored off-line so that if a restore is necessary, an external description exists of what libraries were saved and what tape volumes contain them.

20.16.4   Restore Commands

● RSTSTG - Restore Storage command restores the entire system that was saved by the Save Storage (SAVSTG) command. There is no selective object or library restore. System configuration must be the same as that of the saved system.

● RSTLIB - Restore Library command restores one or all user libraries saved by the Save Library (SAVLIB) command. It allows selective object restore, *OLD, *NEW, *ALL or *FREE.

● RSTOBJ - Restore Object command restores a single or multiple objects in a library that was saved by a single command such as the Save Object (SAVOBJ) or the Save Library (SAVLIB) command. Access paths are restored only if the physical files are restored at the same time. The logical file must be in the same library.

● RSTUSRPRF - Restore User Profile command restores single or multiple profiles that were saved by the Save System (SAVSYS) or the Save Security Data (SAVSECDTA) command. It can also restore authorization lists, authority holders, and mail.

● RSTDLO - Restore Document Library Object command restores documents, folders, and distribution objects (mail) saved with the SAVDLO command.

● RSTCFG - Restores configuration object descriptions saved to tape by the Save System (SAVSYS) or the Save Configuration (SAVCFG) command.

● RSTAUT - Restores user profile private authorities after the user profile and all objects for that profile have been restored.

● RESTORE - This is an S/36EE restore command that restores disk files previously created with the AS/400 SAVE command.

- RESTLIBR - This is an S/36EE restore command that restores an entire library saved with the AS/400 SAVELIBR command.

- RSTS36F - This command restores a file or a group of files saved with the S/36 SAVE or AS/400 SAVS36F.

- RSTS36LIBM - This command restores source and procedure members saved with the S/36 FROMLIBR or AS/400 SAVELIBR.

20.17 Business Recovery Planning

To have a good backup procedure, you must understand what resources are necessary for each of your recovery scenarios. If data cannot be selectively restored, then an outage could have a significant impact on your business.

For example, suppose you decided that SAVSYS and SAVLIB *NONSYS would be your backup procedure. The save takes three tapes, and access paths are not saved. The system is using mirroring. Backups are performed on the weekend because of the time it takes to save the system.

A programmer accidently runs a program that corrupts one of the master files. The master file has a million records with three logical views. What are your options?

- Restore from the backup tape? Which tape is the master file on? How old is the data? How do I recover transactions that have updated the master file since the last save of the file was taken? How long will it take for the master file to be restored and the logical file to be rebuilt?

- Back out the changes that the programmer made? Is there a program written to provide this function? How long will it take to write the program? Will the recovery program run perfectly the first time? How will I recover from recovery program problems?

No one wants a disaster, but a simple error can cause the same impact to a business as a natural disaster. Every company should consider the different outage scenarios and carefully plan the appropriate response to each outage.

Many of today's larger companies are performing disaster recovery planning. All companies should be doing Business Recovery Planning as well. From the Business Recovery Plan, a save strategy can be developed for each possible outage scenario. It is also important to test this plan on a periodic basis. Such tests should use the actual backup data that would be used in a real emergency.

20.17.1 Mission and Objectives

A statement or statements of the mission of the Business Recovery Plan should be provided at the beginning of the development process. An example of the mission and objectives of a Business Recovery Plan could be:

- To provide for the resumption of all CRITICAL MIS services within XX hours following an outage.

- To provide for the resumption of all CRITICAL MIS services within XX hours following the declaration of a disaster.

- To provide for the restoration of all MIS services within XX hours following the declaration of a disaster.

To achieve this mission, the following objectives have been established:

- Periodic review and update of the Business Recovery Plan.

- Document procedures containing specific instructions for the Business Recovery Team to follow in the event of a disaster

- Establish an alternate site to provide for the timely processing of data critical to the continuation of business in a disaster situation.

- Personnel have been trained to implement the Business Recovery Plan.

- Periodic testing of the Business Recovery Plan to ensure disaster recovery readiness.

20.17.2   Assumptions

Any assumptions should be stated clearly, such as:

- The scope of the Business Recovery Plan encompasses the MIS department only. The business functions that do not interface with the MIS department have not been incorporated into this plan.

- People's safety is the first priority.

- Off-site data storage can be retrieved within XX hours.

- Key technical personnel identified in this plan are available during the disaster or outage.

- Replacement hardware will be available within XX hours.

20.17.3   Categorizing Business Functions

Each business function or service can be categorized as Critical, Essential, or Less Essential in the event of a disaster. Within these functions or services, the applications that support them can also be categorized.

- *Critical* functions or applications must be available within a specific time. If this does not occur, the result is a severe negative business impact. In a disaster, these functions or applications must be restored first.

- *Essential* functions or applications are needed. However, the loss of the function or application is less severe to the business than Critical items. In a disaster, these functions are restored after the Critical functions.

- *Less Essential* functions have little impact on the business. In a disaster situation, these functions may be suspended until normal services are resumed.

20.17.4 Identifying a Disaster

A disaster situation can range from a small outage of a few hours to a major outage of several months. The severity of the situation is dependent on its impact to the business. You must quantify the severity of an outage for yourself as it applies to your business and its unique requirements. Generally, the severity is assigned based upon the duration of the outage. This section looks at possible examples of severity levels:

- *Level 1 Outage* - 1 to 4 hours of outage. Critical applications service levels are not being met. Recovery time is less than 4 hours. *ACTION*: This is not a disaster situation. Follow recovery plan X.

- *Level 2 Outage* - 4 to 16 hours of outage. Critical applications are unavailable. Recovery time is less than 16 hours. *ACTION*: Invoke the Business Recovery Plan. A potential disaster is pending.

- *Level 3 Outage* - 16 to 48 hours of outage. Critical applications are unavailable. Recovery time is less than 48 hours. *ACTION*: Invoke the Business Recovery Plan. A disaster is imminent.

- *Level 4 Outage* - 48 or more hours of outage. All applications are unavailable. Recovery time is greater than 48 hours. *ACTION*: Invoke the Business Recovery Plan. Invoke the alternate site. Declare a disaster.

20.17.5 Critical Applications

What are critical applications? How is this different from business functions? Many times, the trend is to think of an application as a business function. Business functions normally encompass a distinct business product, area, or service. Applications form the support systems that enable a business product, area or service to operate. Single applications can cross business function boundaries. Less essential applications automatically becomes critical if they interface to a critical application.

20.17.6   Identifying the Critical Applications

The process to identify the critical applications is similar to understanding the business function.

- Identify all applications supporting each business function.

- Identify the critical point for each application.

- Categorize each application.

- Prioritize each application.

- Identify each application's components.

20.17.7   Critical Point of Applications

Identify how long each business function can survive without this application.   Remember that several different business functions may have dependencies on a single application. Based upon on the business function, the identified times can vary for the same application.

20.17.8   Categorize Each Application

Divide the applications into three categories:

- Critical - Applications must be available within a specific time. If this does not occur, the result is a negative business impact. In a disaster, these applications must be restored first.

- Essential - Applications are needed. However, the loss of the function or application is less severe to the business than critical items. In a disaster, these applications are restored after the critical functions.

- Less Essential - Applications that have little impact on the business. In a disaster situation, these applications may be suspended until normal services are resumed. It is important to get written agreements for such applications and to periodically have such agreements reviewed.

Categorize each application in two ways, application within business function, and application across business function boundaries. Prioritize each application in order of importance. View each application as a single entity. Identify application components such as:

- Online or batch

- Source of input

- Destination of output

- Major databases

- Network requirements

- Alternate and optional software methods of performing application functions

20.17.9   Business Recovery Team

The Business Recovery Team is comprised of individuals from several different areas. In large installations, each of these members are team leaders with specialized teams reporting to them.

Each Business Recovery Team member, their mission and objectives should be described in this section. A detailed example of this section covering the team manager and the various team leader members follows:

Business Recovery Team Manager

<u>Mission</u>

- Ensure that corporate directives are correctly interpreted and incorporated into the Business Recovery Plan.

● Provide for restoration of the business functions and services within the specifications of this Business Recovery Plan.

Pre-Disaster Planning Responsibilities

● Provide overall strategy decisions regarding recovery policies.

● Review completed or revised Business Recovery Plans.

● Ensure the Business Recovery Plan is current.

Disaster Responsibilities

● Declare a disaster and invoke the Business Recovery Plan

● Provide overall leadership and guidance to the Business Recovery Team.

● Advise corporate management on current status.

Business Recovery Team Leader

Mission

● Provide day-to-day management decisions to the Business Recovery Team.

● Assist the Manager in Business Recovery task.

Pre-Disaster Planning Responsibilities

● Implement the corporate policies and strategies as directed by the Business Recovery Team Manager.

● Manage the Business Recovery Team in the Business Recovery planning activities.

Disaster Responsibilities

● Declare a disaster and invoke the Business Recovery Plan when the Business Recovery Team Manager is not available.

- Manage the Business Recovery Team.

- Be the focal point for ALL business recovery activities.

Business Recovery Team Member — Operations

Mission

- Plan for off-site storage of data and operation systems.

- Coordinate the installation of the systems and data at the alternate site.

- Plan and coordinate the telecommunications network tasks at the alternate site.

- Work with the Application team member in the development of backups, restores, and off-site storage of application systems.

- Provide assistance to the application and user teams.

Pre-Disaster Planning Responsibilities

- Develop and maintain backup and restore procedures for the operating systems.

- Develop and maintain backup and restore procedures for the data files.

- Develop and maintain backup and restore procedures for the communications systems.

- Review the backup and restore procedures from the Applications Business Recovery Team Member.

- Develop procedures for the migration of the corporate network to the alternate site.

- Review and update the production schedules as required for migration to the alternate site.

- Identify special forms and other computer supplies that will be required at an alternate site.

Disaster Responsibilities

- Declare a disaster and invoke the Business Recovery Plan when the Business Recovery Team Leader is not available.

- Coordinate the transportation of data, programs, and computer supplies to the alternate site.

- Install the Operating Systems and Program Products at the alternate site.

- Implement the migration procedures for communications at the alternate site.

- Work with other Business Recovery Team Members to resume Critical and Essential business functions within the time frames stated in the Business Recovery Plan.

Business Recovery Team Member — Applications

Mission

- Work with the Operations Team Member to develop plans for the off-site storage of application systems.

- Plan and coordinate the migration of application systems to an alternate site.

Pre-Disaster Planning Responsibilities

- Develop and maintain backup and restore procedures for the application systems.

- Review the backup and restore procedures from the Operations Business Recovery Team Member.

- Develop procedures for the migration of the application systems to the alternate site.

Disaster Responsibilities

- Declare a disaster and invoke the Business Recovery Plan when the Operations Business Recovery Team Member is not available.

- Implement the migration procedures for application systems at the alternate site.

- Work with other Business Recovery Team Members to resume Critical and Essential business functions within the time frames stated in the Business Recovery Plan.

Business Recovery Team Member — Facility and Building Security

Mission

- Work with the Business Recovery Team Manager and Team Leader as required.

- Assess the disaster impact on the facility and the building security as required.

- Ensure the safety of personnel during the disaster situation.

- Provide engineering expertise in the coordination of any rebuilding and/or repair activities.

Pre-Disaster Planning Responsibilities

- Provide assistance to the Business Recovery Team Manager and Team Leader in maintaining and testing the Business Recovery Plan.

- Maintain adequate emergency supplies (first aid, food, water, blankets and hygienic items) and store them in accessible, strategic locations.

- Provide engineering expertise in determining and coordinating Disaster Prevention activities.

<u>Disaster</u> <u>Responsibilities</u>

- Assist Business Recovery Team members during the assessment of a disaster.

- Provide for the safety of personnel.

- Coordinate any rebuilding and/or repair activities as directed by the Business Recovery Team Manager.

- Work with other Business Recovery Team members to resume Critical and Essential business functions within the time frames stated in the Business Recovery Plan.

Other Business Recovery Team Members

Other Business Recovery Team Members may be required for your company. These may include a primary user or other key members of your organization.

20.17.10   Communications During a Disaster

Communications is a vital link in any disaster recovery effort. A command center is identified below for all formal and tactical communications during a disaster. When a disaster has been declared, members of the Business Recovery Team will meet at the command center to begin the coordination of their activities. If the situation makes the command center uninhabitable, the Business Recovery Team members will initially meet at the alternate command center.

In the event of a regional disaster, such as an earthquake, normal telephone communications may be restricted or unavailable. Your Business Recovery Plan should state the procedure for telephone communication and the location of the Command Center. Below is an example:

If the telephone system is restricted:

- Discontinue all non-Business Recovery outgoing phone calls.

● Lines must be available for the Business Recovery Team.

If the telephone system is unavailable:

● Use Business Recovery cellular lines.

The Command Center is in XXX Conference Room, in Building XX located at XXXXX.

The Alternate Command Center is at Company XXXX, Address XXXX, City XXXXX, State XX, Zip-Code XXXXX, Phone Number (XXX) XXX-XXXX.

20.17.11   Executing the Business Recovery Plan

The process of identifying a potential disaster situation, assessing its impact, and determining if a disaster should be declared is a multi-step process. The following section addresses each phase of this process.

When to sound the alarm

If any of the following questions can be answered as *YES*, use the Initial Disaster Notification Procedure.

● Has there been an earthquake or fire?

● Has there been an explosion?

● Can you smell gas?

● Are the police/fire department evacuating the area?

● Is the potential threat life threatening?

● Does the potential threat keep you from entering the building?

● Does the potential threat keep you from entering the computer room?

● Has there been any damage to the computer equipment?

- Has power been lost to the computer room?

- Has the UPS failed?

- Has the air conditioning failed in the computer room?

- Are there unauthorized persons in the computer room?

20.17.12   Initial Disaster Notification Procedure

The following is a sample procedure to be followed by an individual in a disaster situation. You should replace this with your customized version:

- Move to a "safe" area, away from any potential personal danger.

- Call "911" if needed and possible.

- Contact a member of the Business Recovery Team. The phone numbers are listed below:

  The order of contact is:

  Business Recovery Team Manager:
  XXXXXXXXXXXXXXX   (XXX) XXX-XXXX Ext. XXXX

  Business Recovery Team Leader:
  XXXXXXXXXXXXXXX   (XXX) XXX-XXXX Ext. XXXX

  Business Recovery Team Member — Operations:
  XXXXXXXXXXXXXXX   (XXX) XXX-XXXX Ext. XXXX

  Business Recovery Team Member — Applications:
  XXXXXXXXXXXXXXX   (XXX) XXX-XXXX Ext. XXXX

  Continue to call the above list of names until you have reached someone. If you have called the last person on the list and have not been able to speak with anyone, start over with the first person on the list. It is important that at least one person in each organization be reachable via a beeper or cellular telephone. As part of your planning process, you may need to assign this responsibility to an individual.

● Brief the Business Recovery Team member on the current situation, your assessment of the safety of the area/facility, and other information that may be helpful to them.

20.17.13 Disaster Assessment Procedure

The disaster assessment procedure reviews the situation against a criteria list. Its purpose is to help the reviewer analyze the disaster situation to determine the outage level and the appropriate action to be taken.

Key assets which support MIS that must be inspected include:

● Production Data Files

● Operating System

● System Documentation

● System Hardware

● Computer Room

● Environmental Support (air conditioning and power)

● Network Availability

Assess the outage level:

● Determine how long the outage will be.

● Determine whether the critical applications are available.

● Determine the expected recovery time.

● Use the guidelines to determine the outage level and determine which sections of the Business Recovery Plan may need to be invoked.

20.17.14   Disaster Declaration to Alternate Site Procedure

After an assessment has been made, use this procedure if the situation warrants a declaration of a disaster and the use of an alternate site. Replace the following sample with your customized version:

Disaster Declaration Procedure

- Contact the alternate site, providing the required information, identification, and phone numbers.

- Obtain the alternate site information regarding site location, contact person, and phone numbers.

- Arrange for the transportation of the *Vital Data Tapes* to the alternate site.

- If needed, arrange the following for the Business Recovery Team:

  Airline Reservations
  Hotel Arrangements
  Car Rental
  Emergency Funds

20.17.15   Recovery Procedures

Clearly documented recovery procedures contribute significantly to a successful recovery. Detailed recovery procedures that assume the operator has no knowledge of the systems or the company will provide better documentation for the disaster situation.

Include all procedures that will be used to restore the systems at the alternate site in this section. There should be a section on each of the following areas:

- Application Restoration (Data File Restore)

- System Partial Restoration

- Complete Reload of System and Critical Applications

- Remote and Local Network Connection Procedure

20.17.16 Security Procedures

Procedures should consider physical building security requirements as well as MIS needs. For example, some companies may need to secure the damaged area to prevent looting, reduce damage to equipment during cleanup, and secure/recover records. The primary physical building security system may not be operational after the disaster occurs. Document any secondary or manual security procedures in this section.

20.17.17 Backup Procedures

Backup procedures are used for two major requirements. They are:

- System/Application recovery due to system malfunction, hardware failure, data integrity, environmental problems, or utility service interruption.

- Disaster recovery when an alternate site is required. Different procedures may be required when multiple sites are involved.

Although both scenarios require clearly written and detailed documentation, the second scenario may involve personnel who are not familiar with the company's systems or its operations. In this case, it is even more critical that the procedure be periodically tested with the actual people involved who would be involved during a real disaster.

This section contains procedures for backing up all information required for the system recovery. This includes operating systems, applications, and communications. It should describe when backups are taken as well as which type of backup is to be used. It also includes procedures for acquiring and storing emergency supplies and computer supplies as well as off-site storage of tapes. Update this section for your company.

20.17.18   Preparing for a Disaster

Testing your Business Recovery Plan is very important before a disaster occurs. There are three basic categories of testing that are applied to a Business Recovery Plan to assure its success. They are:

- Walk through the plan with Business Recovery Team members.

- Scheduled "simulated" disaster.

- Unscheduled "simulated" disaster.

The walkthrough provides a cost effective method of reviewing the plan for major omissions. These omissions can be changes to the software or hardware environment, changes in the way business is conducted, or simply forgetting information. The synergy of a team review will normally bring out all the major steps required in your Business Recovery Plan. It is important that each team member review, understand, and accept their role in the plan as part of the walkthrough process.

A scheduled simulation of a disaster should combine several types of threats. For example, a scenario could be an earthquake with a minor fire in the supply room adjacent to the computer room. Another example is sabotage, followed by an explosion, then a fire. Different critical resources would be affected by each sequence of events and the basic Business Recovery Plan strategy would be tested.

An unscheduled simulation is similar to a scheduled simulation except the Business Recovery Team is not told of the exercise. This test determines the Business Recovery Team's readiness and their ability to react to unforeseen circumstances.

20.17.19   Training on Business Recovery Plan

All employees should be taught the basic procedures when encountering a potential disaster situation. They should know who on the Business Recovery Team to contact and their phone number. Describe your training program for your employees in this section.

20.17.20   Testing the Business Recovery Plan

The Business Recovery Plan must be tested. Describe the following items for your company in this section:

- Business Recovery Test Plan objectives.

- Test plan criteria.

- Review process during and after the test.

- Procedures to modify the plan if the testing shows that changes are required

- Detailed test scenarios, test data, and individual task assignments.

20.17.21   Business Recovery Plan Updates

It is necessary to periodically review and update the contents of the Business Recovery Plan. Without doing this, even the best plan quickly becomes archaic and unusable. The following events are possible triggers to the update and review of a Business Plan:

- Audit the Business Recovery Plan every six months. Results of the audit must be published to management.

- Test the plan every six months. A test methodology must be defined in order to capture variances, assess their cause, and update the plan.

- Training must occur annually. Details of the Business Recovery Plan and any updates should be included in the training session.

- New release of computer systems, both application and operating system, resulting in substantially different processing. An audit and testing cycle is needed.

- Change in the hardware configuration. Any change in system size or capacity must be reflected in the backup site plan.

- Change in key personnel.

- Significant growth in the basic business. The impact of various functions and applications to the business should be reevaluated to see if any changes need to be made to the Business Recovery Plan.

- Addition of new branches, products, or business functions.

21

Performance Tuning

This chapter looks at tuning OS/400 systems. Note that tuning information is also available in other chapters. Thus, the VTAM chapter contains some information on tuning distributed AS/400 systems that communicate with mainframe host systems. And, the security chapter discusses the performance impact of various security options.

We start with a general look at tuning issues, followed by a discussion of automatic tuning, then look in detail at subjects such as tuning the scheduler, improving I/O, as well as how different coding practices impact performance. The IBM manual *AS/400 Programming: Performance Tools/400 Guide* contains a good general discussion of tuning.

21.1 General Performance Tips

Performance tuning involves balancing the availability of resources against the desired performance levels of your online and batch applications. It is only an issue when you perceive, or your system users perceive, that their objectives are not being met. Thus, you can initiate tuning only when people are unhappy. On the other hand, if tuning is done as part of the ongoing system administration job, then an unexpected performance crisis should not develop. **You are strongly encouraged to tune as you go.**

The elements of system performance are CPU time, memory, and I/Os. If you use too much of any of these resources, your system will perform poorly. Tuning involves reducing the amount of a resource required, or providing enough resource to eliminate/reduce contention. Tuning may involve reducing one resource at the expense of another resource. We will briefly look at each of the three resource tuning areas in the subsections that follow.

21.1.1   Tuning I/O

We start with I/O, because it is often the most important performance problem. A system has an individual capacity for I/O. Once that capacity has been reached, then additional work results in slower and slower processing. Because all I/O occurs in the millisecond range where program instructions execute in the nanosecond and microsecond range, I/O is also the slowest thing each program can do. Our first tuning rule is to eliminate all possible I/O. Our second tuning rule is to make the remaining I/O run as fast as possible.

How do we eliminate I/O? OS/400 automatically makes use of additional system memory to reduce I/O by keeping extra data in memory. The more memory you provide for an application, the better that application will run. You can reserve memory for different categories of users by specifying *storage pools*. This will result in a more consistent level of performance for each group of users, although it may impact the performance of a single such group. You can restrict the number of users by specifying activity levels and by restricting the maximum number of jobs system wide. This reduces I/O conflicts and can result in better total system throughput.

How do we make I/O run faster? One approach is to add more disk controllers. The more controllers, the more simultaneous I/O requests. Modern disk controllers also often involve cache memory that can replace slow I/Os with faster memory accesses. It is important to balance both the disk drives and the I/O accesses across the available controllers. It is also important to balance workload across disk drives through the use of pools. I/O tuning is critical on the AS/400 because of the nature of the AS/400 database as well as the amount and impact of paging I/O that is typically seen on loaded systems.

21.1.2   Tuning Memory

Memory is one of the most important resources to tune, because inadequate memory leads to additional I/O, and I/O waits visibly impact online response time. Like the CPU resource, when you are out of memory, you can add more or use less. These are your only possibilities. However, OS/400 provides a number of parameters to facilitate using less memory. The subject of storage tuning via allocation/reservation is discussed in the *Storage Pools* section that follows.

After all is said and done, the most cost effective way to tune AS/400 memory may simply to be add additional memory until paging problems are no longer seen. The cost of the people time to analyse and tune the AS/400 auxiliary storage pools usually exceeds the cost of additional memory. In this book, we will look at basic tuning steps that require little people time.

You should pay special attention to memory usage when the load on your system increases through increasing the number of online users or through the addition of new applications. Memory problems are involved in more serious performance problems seen in AS/400 downsizing than those of any other resource, with the possible exception of CPU usage.

21.1.3   Tuning CPU Time

Although individual program instructions execute relatively quickly, programs that process a lot of data frequently are limited by the speed of the CPU. When you are running your processor at 100 percent of capacity, you can change to a faster processor, or use less CPU time, or ensure that priority work gets the best processor access. We discuss how coding practices impact the amount of CPU time used in a separate section of this chapter.

The MAXJOBS parameter of your subsystem definition determines how many jobs run in each memory subpool. This parameter affects CPU usage by allowing you to limit the number of CPU intensive jobs that are executing. The QMAXACTLVL system value determines the total number of jobs that may be started system wide. The default value of this parameter is 100 and should be reviewed if you have exhausted available CPU or memory.

21.2 Storage Pools

You can reserve memory for individual storage pools and you can restrict the number of jobs through activity levels. These actions may reduce the amount of work that is simultaneously active, but often improve total system throughput in terms of jobs processed per unit time. However, you should remember that memory is often your cheapest system upgrade, and that because of its virtual architecture, the AS/400 is unusually sensitive to memory constraints. Adequate memory not only reduces paging, but often results in a significant reduction in CPU time.

Storage may be divided into *pools* to ensure that adequate resources are reserved for specific types of work. This is one of the first tuning efforts that should be performed for your AS/400 system. The pools supported and the order you should specify them are:

- Machine pool. Storage reserved for the operating system, common code, and tables.

- *BASE pool. Storage for batch work.

- *INTERACT pool. Storage for online transactions.

- *SPOOL pool. Spool job storage.

21.2.1 Machine Pool

System pool 1 is the machine pool. Note that all paging seen here impacts the entire system. Thus, the machine pool 1 is the first pool you should tune. Tune the machine pool by increasing the size of the pool. This is done by specifying the QMCHPOOL system value.

Note that the proper size for pool 1 is not a constant, but depends upon the amount of memory available as well as the number of jobs you run and the communications configuration of the system. The minimum value that you should specify is processor dependent, but is usually larger than 1400KB.

It is possible to overallocate the machine pool. A machine pool that is too large will increase paging in other pools. If you see excessive paging for pools other than the machine pool, but the machine pool is experiencing less than 0.4 pages per second, then you will wish to reduce the size of the machine pool.

21.2.2   *BASE Pool

All storage not reserved for the machine pool is by default placed in the * BASE pool. When no other pools are defined, then all activity takes place in this pool. For small systems, this may be acceptable. However, the * BASE pool is normally reserved for batch work, with other pools handling the needs of spool (*SPOOL) and interactive (*INTERACT) work.

Jobs running in * BASE should have at least 500KB per activity level for efficient performance. If you have not specified enough storage in the * BASE pool, then you must either increase the size of this pool or reduce the number of jobs by adjusting the activity level. Adjusting the * BASE values is especially important when long running interactive transactions are moved to that pool by the system. If these adjustments do not help, you should specify QTSEPOOL as * NONE and see if that improves performance. If QTSEPOOL was already set to * NONE then you must increase available memory.

21.2.3   *INTERACT Pool

Storage reserved for interactive jobs is placed within the * INTER-ACT storage pool under the QINTER subsystem. When a mix of batch and interactive work is run, it is usually necessary to specify this pool to ensure that online work gets preferential access to storage, and to prevent batch jobs from impacting online work. The amount of storage required for each activity level depends upon application complexity more than other factors, but you may refer to Figure 21.1 for guidelines based upon system storage size.

The value given in the table is divided into the * INTERACT storage to determine the correct activity level for the QINTER pool. Larger values are used for larger storage configurations to ensure consistent performance to the extent possible. The larger sizes also account for the increased complexity of transactions usually seen on larger systems.

Main Storage in MB	KB per Activity Level
12 or less	450
16 - 28	900
32 - 48	1600
64 - 192	2500
208 or larger	3000

Figure 21.1   *INTERACT Pool Guidelines

If you see large spikes in paging for the * INTERACT pool, you will wish to review your pool size and either increase it or reduce your activity levels. The only time that you should be unconcerned about high paging for the * INTERACT pool is when you determine that some transient activity caused the performance spike. One example of such a storage user is interactive compiles. These should be discouraged in a system with high paging as compiles have large storage needs and because they impact all other online transaction work. In a test environment, they should be ignored as the * INTERACT pool is not increased.

21.2.4 *SPOOL Pool

Storage that is reserved for spooling jobs is placed within the * SPOOL storage pool under the QSPL subsystem. Refer to Figure 21.2 for the suggested QSPL pool sizes. Values are given in units of 1KB.

Note that you have no need for a separate QSPL pool unless you perform an appreciable amount of spooling. If spooling jobs are run infrequently or the total volume of spooling is small, then you should not define a separate QSPL storage pool. If you are heavily storage constrained, you may wish to reduce the values given when several spooling jobs are present.

Number of Writers	Activity Level	AFP Size	non-AFP Size
1	1	500	80
2	2	1000	160
3	3	1300	225
4	4	1500	290
>4	5	1700	350

Figure 21.2 QSPL Pool Suggested Sizes

21.2.5 Activity Level Tuning

Adjusting the activity level is usually the best way to tune paging in pools 2 through 16. This is done by taking each pool in turn. If a low page fault rate is seen at the same time as a large number of wait-to-ineligible transitions, you need to increase the activity level for this pool.

High page fault values usually indicate that the activity level is set too high. If other pools appear to be overallocated, you can reduce their size and increase the size of the current pool. Otherwise, you will have to reduce the activity level value of the current pool or add additional hardware resources to the computer system.

21.3 Automatic Tuning

The AS/400 is capable of automatically tuning itself. You enable this tuning as well as control how often the system performs automatic system tuning through various system values. We will look at automatic tuning done at IPL time as well as the dynamic performance parameter tuning that can take place while the system is operating.

21.3.1 Tuning IPL

The AS/400 can automatically check its configuration and establish tuning values at the time of each IPL. This allows adaptation to system changes to exploit the addition or loss of resources, as well as to recognize changes in workload configuration. On the other hand, automatic tuning at IPL time results in the loss of any tuning values you might have established via commands while the system was last operating. You enable IPL tuning by the setting of QPFRADJ. A value of 1 or 2 enables IPL tuning. Other values disable IPL tuning. The system parameters that are set by IPL tuning include:

- QMCHPOOL (system value) machine pool size.

- Shared pool * SPOOL size and activity level. Subsystem QGPL/QSPL pool 2 set to use this shared pool.

- Shared pool * INTERACT size and activity level as well as automatic usage of this pool when necessary.

- QBASACTLVL if the controlling subsystem is QSYS or QGPL / QBASE or QCTL.

The use of shared pools as well as certain system values is determined by the controlling subsystem, so IPL tuning responds to changes in this value. If you make your own adjustments to the pool size or activity level values, then you should disable IPL tuning by setting QPFRADJ to 0.

21.3.2 Dynamic Tuning

The AS/400 can also periodically check how the system is running, and dynamically alter tuning parameters to improve/tune system performance. A QPFRADJ value of 2 or 3 enables dynamic tuning, while other values disable it. A value of 3 enables only dynamic tuning without IPL tuning. This allows values used during prior system operation to be maintained across an IPL, and may be desired especially in certain complex environments.

Dynamic tuning automatically adjusts pool sizes and activity levels. If you make your own adjustments to the pool size or activity level values, then you should disable IPL and dynamic tuning by setting QPFRADJ to 0. Dynamic tuning does the following:

- *MACHINE pool size (QMCHPOOL system value).

- *BASE pool activity level (QBASACTLVL system value).

- Shared pools *SPOOL, *INTERACT, and *SHRPOOL1-10 have their pool size and activity levels adjusted.

Dynamic tuning works by moving storage from underutilized pools to more active pools that can take advantage of it. It also balances resource usage by adjusting the number of jobs based upon pool storage. Wide swings in pool job activity and storage requirements can cause dynamic tuning to impact system performance by causing memory thrashing. Where dynamic tuning is found to be effective only after the system has been up for a while, you may wish to consider setting QPRFADJ to 3 to prevent IPL tuning from resetting values and starting the dynamic tuning learning process over again.

21.4   How AS/400 Scheduling Works

Advanced tuning (manual tuning) of the AS/400 requires a basic understanding of how the system schedules workload. The system attempts to balance work (jobs) against available resources. Let us look at how job states influence this process.

A job can be in an *ineligible, active,* or *wait* state. *Ineligible* means that the job cannot be run because the system cannot accept additional work. This is a result of an activity level specification smaller than the current number of jobs. A job is removed from the ineligible state only when an activity level becomes available.

An *active* job is able to run and does not impact performance except to the extent that it is occupying an activity level some other job could use. Of course, active jobs are also consuming CPU time and occupying memory, which is the reason for activity level specifications. We specify the maximum number of jobs that may be active to ensure we do not exhaust all available memory and

CPU time. It is important that we not run our CPU at 100% and we not use all available memory. Exceeding any resource causes long delays in response time.

A job in a wait state is waiting for a resource. A job in a *wait* state can be in a short wait or a long wait. A job in a *short wait* continues to occupy an activity level, and thus prevents ineligible jobs from starting. A job may remain in a short wait for up to two seconds, then it is moved to a long-term wait. Short waits for remote terminal activity should be avoided to reduce the number of activity levels that are occupied unproductively and to improve system paging performance. A job in a *long wait* does not occupy an activity level. Jobs in long waits are maintained in a queue of waiting jobs, and must bid for an available activity level when their original wait reason has been satisfied. Jobs that are no longer waiting are dispatched from the front of this queue, so queue position is another factor in how long a job must remain in a long wait.

One example of a long wait is a DDM data request. These requests involve processing by the system and frequently include I/Os and may involve waiting for availability of a data management software component. This type of long wait is placed in priority sequence within the queue of jobs that are waiting. Another example of a long wait is a wait for a resource that is currently locked by another job. This type of long wait is kept at the front of the queue of jobs that are waiting to reduce the total time that resources can remain locked.

21.4.1 Priority and Waits

The ineligible queue is maintained in priority sequence. Jobs leave this queue based upon priority and status, so this is a *first-in, first-out, priority queue*. It is important to understand that your priority, and not your ability to run, determines when you leave the ineligible queue. Select your priority by how important it is for your job to regain the system after a long-term wait.

A jobs priority also determines what happens when a timeslice is exhausted. If no jobs of equal or higher priority are available on the ineligible queue, then your job continues to run for another timeslice. If your priority is the same as or lower than that of any other job, then that job gains control on the system. Specifying many jobs at the same priority can increase paging in a storage constrained environment.

21.4.2 Paging and the *PURGE Parameter

When a job is waiting it may remain in main memory or it may be removed to make memory available for other jobs. Jobs in short waits remain in memory, while jobs in long waits are eligible for movement to disk storage in order to free up their main memory. The process of moving the objects required for a job from disk to main storage and from main storage back to disk is called *paging*. The * PURGE work management parameter determines how the AS/400 handles paging. When * PURGE YES is specified, then the method employed is similar to swapping where all of the storage needed for a task is read or written as a group, and where long-term waits generally involve a swap out in a storage constrained environment. You should specify * PURGE YES unless you have excess memory.

When * PURGE NO is specified, then the method employed is similar to demand paging, where the storage used for a job is only read or written as needed, and where only the portion needed is read or written. For nonconstrained environments, * PURGE NO can reduce the amount of CPU time and disk I/O time required for system overhead per transaction and is encouraged. This value should not be used in a storage constrained environment as it increases the amount of storage required and will amplify the existing paging delays.

21.5 Coding Techniques and Performance

In this section we look at the impact different coding approaches have on performance. We look at the overhead associated with program calls between modules, as well as the special considerations of calling CL programs. This information is useful more to prevent performance problems than to fix them, because we often cannot afford the time to redesign applications in order to improve performance. However, a small amount of design work before a program is written can dramatically improve the performance of an application.

21.5.1   Call Overhead

Modular programming is the only logical approach to developing today's complex applications, and to reusing existing code for new development.   However, each call from one program to another introduces an overhead unrelated to the function of the called program.   The performance range for different types of calls is up to two orders of magnitude, so you must pay attention to the type of call if you wish to optimize performance of modular applications.

COBOL calling COBOL or C/400 calling C/400 subprograms are the most efficient types of calls available.   These types of calls may be used with little concern for performance.   RPG calls RPG with somewhat more overhead, while RPG or COBOL call PL/I with a large increase in cost.   The worst type of linkage is RPG or COBOL calling a C/400 main module where the C environment must be created.   This type of call is more than 300 times more expensive than COBOL calling COBOL or C/400 calling C/400.   Note that even calling an existing C/400 environment via QPXXCALL is somewhat more expensive than calling PL/I and is twenty times more expensive than the fastest type of call available.   Clearly, all calls are not created equal.

Even the fastest type of call must be used with care.   Ensure that the total count of calls is kept manageable and does not grow without limits.   For example, designing an application to process a 100MB file where each character of data is accessed by a separate call to a subroutine is always a poor choice.   Here we see a linear performance cost made excessive by the number of calls.   We must also be careful of nonlinear growth in the number of calls.   Thus, activities such as sorting data, inserting entries into tables, and record parsing can result in massive processor costs if called subroutines are used within the operation.

21.5.2   Calling CL Routines

Command Language is a powerful tool, because of its ease of use, and because of the amount of general purpose CL code provided with the AS/400 system.   However, CL routines can be expensive to call.   For example, benchmarks show that the total cost of each use of a CL routine can exceed 10 milliseconds on an entry level F series system. This does not sound like much but can add hours to the processing time for a million records.

The cost of CL is easily avoided through the use of RPG subroutines. This is true because RPG routines can be initialized once then reused, while CL routines must be initialized each time they are invoked. An RPG routine is left active by executing a RETRN without setting the LR indicator. Using RPG routines that are left active can save over 95% of the cost of each call.

21.6   Measuring Performance

A number of facilities are provided as part of the base system to measure performance, and to determine the causes of poor performance. The IBM licensed program *Performance Tools/400* is an additional facility for monitoring/managing performance. For information on the Performance Tools product refer to the book *Programming: Performance Tools/400 Guide* (SC41-8084). In this section we only discuss the native facilities. The three commands provided with the base system we will discuss are:

- WRKSYSSTS — Work with System Status

- WRKDSKSTS — Work with Disk Status

- WRKACTJOB — Work with Active Jobs

When using these commands, you have to allow the system to gather the desired data. This is accomplished by issuing one of the commands, waiting a minimum of five minutes to gather data, then pressing F5 to present the data. This data is what is used to make tuning decisions.

21.6.1   Work with System Status

This display shows the overall status of the system. Use it to identify whether or not the CPU is overcommitted. In general, a CPU percentage of over 90 indicates a strong potential for CPU caused performance problems. The display also includes storage and paging statistics by system pool. Note that system pool 1 is the machine pool and that all paging seen here impacts the entire system. Thus, system pool 1 is the first pool you should tune. You should tune the machine pool if you have more than 1 page fault per second reported for pool 1. Tune the machine pool by increasing the size of the pool. This is done by typing the new size value and pressing enter.

Note that the proper size for pool 1 is not a constant, but depends upon the amount of memory available as well as the number of jobs you run and the communications configuration of the system. Thus, the machine pool size should be evaluated whenever you make changes that affect the number of jobs or communications. Each job requires about 1KB of additional machine pool space. The impact of communication is the largest as a single line requires an extra 125KB of space and each controller an additional 25KB of machine pool space.

Pools other than the machine pool (pool 1) should be reviewed for total paging. If any pool exceeds 15-20 pages per second, tuning may be needed. If total system paging exceeds 30-40 pages, then either additional memory may be required, or the activity levels may need to be reduced. Activity level values may be changed by typing the new values and pressing enter. These are rough guidelines; you are referred to tables in the *Performance Tools/400* IBM manual for more detailed information.

From the initial display, you may press F11 to see job dispatching transition data. This displays the number of jobs in each of the following states:

- Active-to-wait

- Wait-to-ineligible

- Active-to-ineligible

Note that wait-to-ineligible is not necessarily bad. You will see a non-zero value here if you have used activity levels to reduce the number of jobs and thus reduce the amount of paging. In general you want your active-to-wait value to be ten times larger than the wait-to-ineligible value, although values of as little as four times larger may be tolerable. Too large a wait-to-ineligible value usually indicates that your activity levels are too small or that your system does not possess enough main memory.

The active-to-ineligible value should be zero if possible. This means that all transactions completed within a single timeslice. Of course, you may have long running transactions that depend upon timeslice values to ensure that other transactions get adequate service. Even if this is true, you want to have 90% or more of your transactions completed within a single timeslice to reduce system CPU overhead.

21.6.2 Work with Disk Status

This display shows the status of the various disk drives present upon your system. Use it to identify disk drives which are overloaded, and others that are underutilized. Work should be moved from overloaded drives to those which are relatively underutilized.

Before attempting to tune your DASD, you should first tune paging. Since paging contributes to total DASD I/O and because paging I/O has a relatively high priority, eliminate as much paging as possible before looking at the DASD I/O load. Refer to the section entitled *Tuning Memory.*

You should begin DASD tuning by looking at the percent busy column for each device. Each DASD unit (actuator) should be less than 40% busy. Over 40% busy you may see erratic response time. Over 60% busy you cannot get acceptable interactive performance. If your actuators exceed 40% busy after tuning, then you need additional DASD, even if you have not used all available space. Note that it is not uncommon for auxiliary storage pool (ASP) actuators to exceed 40%, and this is not a cause for disk configuration changes.

All rules have exceptions; the exception for this rule is that certain batch operations can drive DASD percent busy very high. So long as these batch jobs do not run at the same time as interactive processing, your percent busy can be any value. Examples of such standalone batch jobs are database reloads, and backups of the entire system. Such jobs will run vastly slower if you attempt them while other system processing continues, and will impact any other processing as well. It is important to remember the issue with database reloads when recovering your system after a DASD failure.

21.6.3 Work with Active Jobs

This display shows the status of jobs. It is used in conjunction with the WRKSYSSTS display to get tuning information. When the system status indicates that your CPU is overcommitted, you can look at the CPU cost of individual jobs on the WRKACTJOB display. You can also spot priority and I/O delay induced problems by using this display.

The initial display for WRKACTJOB includes no usable percent CPU data. Press F11 to get elapsed data. Use this percent CPU value to identify excessive resource consumption problem areas. Interactive throughput and response time data is used to determine whether or not response time is acceptable. Note that users who see wide swings in response time usually perceive that response time is *poor*, even though the average response time may look very good. Thus, our primary objective in tuning interactive systems is to first make response times consistent, and then second to improve the average response time. Consistent response time is achieved by eliminating queuing for resources. In order of importance for the typical AS/400 shop this means to reduce queuing for memory, CPU, and disk I/O. It is a rare AS/400 that does not benefit from additional processor memory.

21.7 REXX Performance

The performance of CL commands issued from REXX may be significantly worse than that of the same CL command issued interactively. In fact, the performance of a CL command issued in a batch job may be vastly better than that of the same command issued from within REXX. This is one factor contributing to an overall poor level of performance for REXX code.

21.8 Application Performance

Application design has the greatest impact on end-user performance. If the application design causes a lock wait condition (all users must read/write lock a record, file, or object) to occur between users, changing the system performance may not change the end-user response time.

21.9   System Performance

The following system values that initially allocate job structure storage should be changed to match your operation or uses of the system.

- QTOTJOB - Total Number of Jobs in the System (IBM shipped value is 30). This value should be larger than the total jobs that will be in the system at any given time. Until the spool output files of a job are printed or deleted, the job is still in the system. Monitor the WRKSYSSTS total job field to determine a good initial value.

- QACTJOB - Total Number of Active Jobs in the System (IBM shipped value is 20). This value should be larger than the total active jobs in the system at any given time. Monitor the WRKACTJOB active job field to determine a good initial value.

System Value QADLTJOB (Additional total number of jobs) and QADLACTJ (Additional number of active jobs) should be small so that if the system crosses one of the thresholds, the impact on the system will be only for a short time. If the system has frequent unexplained slow downs for short periods of time, check the QACTJOB and QTOTJOB system values to determine if the values are too small.

21.9.1   PURGE(*YES) or PURGE(*NO)

Only use PURGE(*NO) in a pool that has plenty of memory. PURGE(*NO) uses demand paging. If the amount of memory the system needs to support the jobs is not available, the system could begin to thrash in that pool. Thrashing is when the system is doing more system work (such as paging) than productive work in the pool. This can be corrected by added more memory to the pool or by reducing the activity level of the pool.

For a low memory condition in the pool, PURGE(*YES) provides the best performance. The system will automatically perform PURGE(*NO) procedure functions if the pool is stable. When paging becomes excessive, the system will revert back to perform PURGE(*YES) procedure functions.

21.9.2   Machine Page Faulting

The machine page fault rate should be less than 1 (page fault per second). The larger the faulting rate, the greater the impact on system performance. The machine page faulting depends on the amount of memory available to the pool. Increasing the amount of memory to the pool will reduce the page faulting rate to a point. At that point more memory will have very little impact. A goal would be to reduce the page faulting rate to less than .5.

21.9.3   Shared vs. Private Pools

Prior to Version 1 Release 3 of the operating system, if a customer wanted to separate users to different subsystems, a private pool would have to be created. The reason for the different subsystems was to be able to take a group of user subsystems down and not affect others. The net effect of creating private pools was the separation of the available memory into smaller pools. This often had a negative effect with small memory sizes by leaving some pools without adequate memory.

Version 1 Release 3 introduced shared pools other than *BASE. Shared pools allow the same pool of memory to be shared between multiple subsystems. Using shared pools and private pools provides the greatest flexibility.

21.9.4   System Tuner

The jury is still out on the IBM dynamic tuner that is supplied with the AS/400 system. Over time, the IBM tuner should become the best available tuning option; however, in the past, IBM has chosen to use other vendors' products instead of improving their own tuning products. Vendors such as Help System have tuning products that many customers prefer.

If you are using the IBM tuning, it is suggested that you try the automatic tuning option, especially on smaller systems. This generally outperforms tuning parameters established statically when the system is booted.

To get the best out of any tuner, you will need to understand the variables that affect the tuner's ability to adjust the system performance. And, even with the best automatic tuner, some manual adjustment of tuner or system parameters may be needed for optimum performance.

21.10   Application Performance

In this section we summarize the issues related to application performance. We concentrate on interactive application design because online performance is normally the most important area for AS/400 users. We also discuss batch I/O performance in some detail. One important rule is to not run applications that can be run in batch as interactive applications.

21.10.1   Interactive Application Design

- Use Shared Open Data Path - SHARE(*YES). Whenever possible create or override the database file to SHARE(*YES). This reduces the time the system takes to open a file used by a job multiple times at different program levels. Example: in JOB Order, File A is used in programs ORD01, ORD02, and ORD03. Program ORD01 calls ORD02, and ORD03. If File A's ODP is shared between ORD01, ORD02, and ORD03, then the file open for File A would be shorter for programs ORD02 and ORD03 the first time, and would be zero (0) for every call thereafter if programs ORD02 and ORD03 did not set on LR (for programs written in RPG).

- Reduce the Number of Database Accesses. Only read the records necessary to display one screen of data. As the number of users increases, each additional I/O has a cumulative effect on performance.

- Allow Program Control of the Roll Up Function (page down function) of Subfile Processing. Only write one more record than can fit in a subfile page. By reducing total I/Os both for the disk read and for the subfile write, user response time is improved.

21.11   Database Design

The following areas affect database performance:

- Number of I/O's to get a complete record. If your database design requires most applications to read multiple files to complete a single transaction, the database design may be to the highest normalization, but the performance will not be good. The design should take into consideration the performance impact. Database design should be to the third normal form.

- Number of Indexes (Logical files). For each add, update, and delete, each affected index (logical file) must be adjusted. As the number of indexes increases, so does the maintenance cost in CPU use, number of disk I/Os, the lock wait time, and the working set. If logical files are necessary, use dynamic select/omit or defer index maintenance. Sometimes a sort may be all that is needed if a snap shot of the data can be used.

- Reduce Key Size. As the key gets larger, the index gets larger and may get deeper. Therefore, as the key gets larger, the cost to use the index increases in CPU use, working set, and number of disk I/Os.

- Reduce Lock Wait Delays. Try to avoid control record processing or update the control record last. Example: Order control record. If every job must read and update this record before it can process an order, as the number of users increases, there is a greater probability that users will have to wait on an update lock.

- Use Relative Record Number processing whenever possible. Relative record number is the fastest method to process a database file on the AS/400.

- Run Batch in Batch. The greatest impact on performance is to run a batch job in the interactive subsystem at the interactive priority level. OS/400 was changed to allow a program to run a maximum of 500 milliseconds before the system checks for other jobs at an equal or higher priority. This change prevents any program from totally dominating the system, but a program at a low priority will not get very many cycles.

21.12 Batch Performance

The AS/400 was designed to enhance interactive performance. Data for a given file may be spread over multiple disk arms. This reduces average latency by increasing the probability that randomly accessed data is near one of the arms. For batch processing you typically read data sequentially with little or no disk seeking beyond that required to traverse the file once. Refer to Figure 21.3 for an overview of AS/400 disk processing.

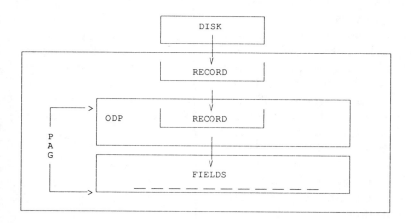

Figure 21.3 Disk Processing Overview

21.12.1 Sequential Processing

Sequential processing is the fastest way to process data on the AS/400. Relative record processing is next. If the system detects that you are processing the records in physical sequence, the system will preread the next record(s) while your program is processing the previous request (adaptive double buffering). To increase the batch performance you must force the processing of the records to physical sequential order. In fact, for large files, it is faster to sort or resequence (RGZPFM Reorganize Physical Member) the records and process the records sequentially than to process the records randomly.

21.12.2   Input and Output Blocking

Most commercial batch jobs are disk I/O bound. This means that the system is most often waiting for data to be read from disk or to be written to disk. By reading more than one record from disk at a time, average I/O time can improve. Of course, blocked input will not improve program performance if the next record the program wants is not the next physical record in the buffer. If a file will be processed sequentially, then increasing the number of records read can greatly improve performance.

If a program reads records randomly, but the records are physically in close proximity to each other, then increasing the number of records read via larger blocking may also improve performance. When files are to be processed in a mixed random/sequential fashion, a review of record blocking is still desirable.

The default blocking buffer size is 4K bytes for most high-level languages. When the system detects that processing is sequential, the system will read the number of records that will fit in a 4K-byte buffer. Especially for faster AS/400 models, this results in frequent waits for disk I/O completion.

To change the number of records that are passed to the program and the number of records that are physically read with one I/O, the OVRDBF command can be used. Refer to Figure 21.4 for NBRRCDS usage. Note: The buffer size should be around 16K bytes for OS/400 Version 1 and 32K bytes for Version 2. Any larger size will not improve batch performance significantly. When more than three or four files are being used, be careful not to exceed the PAG size limitation for OS/400 Version 1. Refer to Figure 21.5 for an example of adaptive double buffering.

SEQONLY(*YES n) is not allowed for

- Update Operations

- Logical file based on two or more physical files

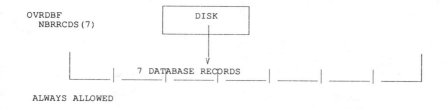

Figure 21.4 OVRDBF NBRRCDS Parameter

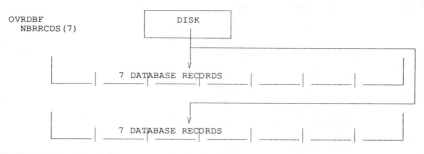

Figure 21.5 Adaptive Double Buffering

● Some output operations

Figure 21.6 covers sequential processing while Figure 21.7 and Figure 21.8 cover indexed input processing and Figure 21.9 covers indexed output processing.

21.12.3 SETOBJACC

New to Version 2 Release 2 is the SETOBJACC command. This command is used to load data objects into memory or purge objects from memory. If an object is loaded into memory via SETOBJACC, a reduction in I/O operations is usually seen, especially for random access file operations. The pool of memory can be a shared or private pool. No jobs can be running in the selected pool and the

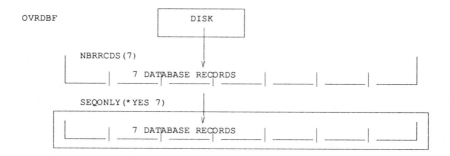

Figure 21.6   Sequential Only

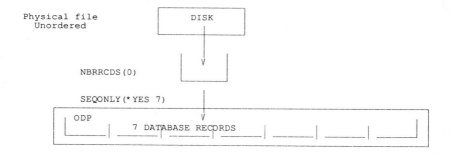

Figure 21.7   Indexed Sequential - Input Only

pool should be cleared with the CLRPOOL command. SETOBJACC Operations are:

- Object and pool are specified on the SETOBJACC command.

- Object will be flushed from main storage. If the object is located in another pool, it will be removed from main storage, then read into the selected pool.

- Object will be loaded from the first byte to the last byte. Deleted record space will also be loaded.

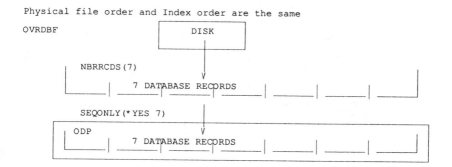

Figure 21.8 Indexed Sequential - Input Only

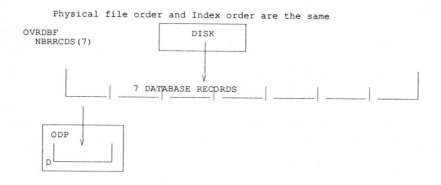

Figure 21.9 Indexed Sequential - Update

- System will report the amount of storage used and the amount that was required for a complete load of the object.

- If the object does not fit in the pool, the system will load the additional data when it is accessed by a job, in the pool of the job.

- Data added to the file will use space in the job pool, not the data pool.

- When the data is no longer needed, the SETOBJACC command can be used to purge the resident objects.

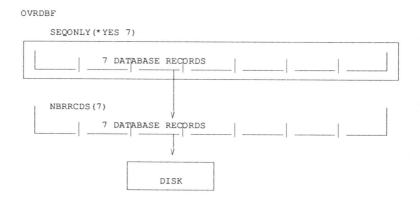

Figure 21.10   Output

The advantages of this command are:

- Faster random processing. Since there are no I/Os performed, the program becomes CPU bound.

- Both the data and access path can be loaded into the pool. This results in faster access path maintenance.

- All jobs have access to the data.

21.13   API vs. Outfile Processing

API processing was provided in the system to improve the ability to write programs to get information from the system without using outfile or needing to override the files command to write the data to a disk file, then reread the disk file for the information that was needed. Another problem with outfile or overriding a print file is that IBM may change the format of the data, which would in turn require the customer program to change. With API processing, a new format can be added leaving the existing format the same.

For a detailed explanation of the use and characteristics of API processing, refer to the IBM manual: *System Programmer's Interface Reference* SC41-8223.

21.14   Numeric Fields

Numeric fields should be defined as packed decimal format. The AS/400 most efficiently handles arithmetic instructions on packed decimal values.

The AS/400 performs arithmetic instructions internally in the following priority: floating-point, if any of the source fields are in floating-point format; packed decimal, if any of the source fields are in zone or packed decimal format; or binary, if any of the source fields are in binary format.

If a field is not in packed decimal format, the system must convert it to that format, perform the arithmetic, and then convert the result to the original data format. Such conversions have a performance impact for each reference to arithmetic data.

Currently only the 35 and 45 models have floating-point hardware. Therefore, if the source fields are in a floating-point format, the arithmetic instructions will be done with software on the higher end models. The best performance with the least impact on the CPU would be packed decimal format. If the field is not in zoned decimal format, the system must convert it to a packed decimal format, perform the arithmetic, and then convert the result to the format of the result field. This conversion has a performance impact each time the system must convert the data.

If the data is defined as an even sized packed decimal format, the system must check the high order four bits in the field to verify that no overflow has occurred during each arithmetic operation. This additional checking causes a performance impact of 7 to 14 times what it would cost to perform the same arithmetic operation on odd length packed decimal fields.

21.15   RPG II Performance Tips

The AS/400 was designed to efficiently process RPG programs more than those in any other language. However, ample room exists for improving the performance of RPG applications. In this section we briefly list some areas:

- Remove subscript variables out of a loop when the variable is not being indexed. The RPG compiler does not perform this common and important optimization.

- Use Data Structures when more than two fields are manipulated. Reduce the use of the MOVEA, MOVEL, and MOVE instructions.

- Use IF rather then COMP.

- Use CAB rather than COMP.

- Use DO for grouping.

- Use a binary search on large tables.

- Avoid the use of the RPG cycle for interactive processing.

- Avoid the use of READE on a sparsely populated format.

- Use RT return for subprograms whenever possible. This allows files opened in the subprogram to remain open. This is especially important on slower AS/400 models where the call initialization overhead is relatively higher. When you employ RT return, be sure to reinitialize any fields that must be the same for every call.

21.16   COBOL Performance Tips

Individual COBOL implementations vary in which programming practices are efficient and which are not. The AS/400 COBOL has its own unique areas of especially poor performance. In this section we look at some general COBOL performance issues as well as those specific to the AS/400 platform. When designing new applications or porting existing COBOL applications, you should pay attention to the following items:

- Use INDEXING rather than SUBSCRIPTING. This is generally true for COBOL implementations, but is an area in which many existing COBOL applications have problems.

- Use SEARCH ALL and order large tables. SEARCH ALL generates a binary search of the table and therefore requires that the table be sorted to find the proper match.

- Use GENOPT(*NORANGE) compiler option. This option is used to eliminate much of the range checking code that is used to assure that the range of a subscript or index variable falls within the range of the dimension of a declared array. Do not use this option during testing/debugging of code.

- Use GENOPT(*OPTIMIZE) compiler option. This option requests the MI Translator to take an additional pass to optimize the pointer addressing for both local code and global pointer assignment.

- Avoid where possible CLASS TEST on DB data.

- Do Not Use Segmentation. This function is not needed on the AS/400.

- Use COMP-3 field with an odd number of decimal digits whenever possible. Odd size packed decimal fields produce two-thirds fewer instructions than zoned decimal data fields.

- Declare all numeric data items as signed. Whenever the compiler does a store into a variable, extra code has to be generated to force the sign to a positive value even though the result is always positive for declared unsigned variables. By only declaring signed numeric variables, the extra hardware instructions on every assignment will not be generated.

- Use Reference Modification to move strings. The use of reference modification is nine times faster to move a 10 character string than moving the 10 characters one byte at a time.

- Use Inline PERFORM whenever possible. Inline PERFORM for looping is approximately three times faster for loop control code than the use of an out-of-line PERFORM.

- Use READ instead of READ INTO whenever possible. On the AS/400 the FD definition is the actual file buffer. If the data does not need to be moved into WORKING STORAGE, then use READ instead of READ INTO.

- Use the QCLSCAN command instead of the STRING and INSPECT builtin functions of the COBOL language. QCLSCAN is much faster than the native COBOL support.

22

Storage Management

This chapter looks at Storage Management issues in OS/400. We look at the *Operational Assistant,* an automated storage management tool, as well as various manual efforts you are responsible for to reduce auxiliary storage usage.

22.1 Operational Assistant

The AS/400 is a sophisticated system able to automatically run much of your regular workload. As such, it also will automatically create a variety of files. Some of these files are temporary in nature, but are kept by the system, and will gradually fill all available auxiliary storage space (DASD space) unless something is done about them. For example, your systems tend to abound with old unprinted spool output, message logs, and unused documents. And, database files often contain a large number of deleted records, whose space is also held until manually released for reuse.

The *Operational Assistant (OA)* was added to OS/400 by IBM to help address these issues. OA provides menus that allow you to specify automated cleanup actions that can dispose of the junk files that are automatically produced by your system. You can most easily access OA by typing GO CLEANUP. You define how often you wish "junk" files purged or whether this is to be done as part of system shutdown using the *Change Cleanup Options* submenu.

You specify when automatic cleanup is to be performed either as a time of day or as *SCDPWROFF to perform cleanup during system power-off processing. You may also specify *NONE to totally disable all automatic cleanup actions. Finally, you specify a different number of days of retention for each of the following types of data:

- User messages

- System and workstation messages

- Job logs and other system output

- System journals and other system logs

- OfficeVision/400 calendar items

For each of the listed items you may specify either a value of KEEP or a number of days of retention. KEEP causes objects of the listed type to not be automatically purged. A number of days ranging from 1 to 366 results in objects older than the number of days specified being purged when cleanup is performed.

22.2 Additional Objects Needing Cleanup

Although the Operational Assistant can be used to clean up a number of types of data, it cannot do the whole job. Some types of data must be manually purged. We will look at how we handle cleanup of data missed by OA in this section.

We can either manually issue the commands to clean up the remaining data, or (better yet) build our own command to perform these cleanup tasks. Our custom command can be either manually issued, or issued as part of OA processing. The types of data not processed by OA that we will concern ourselves with include:

- System temporary data

- Security journals

- Spool file storage

- User defined objects

22.2.1   System Data

The AS/400 manages a lot of transient data including temporary libraries and various control blocks. An IPL of the AS/400 causes storage used for such temporary data to be released for reuse. A periodic IPL should be part of your system schedule. The IPL both makes storage available and results in improved performance. Of course, if you include a system shutdown as part of your automated actions, then the IPL is a regular scheduled item.

An IPL will also cause all current job logs to be closed with new logs started. This permits the old logs of long running jobs to enter your regular cleanup cycle. It also improves performance because appending to a log is faster for small logs than for large ones. If your system has a lot of activity, you should schedule your IPL more often. In general, you should probably IPL your system at least once a week.

Note that damaged objects will occasionally be created as a result of power outages, system failures, and even some job failures. Such damaged objects occupy storage that must be manually reclaimed. The RCLSTG command is used to identify damaged objects and to reclaim their storage. Any reclaimed storage is not immediately available for reuse. Instead the damaged objects are moved to the special QRCL recovery library. This command can only be issued when the AS/400 is idle, and it can run for a significant amount of time. In general, you need only run it when a significant number of damaged objects are present. The Operational Assistant disk reports indicate the space occupied by damaged objects. Refer to the IBM manual *Basic Backup and Recovery Guide* for additional information on the RCLSTG command.

22.2.2   Security Journals

When the Security Audit Journal is active in your system, the log associated with QAUDJRN will grow continually. When many auditing values are selected, this log will grow rapidly. Because many security administrators belong to the "options=all" school, it is not uncommon to find very large security journals on AS/400 systems. Remember, you are responsible for maintaining the security log; the system will not automatically purge it like it will job logs, at least not while the security log is "open."

One way to better manage these logs is to place them in a library separate from QSYS. Although QAUDJRN itself is present in QSYS, the security log does not have to be in the same library. You should define a separate library just to hold these logs. Then, this library can be separately and easily saved/reset. You should also periodically (at least weekly) issue the CHGJRN command to close the current log and begin a new one. Once a log has been closed in this fashion, it becomes eligible for processing by the Operational Assistant under the category *system journals and system logs*. Of course, you should ensure that logs are backed up so that security problems can be tracked down even after the original log has been purged by OA.

22.2.3 Spool File Storage

Although individual spool files are maintained by OA, OS/400 also maintains a database in library QSPL that tracks spool members. This database contains an entry for every spool file, and although the individual entries are purged, the size of the database can grow to a very large size in an active system. Periodic IPLs can assist in reclaiming unused space in the spool tracking database. Unused entries are purged by the system after seven IPLs.

You can also use the system value QRCLSPLSTG to reclaim unused spool tracking members. Set QRCLSPLSTG to the number of days that empty spool members are retained on the system. Once the value is exceeded, the empty member is automatically purged. Or, manually enter the command RCLSPLSTG which will reclaim the space occupied by empty members from the database upon demand. If you specified a retention value for QRCLSPLSTG of *NOMAX then you must periodically issue the RCLSPLSTG command to release space. Your should not specify *NONE as a QRCLSPLSTG value as this causes new members to be created for every spool file.

22.2.4 User Defined Storage

Thus far we have discussed AS/400 system storage cleanup. Of course, we also have storage owned by user-created objects. For example, we routinely produce spool files from our programs. If these files are not printed or otherwise disposed of, then they can occupy significant amounts of storage.

It is important that when programs are created, the procedures to manage their output are also instituted. As an additional measure the AS/400 provides the DLTOLDSPLF utility to purge user spool files older than a designated age. This utility should be periodically used to purge old spool data.

Another type of user storage that can present problems is that occupied by user message queues. Although user message queues are purged of old messages by OA, the message queue itself maintains the storage of its high water mark. The command CLRMSGQ can be used to release unused message queue space. You should issue it periodically for all of your user message queues.

Lastly, we must remember that databases often contain deleted records, and these deleted records occupy space. The space owned by deleted records is not available for reuse except by the owning database. Use the command RGZPFM to reorganize the physical space occupied by a database and release all deleted records. Again, the use of the RGZPFM command should be written into the operational procedures when each new database is designed.

22.3 Automating Manual Cleanup

Although it sounds like a contradiction in terms, you can automate most of the manual cleanup procedures required for your system. Operational Assistant includes a call to the job QEZUSRCLNP whenever its automatic cleanup is performed. IBM provides a template for this job, which you may edit to contain your own cleanup procedures. It is suggested that you insert calls to your own cleanup programs into QEZUSRCLNP and leave the IBM template relatively "clean" rather than modifying it extensively and frequently.

You should compile your own version of QEZUSRCLNP into your own library which is placed prior to QSYS in the system library list. You should not alter the system supplied copy of QEZUSRCLNP itself, as it is replaced along with the rest of QSYS each time you update your system. Modify the system library list to search your library first by altering the QSYSLIBL system value. Of course, you should also carefully test your own cleanup procedures manually in a controlled environment before adding them to your copy of QEZUSRCLNP. There is little worse than automating a procedure that purges "good" data!

22.4   Perform Periodic Maintenance Activities

The Operational Assistant (ASSIST) menu simplifies some of the common operational tasks. Type GO ASSIST to use the Operational Assistant menu (see Figure 22.1).

```
ASSIST              AS/400 Operational Assistant (TM) Menu
                                            System:    XXXXXXXX
To select one of the following, type its number below and press Enter:
    1. Work with printer output
    2. Work with jobs
    3. Work with messages
    4. Send messages
    5. Change your password
   10. Manage your system, users, and devices
   11. Customize your system, users, and devices
   75. Information and problem handling
   80. Temporary sign-off

Type a menu option below
    11

F1=Help    F3=Exit    F9=Command line    F12=Cancel
------------------------------------------------------------------------
MANAGESYS           Manage Your System, Users, and Devices
                                            System:    XXXXXXXX
To select one of the following, type its number below and press Enter:
    1. Display system status
    2. Run a backup
    3. Work with system operator messages
   10. Work with printer output
   11. Work with jobs
   12. Work with signed-on users
   20. Device status tasks
   60. Customize your system, users, and devices

Type a menu option below
    60

F1=Help    F3=Exit    F9=Command line    F12=Cancel
------------------------------------------------------------------------
SETUP               Customize Your System, Users, and Devices
                                            System:    XXXXXXXX
To select an option, type its number below and press Enter:
    1. Change system options
    2. Cleanup tasks
    3. Power on and off tasks
    4. Disk space tasks
    5. Backup tasks
   11. Change passwords for IBM-supplied users
   20. Communications configuration tasks

Type a menu option below

F1=Help    F3=Exit    F9=Command line    F12=Cancel
```

Figure 22.1 Operational Assistance Menu

The following are some of the menu functions available under the Operational Assistant menu that relate to System Management. Refer to Figure 22.2 for examples of these functions.

- CLEANUP. This menu allows starting, ending, or changing automatic cleanup function. The cleanup function deletes old job logs, history logs, messages, office calendar items, and journal receivers that take up storage space.

- SETUP. This menu allows customization of the automatic cleanup function, scheduling of the system power-on and power-off functions, and enrollment of new users.

- SETUPBCKUP. This menu allows changes of the backup options, lists, and schedules.

- POWER. This menu allows displaying and changing of the power-on and power-off schedule.

- BACKUP. This menu supports backup functions. It provides for setup, run, status display, and tape initialize.

- RESTORE. This menu allows restoring of saved information from tape, or save file (SAVF) on the system.

- RUNBCKUP. This menu allows selection of the type of backup to be run (daily, weekly, or monthly).

22.4.1   Cleanup System

Run the CLEANUP function of the Operational Assistant (via an automatic nightly function). CLEANUP processes the following objects:

- User Message queues

- Workstation message queues

- System operator message queue

- QEZJOBLOG output queue (job log output queue)

```
ASSIST                 AS/400 Operational Assistant (TM) Menu
                                               System:   XXXXXXXX
To select one of the following, type its number below and press Enter:
    1. Work with printer output
    2. Work with jobs
    3. Work with messages
    4. Send messages
    5. Change your password
   10. Manage your system, users, and devices
   11. Customize your system, users, and devices
   75. Information and problem handling
   80. Temporary sign-off

Type a menu option below
     11

F1=Help   F3=Exit   F9=Command line   F12=Cancel
-----------------------------------------------------------------------
MANAGESYS             Manage Your System, Users, and Devices
                                               System:   XXXXXXXX
To select one of the following, type its number below and press Enter:
    1. Display system status
    2. Run a backup
    3. Work with system operator messages
   10. Work with printer output
   11. Work with jobs
   12. Work with signed-on users
   20. Device status tasks
   60. Customize your system, users, and devices
Type a menu option below
     60

F1=Help   F3=Exit   F9=Command line   F12=Cancel
-----------------------------------------------------------------------
SETUP                 Customize Your System, Users, and Devices
                                               System:   XXXXXXXX
To select an option, type its number below and press Enter:
    1. Change system options
    2. Cleanup tasks
    3. Power on and off tasks
    4. Disk space tasks
    5. Backup tasks
   11. Change passwords for IBM-supplied users
   20. Communications configuration tasks
Type a menu option below

F1=Help   F3=Exit   F9=Command line   F12=Cancel
```

Figure 22.2   Operational Assistance Menu

- QEZDEBUG output queue (service and program dump output queue)

- Application Program Driver (APD) Journal

- DSNX Journal

- Job Accounting Journal

- OfficeVision/400 Journal

- Performance Adjustment Journal

- Problem Log Journal

- SNADS Journal

- X.400 Journal

- OfficeVision/400 Objects (calendar entries, reorganized folders, reorganized database files, reorganized mail log)

- History Log

- Problem Log and Files

- Alerts Database

- PTF Save Files

- Reclaim temporary storage used by temporarily decompressed objects.

Manual cleanup is still necessary for

- Messages on all other message queues.

- Printer output on all other output queues.

- Security Journal and all user journals.

- Removal of any old items in the mail log or folders.

- Removal of any objects created by applications or users that are no longer needed.

- Reorganization of applications database files.

Part

F

OS/400 Installation and Maintenance

Part F looks at OS/400 operating system installation and maintenance and is intended primarily for systems managers or other
technical staff. Chapter 23 looks at the installation and change
management process. Chapter 24 covers problem determination,
tracking, and management. Chapter 25 covers the IBM PTF
application process.

Chapter

23

OS/400 Installation and Maintenance

This chapter looks at the system management process including the installation and maintenance of the OS/400 operating system. We start by asking the question *What Comprises System Management?* We then progress into issues such as change management and the maintenance cycle. The next chapter looks at problem tracking plus management. The final chapter of Part F covers the PTF application process.

23.1   What Comprises System Management?

To some extent our first chapter consists of answering this question. Let us start by looking at the components of a system management program. In order to manage our system, we must first understand exactly what we have.

- Accurate Documentation of Your System/Staff Responsibilities

    Change Log of All System Changes
    Problem Log of all Problems
    Support Number
    System Configuration
    Recovery Plan
    Maintenance Calendar

- Planned and Regularly Scheduled Maintenance Activities

- Defined Problem Definition and Resolution Procedures

- Defined Change Management Process

- Service Level Contracts

23.2   Document Your System

In order to manage changes to your system it is important that you have a current and accurate description of its current state. You must document both the hardware configuration and the software configuration. We will discuss the components of each of these broad areas, along with the commands you issue to display and modify them.

23.2.1   Hardware Configuration

The documentation of your hardware configuration takes several forms because it is used for multiple purposes. In the event of a disaster, we need the hardware configuration description to tailor our backup site. For performance management and capacity planning, we must be aware of each key resource (processor, memory, and DASD) in terms of where we are now as well as what changes are possible.

- CPU and I/O - WRKHDWPRD command (option 5 on the DEFINE menu) and take option 1 on the Work with Hardware Products menu. Refer to Figure 23.1 for an example of the initial screen. Refer to Figure 23.2 for sample output from the *Work with Rack Configuration* screen that option 1 takes you to. Note that F17 will generate a printout of the rack configuration. It is a good idea to maintain hardcopy records of your configuration, both for your own use and for the use of IBM maintenance personnel.

- Local Devices - PRTDEVADR for each controller. Refer to Figure 23.3 for an example of this display.

```
                    Work with Hardware Products
Select one of the following:

   1. Work with rack configuration
   2. Copy rack configuration
   3. Replace rack configuration


Selection
===>

F3=Exit F12=Previous
```

Figure 23.1   WRKHDWPRD

```
                    Work with Rack Configuration
                                                System: XXXXXXXX
System ID  . . . . :   9406-000XXXX-XXXXXXXX-XXXXXX
Type options, press Enter. 2=Change   4=Remove
                                   ----------Location----------
                             Rack    EIA    Device  Card
Opt  Description         Type-Model  ID  Location  Slot   Slot
     1.6M SPCN Rack       9406       01
       3 Unit Filler Panel           01     30
       Disk Unit Enclosure 9336-000  01     25
        857MB Disk Unit   9336-020   01     25     1
        857MB Disk Unit   9336-020   01     25     2
        857MB Disk Unit   9336-020   01     25     3
        857MB Disk Unit   9336-020   01     25     4
       1 Unit Filler Panel           01     24
       Reel Tape Unit     9348-001   01     19
       9406 System Unit              01     14
       Main Card Enclosure 9406-E50  01      1
         Multi-function IOP 2615      01      1              1
         EIA 232/V.24 Adapter 6152    01      1             1C
           Port 1
         EIA 232/V.24 Adapter 6152    01      1             1B
           Port 1
       Tape Unit IOP      2621       01      1              2
       Token-Ring Adapter 2626      01      1              3
         Port 1
       Token-Ring Adapter 2626      01      1              4
                                                         More...
F3=Exit       F11=Display serial numbers and resource names  F12=Cancel
F17=Print     F18=Work with cables   F24=More keys
------------------------------------------------------------------------
    Date XX/XX/XX          Rack Configuration List          Page 1
 System ID . . . . . . .:  9406-000XXXX-XXXXXXXX-XXXXXX
                        Type-Model      Serial/      Location
                          or      Resource  Part    (Rack ID, EIA
 Description             Feature     ID   Number   location, card Slot)
 1.6M SPCN Rack           9406                      01
   3 Unit Filler Panel                              01    30
   Disk Unit Enclosure   9336-000   DC10  XX-XXXXXXX 01   25
     857MB Disk Unit     9336-020   DD021 XX-XXXXXXX 01   25   1
     857MB Disk Unit     9336-020   DD022 XX-XXXXXXX 01   25   2
     857MB Disk Unit     9336-020   DD023 XX-XXXXXXX 01   25   3
```

Figure 23.2   Work with Rack Configuration and Listing

```
                              Device Addresses for CTL01
Switch
Setting  --> 0        1         2        3        4        5        6

          DSP01    DSP05
Port 0    * DSP    * DSP
          3197 D2  3477 HC


Port 1


                               DSP02    DSP04
Port 2                         * DSP    * DSP
                               3179 2   3477 HC

          DSP03
Port 3    * DSP
          5291 2

                     PRT01    PRT02    PRT03
Port 4               * PRT    * PRT    * PRT
                     3812 2   5225 4   4224  C1


Port 5


Port 6


Port 7
```

Figure 23.3   PRTDEVADR For CTL01

- Device Descriptions DSPDEVD DEVD(...) OUTPUT(*PRINT).

- Communications Configuration
  Line Descriptions - DSPLIND
  Control Unit Descriptions - DSPCTLD
  Device Descriptions - DSPDEVD
  Mode Descriptions - DSPMODD
  Directory Displays - DSPDIR

- Cabling Identification Diagram
  Workstation Controller Ports
  Cable ID Labels (Both Ends)
  Device Information (Name, Address, Type, Location)

23.2.2   Software Configuration

In many ways the software configuration is as important to
document as the hardware configuration. First, your software often
changes more frequently than the hardware does. Second, software
changes are sadly not as easy to track as hardware changes. Third,
subtle software level interdependencies are a too common occurrence.

- System Program Product and Release Level - Go LICPGM
  command and take Option 10 (Display Installed Licensed
  Programs). Refer to Figure 23.4 for an example.

```
                    Display Installed Licensed Programs

Press Enter to continue.
Licensed                                                   Installed
Program        Description                                 Release
5738BA1        AS/400 BASIC                                 V2R2M0
5738CB1        COBOL/400 - Base Support                     V2R2M0
5738CB1        COBOL/400 - System/36-compatible COBOL       V2R2M0
573BCB1        COBOL/400 - System/38-compatible COBOL       V2R2M0
5738DB1        AS/400 System/38 Utilities                   V2R2M0
5738DS1        AS/400 Business Graphics Utility             V2R2M0
5738PC1        AS/400 PC Support - Base Support             V2R2M0
5738PC1        AS/400 PC Support - SBCS Support             V2R2M0
5738PC1        AS/400 PC Support - DBCS Support             V2R2M0
5738PL1        AS/400 PL/I                                  V2R2M0
5738PT1        AS/400 Performance Tools                     V2R2M0
5738PW1        AS/400 Application Development Tools          V2R2M0
5738QU1        AS/400 Query                                 V2R2M0
5738RG1        RPG/400 - Base Support                       V2R2M0
5738RG1        RPG/400 - System/36-compatible RPG II        V2R2M0
5738SS1        OS/400 - Base Support                        V2R2M0
5738SS1        OS/400 - Extended Base Support               V2R2M0
5738SS1        OS/400 - Online Information                  V2R2M0
5738SS1        OS/400 - Online Education                    V2R2M0
5738SS1        OS/400 - S/36 and S/38 Migration             V2R2M0
5738SS1        OS/400 - System/36 Environment               V2R2M0
5738SS1        OS/400 - System/38 Environment               V2R2M0
5738SS1        OS/400 - Example Tools Library                V2R2M0
5738WP1        AS/400 Office                                V2R2M0
5738DCT        US English Dictionary                        V2R2M0

F3=Exit    F12=Previous
```

Figure 23.4   Display Installed Licensed Programs

- System Program Product PTFs - Use the DSPPTF command
  to display all PTFs currently applied to the system (see
  Figure 23.5 for an example of this display).

```
                        Display PTF Status.
                                                   System:   XXXXXXXX
Product ID   . . . . . . :    5738999
IPL source   . . . . . . :    ##MACH#B
Release . . . . . . . . :     V2R2M0

Type options, press Enter.
  5=Display PTF details    6=Print cover letter    8=Display cover letter

     PTF
Opt  ID        Status                              On Order
     TL93173   Temporary applied                   No
     TL93131   Superseded                          No
     TL93089   Superseded                          No
     MF04724   Permanently applied                 No
     MF04671   Permanently applied                 No
     MF04670   Permanently applied                 No
     MF04663   Permanently applied                 No
                                                              More...
F3=Exit    F11=Display alternate view    F12=Cancel
----------------------------------------------------------------------------
                        Display PTF Status.
                                                   System:   XXXXXXXX
Product ID   . . . . . . :    5738SS1
IPL source   . . . . . . :    ##MACH#B
Release . . . . . . . . :     V2R2M0

Type options, press Enter.
  5=Display PTF details    6=Print cover letter    8=Display cover letter
     PTF
Opt  ID        Status                              On Order
     TC93173   Temporarily applied                 No
     TC93131   Superseded                          No
     TC93089   Superseded                          No
     TA93173   Temporarily applied                 No
     TA93131   Superseded                          No
     TA93089   Superseded                          No
     SF98029   Cover letter only                   No
     SF13642   Temporarily applied                 No
     SF13552   Temporarily applied                 No
                                                              More...
F3=Exit    F11=Display alternate view    F12=Cancel
----------------------------------------------------------------------------
                        Display PTF Status.
                                                   System:   XXXXXXXX
Product ID   . . . . . . :    5738AF1
IPL source   . . . . . . :    ##MACH#B
Release . . . . . . . . :     V2R2M0

Type options, press Enter.
  5=Display PTF details    6=Print cover letter    8=Display cover letter
     PTF
Opt  ID        Status                              On Order
     SF11747   Temporarily applied                 No
     SF11185   Temporarily applied                 No
     SF10909   Permanently applied                 No
                                                              Bottom
F3=Exit    F11=Display alternate view    F12=Cancel
```

Figure 23.5   DSPPTF command

- Other Vendor Application Packages - Package Names, Vendor Names, Contacts, Libraries, Local Support Contact, and Remote Support Contacts. Various packages each have their own configuration information that you will have to identify and manually record.

23.2.3 Problem and Change Logs

Many system changes are initiated in response to problems that occur. It is critical to record all problems along with the changes made to correct them. Usually, two separate logs are kept.

The *Problem Log* is a record of all problems encountered. It is used to document any issues that affect the successful operation of your computer system. Examples of problems range from environmental issues such as air conditioning, water leaks, and power failures through hardware failures and finally to software failures. A problem tracking number should be used and referenced in all related incident records.

A *Change Log* is a record of all system changes. It should contain a change tracking number, the date of the change, and a list of affected software/hardware components at a minimum. You should also record backout procedures for changes to critical applications so that you can fall back to the prior (hopefully better) state should problems arise.

23.2.4 Security Control

Securing your system is important, but it is equally important to ensure that the security related information is available in the event of a disaster. Imagine the problems you would encounter if the only person with your top level passwords was to be in the hospital when they were needed most! For this reason it is suggested that all security control data be backed up in hardcopy form for disasters. Of course, you will want to keep this type of information in a secure location. Some of the information in this category includes:

- Keys to System

- Security Password Control

- Outside Support Policy/Procedures

23.2.5   Support/Help Contacts

Although it sounds obvious, a list of the contacts for software/hardware support as well as general help is often over-looked. The *Support/Help* contact sheet should be easily available to all personnel. It should contain the name and phone number of the following:

- Local Contacts

- On-call Contract Personnel

- IBM Support Contacts

Note that the system will assist you in maintaining a record of contacts. Let us look at the tools provided:

- Contact Information - WRKCNTINF command.   Refer to Figure 23.6.

- Work with Service Contact Information - Option 2 on Work with Support Contact Information screen.   On Work with Local Service Information screen, use option 1 to Display Service Contact Information and option to 2 to Change Service Contact Information (see Figure 23.7).

```
              Work with Support Contact Information
                                                    System:   XXXXXXXX
Select one of the following:

    1. Work with question and answer (Q & A) database
    2. Work with local service information
    3. Work with IBM product information
    4. Work with technical information exchange (TIE)
    5. Work with upgrade order information
    6. Work with service providers




Selection or command
===>

F3=Exit    F4=Prompt    F9=Retrieve    F12=Cancel
```

Figure 23.6   WRKCNTINF Screen

```
                    Work with Local Service Information
    Select one of the following:            System:    XXXXXXXX

       1. Display service contact information
       2. Change service contact information

    Selection
       2
    F3=Exit    F12=Cancel
--------------------------------------------------------------------
                    Change Service Contact Information
                                            System:    XXXXXXXX
    Type changes, press Enter.

       Company . . . . . . . . .     _____
       Contact . . . . . . . . .     _____
       Contact telephone numbers:    _____
         Primary . . . . . . . .     _____
         Alternative . . . . . .     _____
       Mailing address:
         Street address  . . . .     _____

         City/State  . . . . . .     _____
         Country . . . . . . . .     _____
         Zip code  . . . . . . .     _____

                                                  More...
    F3=Exit    F4=Prompt   F5=Refresh   F12=Cancel
--------------------------------------------------------------------
                    Change Service Contact Information
                                            System:    XXXXXXXX
    Type changes, press Enter.

       National language version    2924   F4 for list
       Media for mailing PTFs  . .  1      1=Automatic selection
                                           2=Half inch reel, 1600 bpi
                                           3=Half inch reel, 6250 bpi
                                           4=Half inch cartridge
                                           5=8 MM cartridge
                                           6=Quarter inch cartridge
                                                            Bottom
    F3=Exit    F4=Prompt   F5=Refresh   F12=Cancel
```

Figure 23.7   Service Contact Information

- Work with Product Contact Information - Option 3 on Work with Support Contact Information screen takes you to the Work with Product Contact Information screen. Use option 1 to Display information and option 2 to Change information (see Figure 23.8).

- Work with Technical (TIE) Contact Information - Option 4 of the Work with Support Contact Information screen takes you to the Work with TIE Contact Information screen. Use option 1 to Display and option 2 to Change TIE Contact Information (see Figure 23.9).

```
                     Work with IBM Product Information
                                                     System:  XXXXXXXX
         Select one of the following:

            1. Display product contact information
            2. Change product contact information

         Selection
            2
         F3=Exit    F12=Cancel
         ----------------------------------------------------------------------
                       Change Product Contact Information
                                                     System:  XXXXXXXX
         Keyboard identifier
            description . . . . . . . :    United States/Canada

         Type changes, press Enter.

            Remote source:
               Name  . . . . . . . . .    IBM Corporation, Dept. DFL
               Address . . . . . . . .    4111 Northside Parkway

                                          Atlanta, GA  30327

            Telephone number  . . . .     1-800-543-3912
            3270 printer emulation        Y              Y=Yes, N=No
            Double-byte character set     N              Y=Yes, N=No

         F3=Exit    F5=Refresh    F12=Cancel
         F14=Select keyboard identifier description
```

Figure 23.8   Product Contact Information

- Work with Upgrade Contact Information - Option 5 on Work
  with Support Contact Information screen. On Work with
  Upgrade Contact Information screen, use option 1 to Display
  Upgrade Contact Information and option 2 to Change Upgrade
  Contact Information (see Figure 23.10).

- Work with Service Provider Contact Information - Option 6 on
  Work with Support Contact Information screen. On the Work
  with Service Provider Contact Information screen, use option
  1 to Add Service Provider Contact Information and option 2 to
  Change   Service   Provider   Contact   Information   (see
  Figure 23.11).

- Work with Question and Answer (Q&A) database - Option 1 on
  Work with Support Contact Information screen. On Work
  with Q&A Database screen, use option 5 to Display Q&A Database Information and option 2 to Change Q&A Database
  Information (see Figure 23.12).

```
                            Work with TIE
                                            System:   XXXXXXXX
      Select one of the following:

         1. Display TIE contact information
         2. Change TIE contact information

      Selection
         2
      F3=Exit    F12=Cancel
---------------------------------------------------------------------
                      Change TIE Contact Information
                                          System:   XXXXXXXX
      Type changes, press Enter.

         Remote source:
           Name  . . . . . . . .    IBM Corporation, Dept. C7V
           Address . . . . . . .    1 East Kirkwood Boulevard
                                    Roanoke, Texas  76299-0015

           Telephone number  . . .  1-800-543-3912
         Host connection information:
           Account number  . . . .    _____
           Use connect code  . . .    _           Y=Yes, N=No
         Mail box information:
           Support system account
             number  . . . . . . .    _____
           Support system user ID     _____
                                                            Bottom
      F3=Exit    F5=Refresh    F12=Cancel
```

Figure 23.9   TIE Contact Information

23.2.6   Application Operation Procedures

It is essential that written procedures exist for running all applications. It is obvious that this is needed for jobs run infrequently. However, even daily jobs benefit from documentation in the event of application changes, vacations, staff changes, as well as unusual circumstances such as a rerun or a restart. The content of operations procedures varies from site to site, but some information and questions that you should consider include:

- Responsibilities. Who runs the work? Who releases it to be run?

- Input Controls. When is the input ready? How do we know it is accurate?

- Processing Schedule. When is the job run? What other work must complete first?

```
                     Work with Upgrade Order Information
                                             System:    XXXXXXXX
         Select one of the following:

             1. Display upgrade contact information
             2. Change upgrade contact information

         Selection
             2
         F3=Exit    F12=Cancel
         -----------------------------------------------------------------
                         Change Upgrade Contact Information
                                              System:    XXXXXXXX
         Type changes, press Enter.

         File destination information:
             Node . . . . . . . . . . . ._____
             User ID . . . . . . . . . ._____

         Mailing address:
             Company name . . . . . . ._____
             Contact name . . . . . . ._____
             Street address . . . . . .

             City/State . . . . . . . ._____
             Country  . . . . . . . . ._____
             Zip code . . . . . . . . ._____
             Telephone  . . . . . . . ._____

         Country code . . . . . . . .___        F4 for list

         F3=Exit    F4=Prompt    F5=Refresh    F12=Cancel
```

Figure 23.10   Upgrade Contact Information

- Report Distribution. What output is produced? Who does it go to? When must it be received?

- Record Retention. What records are needed? Who needs these records? Who long must they be kept?

- Unusual Circumstances. Is month-end processing special? Is a rerun different from the initial execution?

An overriding concern in all written application procedures should be the *Control Processes*. This refers to the controls that ensure the work is started when it can be, completed in a timely fashion, any output is accurate and is distributed where needed, and necessary security is maintained. Many of our questions above are related to controlling the work process. You will probably have additional questions applicable to your environment and organization that we have not listed.

```
                         Work with Service Providers
                                                    System:   XXXXXXXX
      Position to  . . . . .          Control point
        Network ID . . . . .

      Type options, press Enter.
        1=Add    2=Change    3=Copy    4=Remove    5=Display

               Control
      Opt      Point        Network ID     Description
       2       *IBMSRV                      IBM Service Support

                                                             Bottom
      F3=Exit    F5=Refresh    F12=Cancel    F22=Change IBM service route
      -----------------------------------------------------------------------
                         Change Service Provider
                                                    System:   XXXXXXXX
      Control point . . . . . . . . . . :    *IBMSRV
        Network ID . . . . . . . . . . :
        Description . . . . . . . . . . :     IBM Service Support

      Type changes, press Enter.

        Service support center telephone numbers:
          Hardware service  . . . . . . ._____
          Software service  . . . . . . ._____

                                                             Bottom
      F3=Exit    F5=Refresh    F12=Cancel
```

Figure 23.11   Service Provider Contact Information

23.2.7   Backup Procedures

Although we discuss *Recoverability* in Chapter 20, let's look briefly at the issue of Backup Procedures. Here we are talking about formal written procedures covering backups. Some issues and questions you should consider in establishing your procedures include:

- Schedule of Procedures
  - Daily, Weekly, Monthly, Other (Quarterly, Year End, Other).
  - What may not be running during the backup?

- Who is Responsible for Performing the Backup?

- Where are Local and Off-site Media?

- How long are backups kept?

- How is Media Documented?

```
                            Work with Q & A Database
                                             System:    XXXXXXXX
          Type options, press Enter.
            2=Change Q & A database information  5=Display Q & A database information

          Option    Database      Library       Index
            2        QSYSQST       QUSRSYS        01

                                                              Bottom
          F3=Exit    F12=Cancel
          ---------------------------------------------------------------------
                            Change Q & A Database Information
                                             System:    XXXXXXXX
          Database  . . . . . . . :    QSYSQST
            Library . . . . . . . :    QUSRSYS
          Description . . . . . . :    IBM-supplied Q and A database

          Type choices, press Enter.

            Remote Q & A database:
              Remote data linked to
                local database . . . .   N         Y=Yes, N=No
            Database use:
              Controlled publication     N         Y=Yes, N=No
            Single-byte Character Set:
              Graphic character set ID  101        1-32767
              Code-page ID . . . . . .   37        1-32767
                                                              Bottom
          F3=Exit    F5=Refresh    F12=Cancel
```

Figure 23.12   Q&A Database Information

23.3   Monitor Hardware Status

Hardware management differs in one key way from software management. Hardware can go bad without being touched. For this reason we must establish procedures to monitor hardware status and identify minor problems before they develop into solid failures. Some procedures/tools that can help you identify developing problems include:

- Review QSYSOPR message queue - Important messages about the system are sent to QSYSOPR. Since QSYSOPR also gets informational messages, it may be possible to miss the important messages. If the QSYSMSG messages queue is present, the system will send these high impact messages to both QSYSOPR and QSYSMSG. See *CL Programmer Guide* for detail.

- Print Error Log (Summary) - Use the Go CMDSRV command to display the Service Command Menu. Refer to Figure 23.13

for an example of the screen. Take option 9 for the
PRTERRLOG Command (PRTERRLOG can be issued from the
command line). A sample of the actual PRTERRLOG output
can be seen in Figure 23.14.

```
                        Print Error Log (PRTERRLOG)

Type choices, press Enter.

Type of log data to list . . . . TYPE          > *ALLSUM
Time period for log output:      PERIOD

  Beginning time . . . . . . . .                *AVAIL
  Beginning date . . . . . . . .                *CURRENT

  Ending time  . . . . . . . . .                *AVAIL
  Ending date  . . . . . . . . .                *CURRENT
                                                              Bottom
F3=Exit  F4=Prompt  F5=Refresh  F12=Cancel  F13=How to use this display
F24=More keys
```

Figure 23.13   Service Command Menu & PRTERRLOG

23.4   Perform Periodic Maintenance Activities

The Operational Assistant (ASSIST) menu simplifies some of the
common operational tasks. Type GO ASSIST to use the Operational Assistant menu. Refer to the *Operational Assistant* section of
Chapter 22 for details on use of this facility. In this section we
briefly look at some of the functions we perform as part of scheduled maintenance.

23.4.1   Backup Your System

To ensure that your system can be restored to its running status in
the event of a disaster, periodic system backups are needed.
Chapter 20 discusses the subject of backups and system recovery in
detail. Here we simply list the various type of backups we should
perform. These are comprised of:

● Application Based Backups

```
Error Log Utility                        Page . . . :
                                 Summary of Processor Entries
    From  . . :   XX/XX/XX  00:00:00       To . . :   XX/XX/XX   23:59:59
                                  No Log Entries Found
                              Summary of Magnetic Media Entries
    From  . . :   XX/XX/XX  00:00:00       To . . :   XX/XX/XX   23:59:59
                                           Serial
    Resource              Type       Model    Number       Address          Count
    TAP01                 7208       002      00-00000      0020-0700FFFF        4
    TAP02                 9348       001      00-00000      0020-1700FFFF        1
                                Partial Report for Resource
                                           Serial
    Resource              Type       Model    Number       Address      Total Count
    TAP01                 7208       002      00-00000      0020-0700FFFF        4
    Reference Code                        Error Type               Count
       3002                              Permanent                    1
       FFF6                              Statistic                    3
                                Partial Report for Resource
                                           Serial
    Resource              Type       Model    Number       Address      Total Count
    TAP02                 9348       001      00-00000      0020-1700FFFF        1
    Reference Code                        Error Type               Count
       FFF6                              Statistic                    1
                        Summary of Local Work Station Entries
    From  . . :   XX/XX/XX  00:00:00       To . . :   XX/XX/XX   23:59:59
                                           Serial
    Resource              Type       Model    Number       Address          Count
    PRT06                 4224       000      00-00000      0070-000006FF       21
    VT100                 6141                00-00000      0230-000000FF        2
                                Partial Report for Resource
                                           Serial
    Resource              Type       Model    Number       Address      Total Count
    PRT06                 4224       000      00-00000      0070-000006FF       21
    Reference Code                        Error Type               Count
       0200                              Temporary                    5
       0203                              Temporary                    2
       0204                              Temporary                   13
       0207                              Temporary                    1
                                Partial Report for Resource
                                           Serial
    Resource              Type       Model    Number       Address      Total Count
    VT100                 6141                00-00000      0230-000000FF        2
                         Summary of Communication Entries
    From  . . :   XX/XX/XX  00:00:00       To . . :   XX/XX/XX   23:59:59
    Resource              Type                        Address          Count
    RBAL01                LINE                        0010-E200FFFF        8
    QH1LINRJE             LINE                        0060-E0FFFFFF        5
    TRNLINE1              LINE                        0030-E000FFFF        1
    TRNLINE1              LINE                        0030-E0FFFFFF       12
    TRNLINE2              LINE                        0040-E000FFFF      107
    TRNLINE2              LINE                        0040-E0FFFFFF       29
                             Summary of Line Entries
    Resource              Type                        Address      Total Count
    RBAL01                LINE                        0010-E200FFFF        8
```

Figure 23.14 PRTERRLOG Listing

- SAVDLO (saves your Document Library Objects)

- Entire System Save (Quarterly or Biannually)
  - SAVSYS
  - SAVLAB *NONSYS
  - SAVDLO (System DLO)

23.5   Implementing Software Controls

The term *Controls* conjures up images of bureaucracies applicable only to large companies for many of us. However, any mission-critical work calls for controls to prevent problems and to manage those problems that occur anyway. In this section we discuss the software controls that are part of effective change control procedures for application and system software.

23.5.1   Application Program Changes

Application program changes are responsible for most problems in any given environment. Controlling and tracking changes are important steps in managing such problems. Some areas to consider along with questions to answer include:

- Establish a regular procedure for controlling changes to your application programs. When are changes done? Who approves changes? What work could be impacted by each change? What do I do to backup the change in case of problems?

- Establish standards for program names, database names, field names for all application. How do we know a new name is unique? Can we tell from the name who owns it?

23.5.2   IBM System Products

Just as we carefully control our applications we must manage our system software. The procedures and control you should establish are similar with a few key differences including:

- Release Currency. Move to current release within 6 months of GA (Necessary for Support on Required Releases)

- Program Temporary Fixes (PTFs).
  Cumulative PTF Packages. Every six weeks a new cumulative PTF Package is released containing the previous cumulative PTF Package plus all new fixes. When a system is installed, the most current cumulative PTF Packages should be used.

For a stable system, the cumulative PTF Packages should be installed quarterly. To ensure fewer problems with defective PTFs, use the cumulative PTF Package that was released prior to the most current cumulative PTF Package. Always install this new cumulative PTF package using the temporary apply option. Allow 4 to 6 hours for the install. The most current cumulative PTF Package can be ordered by ECS by requesting PTF number SF99VRM (VRM, V is Version number, R is Release Number, M is Modification number. Example: SF99220 for Version 2 Release 2 Modification 0). Be sure to save the system after the PTFs are loaded.

HIPER (High Impact PERvasive) PTFs. These are PTFs that fix problems that may greatly impact your system. Weekly or biweekly someone should examine the Preventive Service Planning (PSP) report to determine if there are any HIPER fixes available that may impact your system. The report can be requested through ECS by ordering PTF SF98VRM. (This would be SF98220 for Version 2 Release 2 Modification 0.)

Chapter

24

Problem Management

This chapter looks at problem management in a formal fashion. We look at problem determination and the various steps of problem management from initial identification, through the tracking process, and finishing with problem resolution.

24.1 Problem Definition

Different types of problems each have their own subdivisions, each with its own set of applicable actions. The *Problem Definition* process divides problems into a hierarchy of groups for subsequent tracking and resolution.

Hardware Problem Categories:

- Hardware Down. Need to call for service. The IBM Service number is 1-800-IBM-SERV if you have an IBM maintenance contract. Record any System Reference Code (SRC) available on the system.

- Hardware Up. Review any messages in the QSYSOPR message queue. Display the second-level help text for additional information. Press the HELP key (F1) with the cursor on the message you want the second-level help text for. Some messages allow the ANZPRB command to be issued with the F14 command key. The ANZPRB command can be used to analyze any problem on the system. ECS can also be used to send a message about the problem to the IBM Service organization if you have an IBM maintenance contract.

Software Problem Categories:

- End User Application Software Problem. Use the application help support and application help desk support to resolve the problem. STRCPYSCN command allows the help desk to see all screens and input from the user screens.

- Application Programmer Software Problem. There are several tools on the AS/400 to help in resolving programming problems such as DEBUG, Job Logs, System messages, and the ANZPRB command. It is possible that the problem could be cause by a defect in the IBM software products.

- IBM System Software Problem. Use ANZPRB command and ECS to contact the IBM Support Center (Level II) or the voice support to reach IBM Service Support Level I (1-800-237-5511). Be sure to have all logs that describe the problem.

24.2   Problem Determination

During the problem determination phase our task is to identify the cause of the problem. In order to do this we need to have information about what initiated the failure. Since most software failures can be associated with an input screen, let us start with how we can get the screen associated with a specific problem.

The STRCPYSCN command (Start Copy Screen Image) is used to copy all output and input operations from a source device and display the result on a target device. Refer to Figure 24.1 for sample output. This allows the user to repeat their input to the failing application and to provide data so that the help desk can determine which input (or response) was in error in the case of a user error. The STRCPYSCN command can be issued on the receiving device, which appears to create a security exposure. The STRCPYSCN command is secured to prevent a user from "stealing" input data from a terminal other than their own.

```
STRCPYSCN                    Start Copy Screen

Type choices, press Enter.
Source device  . . . . . . . . .   DSP41       Name, *REQUESTER
Output device  . . . . . . . . .   DSPHLP05    Name, *REQUESTER, *NONE
Job queue  . . . . . . . . . . .   QCTL        Name
  Library  . . . . . . . . . . .     *LIBL     Name, *LIBL, *CURLIB
File to receive output  . . . .    *NONE       Name, *NONE
  Library  . . . . . . . . . . .               Name, *LIBL, *CURLIB
Output member options:
  Member to receive output  . .    *FIRST      Name, *FIRST
  Replace or add records  . . .    *REPLACE    *REPLACE, *ADD
                                                                  Bottom
F3=Exit   F4=List   F5=Refresh   F11=keywords   F12=Previous
F13=how to use this display
```

Figure 24.1   STRCPYSCN - Copy Screen Image

When the STRCPYSCN command is issued on the target device, a message is sent to the source device requesting if the copy screen function should be allowed.   If the reply is **C**, then the STRCPYSCN function will be canceled. A reply of **G** will allow the function to complete (see Figure 24.2).

```
                Display Messages
                                              System: XXXXXXXX
Queue . . . . . :  DSP41           Program . . . . :   *DSPMSG
  Library . . . :    QSYS            Library . . . :
  Severity  . . :  00              Delivery  . . . :   NOTIFY
Type reply, press Enter.
  From  . . . :  HELPJLG     XX/XX.XX    XX:XX:XX
  Cause . . . . . . :  Start copy screen has been requested with output to
    DSP41. Reply C to prevent copy screen or G to allow it. (C G)
  Reply . . .  g
                                                              Bottom
F3=Exit         F10=Display all      F11=Remove a message
F12=Previous    F13=Remove all
```

Figure 24.2   Example Message on Source Device

When the user at the Source device presses enter, the screens appear at the output device. The copy screen function can be ended from either the source or target user. The source user can end the function by either signing off or issuing the ENDCPYSCN command.   For the target user to end the copy screen function, the target user must enter the system request menu, key in the ENDCPYSCR command, and press Enter.

- Help Text of QSYSOPR message (see Figure 24.3).
  In the example shown in ?, there is a data set read problem.
  The modem may be powered off.

```
                          Display Messages
                                              System: XXXXXXXX
Queue . . . . . :   QYSOPR            Program . . . . :  *DSPMSG
   Library . . . :   QSYS                Library . . . :
Severity  . . . : 50                  Delivery . . . :  *BREAK
Type reply, press Enter.
*  Line OPNSDLC01 failed. Probable local hardware problem. (C G R)
     Reply . . .
F3=Exit          F10=Display all      F11=Remove a message
F12=Previous     F13=Remove all       F14=Run problem analysis
   * - Problem analysis allowed for message.
----------------------------------------------------------------------
                    Additional Message Information
Message ID . . . . . . :  CPA5817        Severity . . . . . . : 99
Message type . . . . . :  INQUIRY
Job . . : QSYSARB        User . . : QSYS        Number . . : 001345
Date sent . . . . . . . :  XX/XX/XX     Time sent . . . . . : XX:XX:XX
From program . . . . . :  QSSNDMDS      Instruction . . . . : 0000
Message . . : Line OPNSDLC01 failed. Probable local hardware problem. (C G)
Cause . . . : The system is trying to start a remote session and the local
modem is not responding in time.  The probable cause are:
  -- The sign-on record may not be correct in the binary synchronous
     communications (BSC), remote job entry (RJE) environment.
  -- A remote system problem.
  -- A remote modem problem.
  -- A local modem problem.
  -- A line problem.

Recovery  . . . :   Do the following:
  -- If the system is running RJE operations, verify that the sign-on
     record is correct.
  -- Have the remote system operator verify that the controller and modem
     are operational.
  -- Verify that the local modem is powered on
Then do one of the following:
  -- Type C to cancel recovery and to inform any applications that are
     waiting for an operation that the recovery has been canceled.
  -- Type G to start the automatic communications recovery again as
     defined by the system communications recovery limit (QCMNRCYLMT).
  -- Type R to try the operation one more time.
If the problem continues, press F14 to run problem analysis.
Possible choices for replying to message . . . . . . . . . . . . . . :
   C -- Cancel.
   G -- Start automatic recovery again.
   R -- Try again one more time
Technical description . . . . :   The error log identifier is X'40003123'.
The reason code is X'44001658'.  The reason codes and their meanings
   follow:
   44001658 -- A data set ready (DSR) timeout has occurred.  The DSR signal
     was not received in the required time after a data terminal ready (DTR)
     signal was sent.
   54001490 -- DSR has dropped.

The DSRETO parameter in the port monitor configuration record may not be
correct for leased-local attach call, or the CNTTO parameter in the port
monitor configuration record may not be correct for switched-call.

F3=Exit              F12=Previous         F14=Run problem analysis
```

Figure 24.3 Message in QSYSOPR and Second-level Help

- Problem Analysis Screen. Run ANZPRB or F14 to run problem analysis. Refer to Figure 24.4 for the initial display. These initial checks identify simple but frequent sources of problem failure, such as loose or defective cables. Next, refer to Figure 24.5 and Figure 24.6 for the rest of the process.

- Press F6 to prepare a service request. Perform this step only if you have identified a hardware component as the source of the failure and need outside service.

```
AJCUJOMA                Communications Problem Analysis
You may be directed to check, connect, or disconnect cables or connectors.
Please read these notices before you continue.
DANGER
During an electrical storm, do not connect cables or station protectors
for communication lines, display stations, printers, or telephones.
DANGER
Use one hand, when possible, to connect or disconnect signal cables to
prevent a possible shock from touching two surfaces with different
electrical grounds.
Press Enter continue.
F3=Exit
--------------------------------------------------------------------------
AJCUJ02C                Communications Problem Analysis
The problem could be caused by the external cable or the data communication
equipment (DCE)/modem attached to the following location:
   Line . . . . . . . . . . . . . . .    OPNSDLC01
   Card address . . . . . . . . . . .    0011 E2FF
   Port . . . . . . . . . . . . . . .    1
Do the following:
   - Make sure that the external cable that attaches the DCE/modem to the
     system is the correct cable for the communications interface.
   - Make sure that this cable is tightly connected at both ends.
   - Also make sure that the cable between the DCE/modem and the telephone
     line is tightly connected at both ends.
   - Reset the DCE/modem by powering it off and the powering it on again.
   - Make sure that the DCE/Modem is in operate mode
   - Press Enter to continue.
   F3=Exit
--------------------------------------------------------------------------
AJCUJ02D                Communications Problem Analysis
If you found and corrected a problem with the external cable or the
DCE/modem, do the following:
   - Select option 1 to end problem analysis
   - If you started problem analysis from a message in the operator queue
     (QSYSOPR) and it has an R reply, type R to answer the message and try
     the job again.
   -OR-
   - If the problem still exists, select option 2 to continue problem
     analysis.
Is the problem corrected?
      1. Yes
      2. No
Selection ==> 2
F3=Exit                 F12=Previous
```

Figure 24.4 Problem Analysis Screen

AJCUJOHP   Communications Problem Analysis

System   Local   Remote   Remote System

Configuration values:
    Line OPNSDLC01
    Protocol . . . . SDLC
    Network . . . . Multi-point
                                             Nonswitched
    Modem . . . . Normal
    Station . . . . Control
Press Enter to test the line.
F3=Exit

AJCUJ0M2   Communications Problem Analysis

Before a test can run to check your system's communications cable, you must
install a wrap plug on the end of the external cable that is attached to the
following system location:
    Line . . . . : OPNSDLC01
    Card address . . . . : 0011 E2FF
    Port . . . . : 1
Without powering off any units, do the following:
    1. Use the system planning charts or manually trace the cable
       to find the opposite end of the cable from the system.
    2. Disconnect the end of the cable that is farthest form the system.
    3. Connect the wrap plug to the end of the cable.
    4. Press Enter to start the test.
F3=Exit

AJCUJ0M4   Communications Problem Analysis
The communication cable test is complete.
Do the following:
    1. Disconnect the communications cable from the wrap plug.
    2. Connect the cable into the socket where it was before you ran the test.
    3. Press Enter to continue.
F3=Exit

AJCUJ094   Communications Problem Analysis

Line . . . . : OPNSDLC01
Card address . . . . : 0011 E2FF
Port . . . . : 1
System   Local   Remote   Remote System

****************=====
The devices underlined with asterisks (***) were tested with no problems.
The devices underlined with equal signs (+++) are possible causes of the
problem, but could not be tested.
Press Enter to continue:
F3=Exit

Figure 24.5 Problem Analysis Part 2

```
AJCUJ096                  Communications Problem Analysis
The system may not be able to test all devices.  If the failure that is
occurring could be caused by an untested device, the system will display
that device as a possible cause of the problem.  This problem can also be
caused by errors in the communications attachment software.
if you can do problem analysis on such an untested device, do the following:
  - If you determine that the device is not failing:
    - Remove the device from the list of possible causes.  Do not report the
      device when you call for service.
  - If you determine that the device is failing:
    - Call for service on the device.
  - Press Enter to continue.
F3=Exit                        F12=Previous
--------------------------------------------------------------------------
                         Problem Analysis Complete
Problem analysis has completed with the possible cause shown below.
Type options, press Enter.  To prepare a service request, press F6.
   5=Display detail
            Possibility
  Option      ( % )    Possible Cause of Problem
    5           96      Local attached data communications equipment/modem
                3       Operating system program
                                                                    Bottom

  F3=Exit      F6=Prepare service request
--------------------------------------------------------------------------
                        Display Detail - Hardware Part
  Possible cause  . . . :  Local attached data communications equipment/modem
  Possibility . . . . . :  96   %
  Error log ID  . . . . :  40003123
  Part number . . . . . :  FI00704
    Location  . . . . . :
  Attached to:
  Device  . . . . . . . :
    Type-Model  . . . . :  6152-001
    Serial  . . . . . . :  XX-XXXXXXX
    Port  . . . . . . . :  1
    Resource  . . . . . :  LIN041
    Location  . . . . . :  XXXX XXXXXXXXXXXXX XXXXXXXXX XXXXXXXX
  Rack serial . . . . . :  XX-XXXXXXX
  Card address  . . . . :
  Reference . . . . . . :
  Press Enter to continue.
  F3=Exit           F12=Previous
```

Figure 24.6   Problem Analysis Part 3

24.3   Problem Management Phases

Once problems have been separated into groups, we follow procedures specific to each type of problem that lead to a resolution. In
this section we look at one set of problem management procedures
for purposes of illustration. The actual procedures you use may
vary from those we look at as examples. However, in all cases we
will *document the problem* because documentation is key to
avoiding problems in the future and reducing the time to resolution
when problems do recur.

24.3.1   Document Problem

The first step in problem management is to document each problem. A formal hardcopy log is encouraged. You should use a standard form to document and track problems. This form may be online or a paper document. Refer to Figure 24.7 for one sample of a problem log.

Date	Time	Reported by	Description of Problem	HW/ SW/	Date Rep.	Date Fixed	Current Status	Resolution

Figure 24.7   Problem Log

24.3.2   Prepare Service Request

The next step is to prepare a request for service. Refer to Figure 24.8 for a sample of the various screens involved in generating a service request. You provide information of a static nature about your company and the system plus basic information about the problem encountered. You finish by specifying whether or not the problem should be automatically turned over to your service provider.

24.3.3   Monitor Service Provider

Once you have turned a problem over to your service provider, you need to monitor progress in correcting the problem. Some of the steps in this include:

- Determine and communicate timeframe for correction

- Initiate escalation as required

- Notify users as required

```
                    Prepare Service Request
Type changes to information as needed, press Enter.
  Company name . . . . . . . . XXXXXXXXXXXXXX
  Contact name . . . . . . . . XXXXXXXXXXXXXX
  Mailing address:
    Street address . . . . . . XXXXXXXXXXXXXX

    City/State . . . . . . . . XXXXXXXXXXXXXX
    Country  . . . . . . . . . XXX
    Zip code . . . . . . . . . XXXXX
  Telephone numbers:
    Primary  . . . . . . . . . XXX XXX-XXXX
    Alternative  . . . . . . . XXX XXX-XXXX

  F3=Exit F5=Refresh F12=Previous F14=Select different language
-------------------------------------------------------------------------------
                    Select Effect on the System
Problem description . . : Line failed. Probable local hardware problem.

Select one of the following:
    1. High - Problem requires immediate solution
    2. Medium - System operates with restricted function
    3. Low - System operates with limited function
    4. None - System operates with full function
Selection

F3=Exit F12=Previous
-------------------------------------------------------------------------------
                    Select Reporting Option
Select one of the following:
    1. Send service request now
    2. Do not send service request
    3. Report service request by voice
Selection

  F3=Exit    F12=Previous
```

Figure 24.8   Prepare Service Request

24.3.4   Problem Solved

Even when the problem has been solved, your system management tasks are not complete. Suggestions for post-solution steps include:

- Document Solution

    - Work Problem Log (System)
    - Update Problem Log (Hardcopy)

- Initiate Recovery Procedures as Required

- Notify Users as Required

Chapter

25

PTF Application Process

In this chapter we look at the PTF application process. We use many of the actual menu screens that you will encounter when applying IBM maintenance. We also discuss the available options for PTF application as well as recommendations for various types of maintenance. Two forms of PTF are provided by IBM. These are individual PTFs and PTF packages. Let us look at the characteristics of each type of PTF as well as the IBM provided menus/screens to display PTF information and to manage the application process.

25.1 Individual PTF

An *Individual PTF* is a fix for one or more problems. It may also be an enhancement to the functionality of specific program modules. Always check the cover letter for Prerequisite PTFs and Corequisite PTFs. Use ECS to download individual PTFs. If a PTF is too large to be downloaded through ECS, the system will mark that PTF to be sent by overnight express mail if the Delivery Method parameter is (*ANY); otherwise the request will fail and will need to be reprocessed.

For each individual PTF, IBM provides information as to the purpose and type. No matter which type of PTF you process, you should review the available information on it. Refer to Figure 25.1 for the basic displays of individual PTF information.

```
                        Display PTF Status.
                                                   System:  XXXXXXXXXX
     Product ID  . . . . . . :    5738SS1
     IPL source  . . . . . . :    ##MACH#B
     Release . . . . . . . . :    V2R2M0

     Type options, press Enter.
       5=Display PTF details    6=Print cover letter    8=Display cover letter
           PTF
     Opt   ID      Status                            On Order
           SF13392  On order only                    Yes
      5    SF13322  Temporarily applied              No
           SF13299  Superseded                       No

     More...
       F3=Exit   F11=Display alternate view   F12=Cancel
-----------------------------------------------------------------------------
                        Display PTF Details

     Product ID/PTF ID . . . . . . . . . :    5738SS1  SF13322
     Release . . . . . . . . . . . . . . :    V2R2M0

     Select one of the following:

          1. General information

          3. Prerequisite Licensed Internal code fixes
          4. Superseded PTFs

          6. PTF Objects
          7. Symptom strings

          9. APARs fixed

          20. All of the above

     Selection
        20

     F3=Exit   F12=Cancel
-----------------------------------------------------------------------------
                        General information

     Product ID/PTF ID . . . . . . . . . :    5738SS1  SF13322
     Release . . . . . . . . . . . . . . :    V2R2M0

     On order . . . . . . . . . . . . . . :    No
     PTF save file . . . . . . . . . . . :    Yes
     PTF status . . . . . . . . . . . . . :    Temporarily applied
     Status date/time . . . . . . . . . . :    08/01/93   11:27:29
     Type . . . . . . . . . . . . . . . . :    Delayed
     Unattended IPL action . . . . . . . :    None
     Language . . . . . . . . . . . . . . :    None
     Optional part . . . . . . . . . . . :    *BASE
     PTF library . . . . . . . . . . . . :    QSYS
     Cover letter . . . . . . . . . . . . :    Yes
     Mandatory instructions . . . . . . . :    No
     Test Fix . . . . . . . . . . . . . . :    No
                                                              Bottom
     Press Enter to continue
     F3=Exit   F12=Cancel
```

Figure 25.1   Individual PTF Part 1

Figure 25.2 displays prerequisite internal license code PTFS, PTFs superseded by the current PTF, as well as lists any objects affected by the PTF.

```
                    Required Lic Int Code Fixes

Product ID/PTF ID . . . . . . . . . :   5738SS1  SF13322
Release . . . . . . . . . . . . . . :   V2R2M0

            Product                          Product
PTF ID      ID                    PTF ID     ID
MF04104     5738999

                                                        Bottom
Press Enter to continue
F3=Exit    F12=Cancel
------------------------------------------------------------------
                    Display Superseded PTFs

Product ID/PTF ID . . . . . . . . . :   5738SS1  SF13322
Release . . . . . . . . . . . . . . :   V2R2M0

PTF ID                              PTF ID
SF12624                             SF12198
SF13299                             SF12138
SF12589                             SF12136
SF12585                             SF12074
SF12539                             SF12047
SF12549                             SF11985
SF12492                             SF11943
SF12426                             SF11933
SF12379                             SF11913
SF12374                             SF11901
SF12373                             SF11903
SF12315                             SF11897
                                                        More...
Press Enter to continue
F3=Exit    F12=Cancel
------------------------------------------------------------------
                    Display PTF Objects

Product ID/PTF ID . . . . . . . . . :   5738SS1  SF13322
Release . . . . . . . . . . . . . . :   V2R2M0

Object      Type                    Object     Type
QQQVSEL     *PGM
QQQQUERY    *PGM
QQQVALID    *PGM
QQQVAP      *PGM
QQQVFMT     *PGM
QQQVJOIN    *PGM
QQQOPTIM    *PGM

                                                        Bottom
Press Enter to continue
F3=Exit    F12=Cancel
```

Figure 25.2 Individual PTF Part 2

Figure 25.3 displays the symptom strings for problems associated with the PTF as well as the APAR numbers of those problems that are corrected by the PTF.

```
                              Symptom strings

Product ID/PTF ID  . . . . . . . . . :    5738SS1   SF13322
Release  . . . . . . . . . . . . . . :    V2R2M0

Symptom string
OSP MSGMCH1820 WHEN A SUM OF A PRODUCT IS USED IN SQL QUERY
OSP F/QQQOPTIM MSGCPD4365 SQL PROGRAM   QUERY RESOURCE LIMIT
SQL RUN MSGCPD4365 RC4 F/QQQQUERY T/QSQOPEN VIEW WITH SUBSEL
SQL CMPL CURR MSGSQL100 VIEW CORRUPTED AFTER RECOMPILE
OSP INCORROUT TWO SETS OF OVRDBF/OPNQRYF TO SAME FILE, DIFF
QRY QRYRUN MSGMCH1219 QUERY CAN NOT BE RUN OR SAVED
OSP OPNQRYF QUERY OPTIMIZER PERFORMANCE DEGRADATION
SQL RUN MSGMCH3601 T/QQQGET X' 02CE'   USING A SUBSTRING WITHI
SQL PERFM OPTIMIZER IS NOT USING INDEX PROPERLY
OSP RSTLIB INCORROUT UNPRED CCSID OF SQL VIEW COLUMNS
OSP EMBEDDED SQL PERFORMANCE
QRY QRYRUN INCORROUT WRKQRY, OPT 2 CHANGE, F3 SAVE & RUN QUE

                                                           More...

Press Enter to continue

F3=Exit   F12=Cancel
----------------------------------------------------------------------
                         Display APARs fixed

Product ID/PTF ID  . . . . . . . . . :    5738SS1   SF13322
Release  . . . . . . . . . . . . . . :    V2R2M0

APAR Fixed                            APAR Fixed
  SA27873                               SA27217
  SA28677                               SA26405
  SA27742                               SA27303
  SA27294                               SA27197
  SA27286                               SA26928
  SA27262                               SA27016
  SA26619                               SA25715
  SA26105                               SA26749
  SA26062                               SA26800
  SA28733                               SA26862
  SA27143                               SA26835
  SA26513                               SA26554

                                                           More...

Press Enter to continue

F3=Exit   F12=Cancel
```

Figure 25.3   Individual PTF Part 3

25.1.1 Cumulative PTF Package

A *Cumulative PTF Package* contains IBM fixes that are packaged about every six weeks. The latest package include all PTFs from the previous period's packages and any individual PTFs that been marked for distribution during the past six weeks. All available PTFs are not on the Cumulative Tape. Check the PTF Summary List for any PTFs that should be loaded on your system. ECS can be used to request the latest Cumulative Package via SF99VRM where V is the version, R is the release, and M is the modification level (an example would be SF99220 for the package related to Version 2 Release 2 Modification 0).

Let us now discuss then look at examples of the types of PTF support materials we have available to order:

- High Impact Pervasive (HIPER) - PTFs that fix problems that may greatly impact your system. Use SF98220 or SF98029 for Version 2 Release 2 Modification 0 to determine if any of the HIPER PTFs are needed on your system (refer to Figure 25.5). This report should be checked every two weeks. SF98027 is a summary of HIPER PTFS as well as PTFs flagged as in error by date/release (see Figure 25.4).

- Cover Letters - Detailed Information on PTFs. Refer to Figure 25.5 for an example.

- Preventive Service Planning (PSP) Information - Check this information before installing new hardware or software. For a release upgrade, review MF98VRM as well as the Memo to User Guide.

- PTF Summary List (refer to Figure 25.9).

Figures 25.4, 25.5, 25.6, 25.7, 25.8, and 25.9 on the following pages contain examples of the various reports you might receive while working with maintenance. Some of the material in these figures has been edited for improved readability and to fit in the space available.

This section provides a summary of High Impact or Pervasive
(HIPER) problems that have been discovered in the base Version 2
Release 2.0 code since shipment. The PTFs that fix the problems
identified in this section are available as individual PTFs.

Users who regularly order and apply individual PTFs should
periodically review PSP SF98029.

NOTE: HIPERs that were included in the first cumulative PTF
package are not included in this list. All users are
expected to have installed at least one cumulative package
so those PTFs will already be applied to their systems.

	DATE	APAR	PTF/LIC FIX	LIC PGM	CUM PKG
1.	92/08/24	MA05588	MF03866	5738999	C2253220
2.	92/09/02	MA05788	MF03952	5738999	C2253220
		MA05810	MF03952	5738999	C2253220
		MA06041	MF03952	5738999	C2253220
3.	92/09/02	MA06172	MF03955	5738999	C2253220
		MA06173	MF03955	5738999	C2253220
		MA06174	MF03955	5738999	C2253220
4.	92/09/03	MA06169	MF03954	5738999	C2253220
		MA06170	MF03954	5738999	C2253220
		MA06171	MF03954	5738999	C2253220
5.	92/09/03	MA06101	MF03882	5738999	C2253220

P T F S   I N   E R R O R

This section provides a summary of the PTFs that have been
found to cause problems for some users.

Users who regularly order and apply individual PTFs should
periodically review PSP SF98028.

Under certain conditions, we recommend that a PTF applied to your system
be removed or that PTFs be omitted when applying a cumulative package.

	DATE	PE PTF	PE APAR	FIXING PTF	LIC PGM	FIX ON CUM PKG
1.	92/09/14	SF11135	SA24612	SF11393	5738SS1	
2.	92/10/09	MF03966	MA06370	MF04090	5738999	C2330220
3.	92/11/18	SF10799	SA25335	SF11696	5738SS1	
4.	92/11/20	MF03973	MA06537	MF04184	5738999	C3018220
5.	92/12/11	Item Updated, see item 6.				
6.	92/12/16	SF11039	SA24533	SF11205	5738SS1	C2349220
7.	92/12/17	SF11527	SA26349	SF12159	5738SS1	C3089220
8.	93/01/14	SF12154	SA26720	SF12186	5738SS1	C3089220
		SF11984	SA26720	SF12186	5738SS1	C3089220
9.	93/03/01	MF04419	MA07021	MF04437	5738999	C3089220
10.	93/03/16	SF12330	SA27715	SF12578	5738SS1	
		SF12473	SA27715	SF12578	5738SS1	
11.	93/03/24	MF04464	MA07150	MF04500	5738999	C3131220
		MF04491	MA07150	MF04500	5738999	C3131220
12.	93/03/26	SF12601	SA27832	SF12753	5738PC1	
13.	93/05/25	SF12515	SA27686	SF13177	5738PC1	
		SF12753	SA27686	SF13177	5738PC1	
14.	93/05/25	MF04579	MA07391	MF04663	5738999	C3173220
15.	93/05/25	MF04618	MA07435	MF04657	5738999	C3173220
16.	93/05/27	SF13146	SA28914	SF13392	5738SS1	C3173220
17.	93/06/04	MF04513	MA07360	MF04623	5738999	C3173220
18.	93/06/30	Item updated, see item 19.				
19.	93/07/01	SF13433	SA29286	SF13568	5738PC1	C3222220
		SF13419	SA29286	SF13568	5738PC1	C3222220
20.	93/07/01	SF13348	SA29325	SF13572	5738PC1	C3222220
		SF13422	SA29325	SF13572	5738PC1	C3222220
21.	93/07/21	Item updated, see item 27.				
22.	93/08/03	MF04536	MA07502	MF04695	5738999	C3222220
		MF04612	MA07502	MF04695	5738999	C3222220
		MF04648	MA07502	MF04695	5738999	C3222220

Figure 25.4   SF98027 HIPER and PTF in Error Summary

```
                          SF98029
AS / 400    PREVENTIVE SERVICE PLANNING INFORMATION

S E R V I C E   R E C O M M E N D A T I O N S
This section provides details on High Impact or Pervasive (HIPER) problems
that have been discovered in the base Version 2 Release 2.0 code since
shipment.  The PTFs that fix the problems identified in this section are
available as individual PTFs.

NOTE: HIPERs that were included in the first cumulative PTF package are
not included in this list.  All users are expected to have installed at least
one cumulative package so those PTFs will already be applied to their systems.

- ' PROBLEM'          - This field provides a reference to the APAR
                         that addresses the problem (ie: SA01234),
                         the Licensed Program Number, and a brief
                         description of the problem.

- ' USERS AFFECTED'   - This field describes the users who are
                         exposed to this problem.

- ' RECOMMENDATION'   - This field describes the action you should
                         take to avoid the problem.

NOTE: You should evaluate each entry to determine the impact of the
      problem to your operations.  Depending on your environment and
      the requirements of your users, you may need to follow the
      recommendation immediately or you may be able to incorporate the
      recommendation into future system maintenance.

      1. 92/08/24 PROBLEM: (MA05588) Licensed Program = 5738999
                           Messages MCH1604 and CPF3289 may be issued
                           when performing various operations on a
                           logical file.  In some cases, message MCH3203
                           with function error x' 1716' may also be issued.
                  USERS AFFECTED: All AS/400 users with logical file
                           access paths that were created prior
                           to Version 2 Release 1.0.
                  RECOMMENDATION: Apply LIC fix MF03866.

        PTF
Opt     ID        Status                        On Order
        SF13392   On order only                 Yes
 8      SF13322   Temporarily applied           No
        SF13299   Superseded                    No
        SF13293   Temporarily applied           No
        SF13246   Temporarily applied           No

PTF/FIX #: SF13322 - OPERATING SYSTEM/400
LICENSED PROGRAM: 5738SS1
-----------------------------------------------------------------------
: SYSTEM : MODELS : RELEASE : RECOMPILE : LIBRARY  :  MRI    : APAR    :
:        :        :         :           :          : FEATURE : FIXED   :
:        :        :         :           :          :         :         :
: AS/400 :  *ALL  : V2R2M0  :     N     :  QSYS    :  NONE   : SA27873 :
-----------------------------------------------------------------------

PRE/CO-REQUISITE PTF/FIX LIST
   REQ    LICENSED  PTF/FIX
   TYPE   PROGRAM   NUMBER    LICENSED PROGRAM DESCRIPTION
   ----   --------  -------   ----------------------------

   PRE    5738999   MF04104   OPERATING SYSTEM/400
   CO     5738SS1   SF12704   OPERATING SYSTEM/400
   CO     5738SS1   SF12551   OPERATING SYSTEM/400
   CO     5738SS1   SF12550   OPERATING SYSTEM/400
   CO     5738SS1   SF12532   OPERATING SYSTEM/400
   CO     5738SS1   SF12316   OPERATING SYSTEM/400
   CO     5738SS1   SF11225   OPERATING SYSTEM/400

DESCRIPTION OF PROBLEM FIXED FOR APAR SA27873 :

    The customer runs the query listed below and receives message
MCH1820 - Error detected in selection template type X' 00'.  The
query uses join, grouping, ordering and sum of a product.

        SELECT      db220pf.mnl,
                    db220pf.mstnr,
                    sum(mmgere*mufak1)
        FROM        db220pf, db340pf
        WHERE       mga<>3 AND
                    mga<>4 AND
                    db220pf.mjahr=1993 AND
                    db220pf.monat = 01 AND
                    db220pf.mnl=db340pf.mnl AND
                    db220pf.mstnr=db340pf.mstnr AND
                    db220pf.monat=db340pf.monat AND
                    db220pf.mjahr=db340pf.mjahr AND
                    martnr between 100 and 6999 AND
                    mgrcd1 = ' A'
        GROUP BY    db220pf.mnl, db220pf.mstnr
        HAVING      sum(mmgere*mufak1) >= 10
        ORDER BY    db220pf.mnl, 3 DESC

CORRECTION FOR APAR SA27873 :

    The MCH1820 was due to the customer query performing ordering
on field sum(mmgere*mufak1) is ordered in descending order.
The PTF will correct the MCH1820 problem.

CIRCUMVENTION FOR APAR SA27873 : none.
```

Figure 25.5   SF98029 HIPER and PTF in Error Listing

```
        A S / 4 0 0   P R E V E N T I V E   S E R V I C E   P L A N N I N G
                          I N F O R M A T I O N
                       Copyright IBM Corporation 1993
     - The information in this document was last updated:
                          NOVEMBER 18, 1993
     - The latest cumulative package for Version 2 Release 2.0 is: C3285220
     - Cumulative package C3285220 began shipping in the USA and all other
       non European countries on October 28, 1993.
     - Cumulative package C3285220 is expected to ship in Europe on November 5, 1993.
         NOTE: Due to variations in world wide distribution schedules,
               this package may not be available in some countries
               until several weeks after this date.
     - The next cumulative package in the USA and all other non European
       countries is scheduled for February 01, 1994.
     - The next cumulative package in Europe is expected to be available
       February 08, 1994.
         NOTE: THIS DATE MAY CHANGE WITHOUT NOTICE, CHECK THIS FILE
               BEFORE ORDERING.
     - The following is a summary of the Version 2 Release 2.0 information
       that is available through Electronic Customer Support (ECS).
    ------------------------------------------------------------------------
    : INFORMATION                                             : PTF #    :
    :--------------------------------------------------------------------:
    : Order the latest cumulative PTF package                 : SF99220  :
    :--------------------------------------------------------------------:
    : PSP information for cumulative package:       C3285220   : SF98220  :
    :--------------------------------------------------------------------:
    : PSP information for cumulative package:       C3222220   : SF98023  :
    :--------------------------------------------------------------------:
    : PSP information for cumulative package:       C3173220   : SF98024  :
    :--------------------------------------------------------------------:
    : PSP information for cumulative package:       C3131220   : SF98025  :
    :--------------------------------------------------------------------:
    : PSP information for installing Version 2 Release 2.0     : SF98020  :
    : including AS/400 PRPQ service recommendations            :          :
    :--------------------------------------------------------------------:
    : Version 2 Release 2.0 Installation - "Read This First"   : SF98026  :
    : Version 2 Release 2.0 Installation - "Memo to Users"     :          :
    :--------------------------------------------------------------------:
    : Summary of the Version 2 Release 2.0 High Impact/Pervasive : SF98027  :
    : (HIPER) PTFs and PTFs that are in error (PE)             :          :
    :--------------------------------------------------------------------:
    : PSP information for installing Version 2 Release 2.0     : MF98220  :
    : Licensed Internal Code and hardware devices.            :          :
    :--------------------------------------------------------------------:
    : PTF Cross Reference Summary - V1R3M0 to V2R2M0           : SF97032  :
    :--------------------------------------------------------------------:
    : PTF Cross Reference Summary - V2R1M0 to V2R2M0           : SF97041  :
    :--------------------------------------------------------------------:
    : PTF Cross Reference Summary - V2R1M1 to V2R2M0           : SF97050  :
    :--------------------------------------------------------------------:
    : Complete detailed list of the Version 2 Release 2.0     : SF98029  :
    : High Impact/Pervasive (HIPER) problems                   :          :
    :--------------------------------------------------------------------:
    : PSP information for cumulative package:       C3285220   : SF98220  :
    :--------------------------------------------------------------------:
    : PSP information for cumulative package:       C3222220   : SF98023  :
    :--------------------------------------------------------------------:
    : PSP information for cumulative package:       C3173220   : SF98024  :
    :--------------------------------------------------------------------:
    : PSP information for cumulative package:       C3131220   : SF98025  :
    :--------------------------------------------------------------------:
    : PSP information for installing Version 2 Release 2.0     : SF98020  :
    : including AS/400 PRPQ service recommendations            :          :
    :--------------------------------------------------------------------:
    : Version 2 Release 2.0 Installation - "Read This First"   : SF98026  :
    : Version 2 Release 2.0 Installation - "Memo to Users"     :          :
    :--------------------------------------------------------------------:
    : Summary of the Version 2 Release 2.0 High Impact/Pervasive : SF98027  :
    : (HIPER) PTFs and PTFs that are in error (PE)             :          :
    :--------------------------------------------------------------------:
    : PSP information for installing Version 2 Release 2.0     : MF98220  :
    : Licensed Internal Code and hardware devices.            :          :
    :--------------------------------------------------------------------:
    : PTF Cross Reference Summary - V1R3M0 to V2R2M0           : SF97032  :
    :--------------------------------------------------------------------:
    : PTF Cross Reference Summary - V2R1M0 to V2R2M0           : SF97041  :
    :--------------------------------------------------------------------:
    : PTF Cross Reference Summary - V2R1M1 to V2R2M0           : SF97050  :
    :--------------------------------------------------------------------:
    : Complete detailed list of the Version 2 Release 2.0     : SF98028  :
    : PTFs that are in error (PE)                              :          :
    :--------------------------------------------------------------------:
    : Complete detailed list of the Version 2 Release 2.0     : SF98029  :
    : High Impact/Pervasive (HIPER) problems                   :          :
    :--------------------------------------------------------------------:
    : Summary of the generally available Version 2 Rel 2.0 PTFs : SF97220  :
    ------------------------------------------------------------------------
    DETAILED DESCRIPTIONS:
    ----------------------
    SF99220 - Order this PTF number when you would like to receive the
              latest cumulative PTF package that is available in your
              country.

    SF98220 - These PSPs provide information for a specific cumulative
    SF98021   PTF package level.  The summary table (above) cross references
    SF98022   the PSP number to the cumulative package level.  Order the
    SF98023   PSP number that corresponds to the cumulative package you
    SF98024   are installing or last installed.  The file you receive
    SF98025   contains information on all known PTFs included in this
              package that were found to cause problems for some users
              after this package began shipping.  These PSPs also
              contain information on all known high impact and
              pervasive problems that may affect your operation.

              The PSP for the cumulative package you have installed
              should be ordered periodically and reviewed for the latest
              information on known problems.
```

Figure 25.6   SF98220 PSP V2R2M0 Part 1

SF98020 - This PSP provides information that should be reviewed
before installing Version 2 Release 2.0 or before adding
new program products. Information in this PSP is grouped
by product area such as the operating system, languages,
communications, etc. Problems that may affect you
during installation are documented in this PSP.

SF98010 also contains service recommendations relating to
AS/400 PRPQ's. See the PRPQ Information Section of the
Preventive Service Planning Information for installing
Version 2 Release 2.0.

SF98026 - A file containing the "Memo To Users" and the "Read This
First" documents is available by ordering this PTF number.
A printed copy of these documents is included with every
Version 2 Release 2.0 shipment. This file is available
as a convenience for those users who misplace their
original copy.

SF98027 - This PSP contains a summary of PTFs that have been identified
as high impact or pervasive problems and a summary of PTFs
that have been found to be in error.

MF98220 - This PSP provides information that should be reviewed before
installing new systems or hardware devices. Information in
this PSP is grouped by system device type such 9402, 9404,
and 9406. Problems that may affect the installation or
operation of hardware devices are documented here.

SF98028 - This PSP provides a complete list of Version 2 Release 2.0
PTFs in Error. Users who regularly order and apply
individual PTFs should periodically review this PSP.

SF98029 - This PSP provides a complete list of all the high impact or
pervasive problems that have been discovered for Version 2
Release 2.0. Those users who support several systems at
different cumulative package levels may find this PSP useful.

SF97032 - This PSP provides a listing to assist you when upgrading
from Version 1 Release 3.0 to Version 2 Release 2.0. This
listing allows you to analyze the PTFs/Fixes you currently
have installed on your Version 1 Release 3.0 system and
determine which Version 2 Release 2.0 PTFs/Fixes you need
to order to maintain the same or higher PTF/Fix level
as you upgrade to Version 2 Release 2.0.

SF97041 - This PSP provides a listing to assist you when upgrading
from Version 2 Release 1.0 to Version 2 Release 2.0. This
listing allows you to analyze the PTFs/Fixes you currently
have installed on your Version 2 Release 1.0 system and
determine which Version 2 Release 2.0 PTFs/Fixes you need
to order to maintain the same or higher PTF/Fix level
as you upgrade to Version 2 Release 2.0.

SF97050 - This PSP provides a listing to assist you when upgrading
from Version 2 Release 1.1 to Version 2 Release 2.0. This
listing allows you to analyze the PTFs/Fixes you currently
have installed on your Version 2 Release 1.1 system and
determine which Version 2 Release 2.0 PTFs/Fixes you need
to order to maintain the same or higher PTF/Fix level
as you upgrade to Version 2 Release 2.0.

Figure 25.7   SF98220 PSP V2R2M0 Part 2

```
C H A N G E    S U M M A R Y
---------------------------
Section                        Last Update
-----------------------        -----------
General Information            93/09/24

Service Recommendations        93/11/18
PTFS in Error                  no entries

G E N E R A L    I N F O R M A T I O N
---------------------------------------
     This section contains general information concerning the
     installation of this cumulative PTF package.
```

1. 92/09/11 The Expanded Memory Specification (EMS) support in
             Microsoft Windows 3.X running in 386 Enhanced Mode
             is intended for DOS applications executed at a DOS
             prompt. Use of EMS outside of this environment is
             not supported by Microsoft. Because PC Support/400
             (Base DOS and Extended DOS) does not meet the Microsoft
             Windows 3.X 386 Enhanced Mode EMS requirements, PC
             Support/400 cannot support the use of EMS while running
             Windows 3.X in 386 Enhanced Mode.

             PC Support/400 must be configured without EMS when
             running Microsoft Windows 3.X in 386 Enhanced Mode.
             The EMS Interface Manager (EIMPCS) and Session Manager
             (SM5250) must be configured for conventional memory
             to prevent PC Support/400 from using EMS. EIMPCS will
             use conventional memory if the P=0 parameter is specified
             on the DEVICE statement in the CONFIG.SYS file. For
             example: DEVICE=C:\PCS\EIMPCS.SYS P=0

             Session Manager will use conventional memory if the /X
             parameter is specified on the command line. For example:
             SM5250 /X

             If Session Manager is run automatically from the STARTPCS
             batch file, the PC Support/400 Configurator (CFGPCS)
             should be used to modify the Session Manager profile
             using the following steps:
             1) Run the CFGPCS command
             2) Choose the "Work station function" option
             3) Choose the "Work with session windows" option
             4) Choose the "Change session options" option
             5) Set the "Always use expanded memory if available"
                option to "No".
             6) Save the file and exit.

Figure 25.8   SF98220 PSP V2R2M0 Part 3

25.2   Using PTF Commands

- GO PTF Menu

- Requesting ECS download of PTFs. Only request PTFs for one library in the SNDPTFORD command. PTFs can be sent to batch by using the SNDSRVRQS command. The SNDSRVRQS

```
                FIX SUMMARY LISTING  -  PTF # SF97220
1.  PURPOSE OF FIX SUMMARY LISTING:
    THE PURPOSE OF THIS LISTING IS TO PROVIDE YOU A CONVENIENT REFERENCE
    OF THE LICENSED INTERNAL CODE FIXES (FIXES) AND PROGRAM TEMPORARY
    FIXES (PTFS) THAT ARE AVAILABLE BY IBM LICENSED PROGRAM CATEGORY.
    THIS LISTING IS UPDATED REGULARLY.  YOU MAY CHOOSE TO ORDER A
    PTF/FIX THAT WOULD EFFECT ONE OF YOUR IBM LICENSED PROGRAMS.
2.  PRODUCT NAME. PTFS ARE LISTED BY IBM LICENSED PROGRAM ID SEQUENCE (PER
    SYSTEMS OPERATOR'S GUIDE SC41-8082 - CHAPTER 6 USING CUSTOMER SUPPORT).
3.  PTF/FIX# EACH AS/400 SYSTEM PROGRAMMING FIX IS RELEASED WITH A UNIQUE
    NUMBER.  PTF (PROGRAM TEMPORARY FIX) REFERS TO FIXES ASSOCIATED
    WITH SOFTWARE AND FIX (LICENSED INTERNAL CODE FIX) REFERS TO FIXES
    ASSOCIATED WITH LICENSED INTERNAL CODE.  WE NORMALLY REFER TO PTF
    AS A GENERAL TERM TO INCLUDE BOTH PTFS AND LICENSED INTERNAL CODE FIXES
4.  PKG #. PTF PACKAGES ARE RELEASED ON A SCHEDULED BASIS FOR THE CUSTOMER
    THAT WANTS TO INSTALL PTFS/FIXES FOR PREVENTIVE PURPOSES (MINIMIZE
    POTENTIAL PROBLEMS).  THE PTF PACKAGE IS AN ACCUMULATION OF MOST
    OF THE PTFS/FIXES SINCE THE BEGINNING OF A RELEASE.
    IF YOU CHOOSE TO ORDER AND INSTALL THIS PACKAGE ON A REGULAR BASIS,
    WE SUGGEST THAT YOU DO IT ON A QUARTERLY BASIS.  YOU CAN ORDER
    IT BY USING THE COMMAND "SNDPTFORD SF99220".
    THE PKG # IS THE YEAR/JULIAN DATE OF THE PTF PACKAGE RELEASE. IN
    THIS LISTING IT IDENTIFIES WHEN A SPECIFIC PTF/FIX WAS INCLUDED IN
    THE PTF PACKAGE.  IF NO PKG # IS LISTED, IT MEANS THAT THE PTF/FIX
    HAS NOT BEEN INCLUDED IN A PTF PACKAGE YET.  IF A PKG # OF 'BASE'
    IS LISTED, IT MEANS THAT THE PTF/FIX IS PERMANENTLY APPLIED TO THE
    V2R2 GA BASE CODE.  IT IS NOT NECESSARY TO ORDER AND APPLY THIS
    PTF AFTER INSTALLING V2R2.  THIS PTF WILL CONTINUE TO BE ORDERABLE
    TO SUPPORT PRE-GA V2R2 CUSTOMERS PRIOR TO THEIR INSTALLATION OF
    THE V2R2 GA BASE CODE.
5.  THE "AVAIL. DATE" IS THE DATE WHEN THE SPECIFIC PTF/FIX WAS RELEASED
    AS AN ORDERABLE PTF/FIX.  THESE SINGLE PTFS/FIXES CAN BE ORDERED
6.  THE "ABSTRACT" IS A BRIEF DESCRIPTION OF THE PTF/FIX THAT SHOULD
    ASSIST IN DETERMINING WHAT PROBLEM IT CORRECTS.
7.  THE "REPLACED BY" REFERS TO A PTF/FIX THAT HAS SUPERSEDED OR REPLACED
    THE LISTED PTF/FIX.  IN THIS CASE YOU MAY WANT TO ORDER THE NEWER FIX.
************** PRODUCT NAME: 5738999 - LICENSED INTERNAL CODE *************
|PTF/    |        | AVAIL. |                                    |REPLACED
|PKG# |  DATE  |ABSTRACT                         |  BY
 MF03818   NONE  03/08/93 RWS-INCORROUT 3174 NETWORK NODE         MF04505
                          DOWNSTREAM FROM AS/400
 MF03823   BASE  08/25/92 INCORROUT-DISK-D/T9336-HLIC-9406DISK     MF06227
                          INCORROUT-DISK-D/T9336-HLIC-9406DISK
                          INCORROUT-DISK-D/T9336-HLIC-9406DISK
 MF03828   2253  09/03/92 INCORROUT-HLIC-940XCOM BUS TIMEOUT ON    MF04439
                          2619 DUMP
 MF03829   2261  09/16/92 INCORROUT-HLIC-940XCOM SUPPORT FOR NEW
                          2605 ADAPTER SRC26050403
 MF03830   2253  09/03/92 OSP-CRTLF-MSGCMCH3203-F/#DBCCR-T/QDBCRTME  MF06330
                          VL02000307 IXPTN40
 MF03833   3018  12/17/92 TCPIPRTL-INCORROUT-RWS-D/T3270DBCS SO/SI  MF04116
                          CHANGED TO NULLS
 MF03834   2253  09/03/92 OSP-SAVLIB-WAIT-SAVE WHILE ACTIVE JOB     MF06343
 MF04257   3047  01/07/93 DDM-PERFM SEVERE PERFORMANCE DEGRADATION
                          RECEIVING RECORDS
 MF04258   3173  04/05/93 NEW FUNCTION                             MF06016
 MF04259   3047  02/17/93 NEW FUNCTION
 MF04260   3285  08/09/93 NEW FUNCTION                             MF06307
 MF04261   3285  07/15/93 NEW FUNCTION
************** PRODUCT NAME: 5738SS1 - OPERATING SYSTEM/400 *************
|PTF/ |        | AVAIL. |                                    |REPLACED
|FIX # |  |PKG# |  DATE  |ABSTRACT                         |  BY
 SF10700   2253  09/03/92 3270EM-LOOP INTERMITTENT LOOP AFTER      SF14220
 SF12173   NONE  03/15/93 IPDS-INCORROUT-PRT-D/T3835 PRINTING A    SF14196
                          SPOOL FILE WITH MULTIU
 SF12180   NONE  04/05/93 NEW FUNCTION                             SF13006
 SF12182   NONE  04/05/93 NEW FUNCTION                             SF14344
 SF12183   NONE  04/05/93 NEW FUNCTION                             SF14480
 SF12185   3089  01/18/93 OSP-BACKUP-MSGCPF6772-F/QTAERR-T/QEZINIT SF12507
                          USING OPTION 21 IN
 SF12186   3089  02/04/93 OSP-DSPDOC-MSGCPF5192 RC1005011B         SF14344
                          F/QWSGET WHEN BREAK MSG PGM
```

Figure 25.9 SF97220 PTF Summary List V2R2M0 Part 1

command will send all problem log entries that are in either
*PREPARE or *OPEN status. Use the *PREPARE option on
the SNDSRVRQS command. Be sure to order all prerequi-

```
PTF                     Program Temporary Fix (PTF)
                                                     System:  XXXXXXXX
Select one of the following:

     1. Load a program temporary fix
     2. Apply a program temporary fix
     3. Copy a program temporary fix
     4. Remove a program temporary fix
     5. Display a program temporary fix
  6. Order a program temporary fix
     7. Install a program temporary fix from a list
     8. Install program temporary fix package

    70. Related commands


Selection or command
===>

F3=Exit   F4=Prompt   F9=Retrieve   F12=Cancel   F13=User support
F16=AS/400 Main menu
```

Figure 25.10 PTF Menu

sites. When requesting PTFs in batch, the ORDER parameter should be *PTFID. If any of the prerequisites are allay loaded on the system and the ORDER parameter is (*REQUIRED), the batch request will fail. When requesting the PTF with an interactive job, the ORDER parameter should be (*REQUIRED) to get any prerequisite PTFs.

```
                    Send Service Request (SNDSRVRQS)
Type choices, press Enter.

Action . . . . . . . . . . . .  *PREPARED     *PREPARED, *OPENED, *TEST
Remote control point . . . . .  *IBMSRV       Name, *IBMSRV, *SELECT
Remote network identifier  . .  *NETATR       Name, *NETATR




                                                             Bottom
F3=Exit   F4=Prompt   F5=Refresh   F12=Cancel   F13=How to use this display
F24=More keys
```

Figure 25.12 SNDSRVRQS - Batch Request FOR SNDPTFORD

● PTF Installation - All new PTFs should be applied as temporary. PTFs are a complete program replacement. The PTF application process will keep a copy of the old program, if the PTF is applied as temporary. This will allow the old program

```
                    Send PTF Order (SNDPTFORD)
Type choices, press Enter.

PTF description:
  PTF identifier . . . . . . . . > SF98220       Character value
  Product  . . . . . . . . . . .   *ONLYPRD      F4 for list
  Release  . . . . . . . . . . .   *ONLYRLS      *ONLYRLS, VxRxMx
                 + for more values
PTF parts  . . . . . . . . . . .   *ALL          *ALL, *CVRLTR
Remote control point . . . . . .   *IBMSRV       Name, *IBMSRV, *SELECT
Remote network identifier  . . .   *NETATR       Name, *NETATR

                  Additional Parameters

Delivery method  . . . . . . . .   *LINKONLY     *ANY, *LINKONLY
Order  . . . . . . . . . . . . .   *REQUIRED     *REQUIRED, *PTFID
Reorder  . . . . . . . . . . . .   *NO           *NO, *YES

                                                            Bottom
F3=Exit   F4=Prompt   F5=Refresh   F12=Cancel   F13=How to use this display
F24=More keys
-------------------------------------------------------------------------
                  Verify Contact Information
                                          System:  XXXXXXXX
Type changes, press Enter.

   Company . . . . . . . . .   XXXXXXXXXXXXXXXXXXXXXXXXXXXXXXXXXXXX
   Contact . . . . . . . . .   XXXXXXXXXXXXXXXXXXX
   Mailing address:
     Street address  . . . . .   XXXXXXXXXXXXXXXXXXXXXXXXXXXXX

     City/State  . . . . . . .   XXXXXXXXXXXXXXXXXXXXXX
     Country . . . . . . . . .   XXXXXX
     Zip code  . . . . . . . .   XXXXX
   Telephone numbers:
     Primary . . . . . . . . .   XXX-XXX-XXXX
     Alternative . . . . . . .   XXX-XXX-XXXX
   National language version   2924   F4 for list

                                                            Bottom
F3=Exit   F4=Prompt   F5=Refresh   F12=Cancel
-------------------------------------------------------------------------
                  Select Reporting Option
                                          System:  XXXXXXXX
Problem ID . . . . . . :  9332532220
Current status . . . . :  READY
Problem  . . . . . . . :  Preventive service planning information requested.

Select one of the following:

   1. Send service request now
   2. Do not send service request
   3. Report service request by voice

Selection  2
```

Figure 25.11 SF98220 Request

to be copied back into production should the PTF have to be removed from the system. When a PTF is applied permanently, the old program version is deleted from the system. Most of QSYS's PTFs must be applied in delayed mode (QSYS cannot be running when the PTF is applied). Licensed

Internal Code PTFs must be applied when the system has been IPLed on the A side. There are two copies of the Licensed Internal Code, side A and side B. Side A contains only permanently applied PTFs. Side B contains both temporary and permanently applied PTFs. To simplify the install process, option 8 on the GO PTF menu will automatically install all of the PTFs on the cumulative tape with an automatic IPL if necessary. Of course, it is always a good idea to take a separate full system backup before applying large amounts of maintenance.

```
                 Install Options for Program Temporary Fixes
                                                  System: XXXXXXXX
Type choices, press Enter.

  Device . . . . . . . . . .          Name, *SERVICE

  Automatic IPL  . . . . . .  Y       Y=Yes
                                      N=No

  PTF type . . . . . . . . .  1       1=All PTFs
                                      2=HIPER PTFs and HIPER LIC fixes
                                        only
                                      3=HIPER LIC fixes only




  F3=Exit    F12=Cancel
```

Figure 25.13 Install Cumulative Tape Screen

● Manual Install of PTFs - Requires a load and apply for each library that contains PTFs on the tape or diskette. Any new PTFs should be temporarily applied and tested. All PTFs that are in production should be installed permanently. The figures on the next two pages cover manual PTF processes.

The DSPPTF command is used to create a manual display of information available for PTFs. Refer to Figure 25.14 for the parameter screen for this command.

The LODPTF command is used to load a PTF. Refer to Figure 25.15 for the parameter screen for this command.

```
                 Display Program Temporary Fix (DSPPTF)

Type choices, press Enter.

Product . . . . . . . . . . . .  *ALL        F4 for list
PTF numbers to select . . . . .  *ALL        Character value, *ALL...
Release . . . . . . . . . . . .  *ALL        *ALL, VxRxMx
Cover letter only . . . . . . .  *NO         *NO, *YES
Output . . . . . . . . . . . .   *           *, *PRINT, *OUTFILE




                                                             Bottom
F3=Exit   F4=Prompt   F5=Refresh   F12=Cancel  F13=How to use this display
F24=More keys
```

Figure 25.14   DSPPTF Command

```
                 Load Program Temporary Fix (LODPTF)

Type choices, press Enter.

Product . . . . . . . . . . . .  5738SS1     F4 for list
Device . . . . . . . . . . . .   *SERVICE    Name, *SERVICE, *SAVF
PTF numbers to select . . . . .  *ALL        Character value, *ALL
              + for more values
PTF numbers to omit . . . . . .              Character value
              + for more values
Superseded PTFs . . . . . . . .  *APYPERM    *APYPERM, *NOAPY
Release . . . . . . . . . . . .  *ONLY       *ONLY, VxRxMx



                                                             Bottom
F3=Exit   F4=Prompt   F5=Refresh   F12=Cancel  F13=How to use this display
F24=More keys
```

Figure 25.15   LODPTF Command

The APYPTF command is used to apply a PTF. Refer to Figure 25.16 for the parameter screen for this command.

The RMVPTF command is used to remove a PTF. Refer to Figure 25.17 for the parameter screen for this command.

```
                     Apply Program Temporary Fix (APYPTF)

Type choices, press Enter.

Product  . . . . . . . . . . . . > 5739SS1        F4 for list
Release  . . . . . . . . . . . .   *ONLY          *ONLY, VxRxMx
PTF numbers to select  . . . . .   *ALL           Character value, *ALL
              + for more values
PTF numbers to omit  . . . . . .                  Character value
              + for more values
Extent of change . . . . . . . .   *TEMP          *TEMP, *PERM
Delayed PTFs . . . . . . . . . .   *YES           *NO, *YES


                                                               Bottom
F3=Exit    F4=Prompt    F5=Refresh    F12=Cancel    F13=How to use this display
F24=More keys
```

Figure 25.16   APYPTF Command


```
                     Remove Program Temporary Fix (RMVPTF)

Type choices, press Enter.

Product  . . . . . . . . . . . .                  F4 for list
Release  . . . . . . . . . . . .   *ONLY          *ONLY, VxRxMx
PTF numbers to select  . . . . .   *ALL           Character value, *ALL
              + for more values
PTF numbers to omit  . . . . . .                  Character value
              + for more values
Extent of change . . . . . . . .   *TEMP          *TEMP, *PERM
Delayed PTFs . . . . . . . . . .   *NO            *NO, *YES



                                                               Bottom
F3=Exit    F4=Prompt    F5=Refresh    F12=Cancel    F13=How to use this display
F24=More keys
```

Figure 25.17   RMVPTF Command

Bibliography

In this bibliography we list IBM manuals and various books that were used as technical sources for this book, or that you may wish to consider for additional information. The manuals and books are listed under the main subject areas used within the book. Where an IBM manual is referenced, the manual title is followed by the IBM order number (in parentheses). The IBM manuals listed here are generally those applicable to OS/400 Version 2 Release 2 systems. Later versions of the operating system may have different manual numbers. Some of the manuals for older OS/400 systems have different order numbers and some have different titles.

All of the IBM manuals for the AS/400 are provided in softcopy form on a single CD ROM in BookManager Read format. The AS/400 CD ROM is an excellent delivery vehicle, and the IBM BookManager Read product offers powerful search and retrieval capabilities. The search engine was instrumental in finding some of the more obscure items presented in this book. Try the Book-Manager Read product if you have not yet encountered it.

One important source of information for any AS/400 site is the magazine *News 3X/400* which is published monthly (plus quarterly product specials) by Duke Communications International. For subscription information, call (800) 621-1544. Duke Communication also publishes a number of books on the AS/400. Although somewhat pricey, these books have information that is difficult or impossible to get from other sources.

AS/400

Architecture and Applications by Jill T. Lawrence (ISBN 0-89435-434-5).

A Practical Guide to Programming and Operations by Donald Zeilenga and Donna Lenczycki (ISBN 0-89435-433-7).

AS/400: Advanced Backup and Recovery Guide Version 2 (SC41-8079).

AS/400: Control Language Guide by Brian Fu.

AS/400: Concepts and Facilities by Tony Baritz and David Dunne (ISBN 0-07-018301-5).

AS/400: Product Specifications (SA41-9983).

AS/400: Operator's Guide (SC41-8082).

AS/400: System Programmer's Interface Reference (SC41-8223).

IBM AS/400: A Business Perspective by Jim Hoskins (ISBN 0-471-58063-5).

Programming: Control Language Programmer's Guide (SC41-8077).

Programming: Control Language Reference (SC41-0030).

Programming: Performance Tools/400 Guide (SC41-8084).

CICS

CICS: A Practical Guide to System Fine Tuning by S. Piggott (ISBN 0-07-050054-1).

CICS/VSE: CICS-Supplied Transactions (SC33-0710).

Glossary

This glossary defines the technical terms used in this book. The definitions are based on the IBM manual *Vocabulary for Data Processing, Telecommunications, and Office Systems* (GC20-1699), and on additional information from a number of AS/400 specific manuals.

AFP
Advanced Function Printing. AFP is the facility that allows programs to use the all points addressable feature of IBM printers for printing graphic images and to support downloaded fonts.

API
Application Program Interface. An API is used to define a formal interface to a process. The use of an API isolates programs with the details of the implementation of a process. This allows the process to be enhanced or replaced without affecting the programs using its services.

APPC
Advanced Peer-to-Peer Communications. APPC implements the VTAM LU 6.2 protocol. It is commonly used for communications with PCs and LANs, and is becoming more frequently used for mainframe-to-mainframe communications.

APPN
Advanced Peer-to-Peer Networking. APPN is the name of the AS/400 system implementation of SNA LU 6.2 and note type 2.1

architectures. Where APPC refers to the programming API, APPN is the actual architectural implementation of LU 6.2 SNA.

Auxiliary Storage Pool (ASP)
An ASP is a group of DASD units defined from all units available on the system. ASPs are used to isolated data to reduce the amount of data lost when a single drive fails, and also to reserve DASD resources for a given use.

Client/Server
The term client/server describes a system where a process is divided into programs executed on multiple computer systems. Each process is invoked via a formal API. A CICS application employing MRO function shipping is a classic example of client/server processing.

Command Language (CL)
CL is used to write OS/400 commands. It is also used to manage the execution of programs in the AS/400 environment. As such, it functions in a role similar to Job Control Language (JCL) for mainframe operating systems.

Cooperative Processing
Cooperative processing is used to describe a system where a task is split and partially performed by each of several systems. For example, a transaction split between CICS/OS2 and CICS/400 utilizes cooperative processing. Also see *Distributed Processing.*

Distributed Computing Environment (DCE)
DCE is a set of services that facilitate the creation, use, and maintenance of distributed applications. These fall into distributed directory, security, and time services that allow independent applications to work together, as well as a Remote Procedure Call (RPC) mechanism that facilitates splitting the code of an application across processors.

Data Description Specification (DDS)
DDS is used to define data to be processed by a program. The data can be present on the AS/400 in a dataset or created via the DDS or provided by another system via SNUF. One use of DDS is to define screen images via a local display file.

Distributed Data Management (DDM)

DDM is a function of OS/400 that allows database files on one system to be accessed by programs running on another system. DDM support remote access to data on AS/400s as well as other IBM systems that support DRDA.

Distributed Processing

Distributed processing is a general term used to describe any function performed upon multiple systems, even where a single task may be completed upon one processor. For example, several VSE systems with a shared POWER queue are employing distributed processing. Also see *Cooperative Processing* and *Client/Server*.

Distributed Relational Database Access (DRDA)

DRDA is a protocol that supports SQL statement access to data residing on processors other than that of the SQL request issuing program. AS/400 systems support the DRDA concept of a Remote Unit of Work.

Downsizing

The term *downsizing* (and its close relative *rightsizing*) is often used to describe the replacement of a mainframe computer with one or more smaller systems. MVS, VSE, and VM systems have been replaced by AS/400s or PC/LANs in combination with AS/400s. They have also been replaced by RS/6000s and other UNIX systems. This differs from client/server solutions where mainframes are used in conjunction with a variety of other computer systems.

Dumb terminals

The term *dumb terminal* is applied to terminal devices without local intelligence. Mainframe terminals such as 3270s are the classic dumb terminals. The AS/400 5250 terminal is also a dumb terminal. The term is used to separate programmable work stations from the older style terminals. Note that programmable work stations (PCs) are often used to emulate dumb terminals.

ESA / Enterprise System Architecture

The term *ESA* refers to Enterprise System Architecture. The System/390 computers all implement ESA. It is supported by mainframe operating systems VSE/ESA, MVS/ESA, and VM/ESA.

ESCON / Enterprise System Connection

The term *ESCON* is associated with the System/390 architecture. It is an acronym for Enterprise System Architecture and refers to the new I/O channels implemented on S/390 processors. It uses high speed serial channels that exploit fiber optic technology.

IPL / Initial Program Load

The IPL process initializes the AS/400 system by resetting memory, loading the operating system nucleus, and defining tables used to control the system.

LAN / Local Area Network

A Local Area Network is a group of PCs connected via a communications channel where direct data sharing is supported. Data present on a *file server* may be accessed as though it was on a local disk drive by specifying the correct drive letter. PC Support/400 supports access to AS/400 data from PCs.

Multiprocessing

Multiprocessing is the simultaneous processing of two or more portions of the same program or of different programs by two or more processing units or CPUs. The AS/400 family includes high end units with several CPUs, and is capable of multiprocessing.

Multiprogramming

Multiprogramming allows multiple applications to be executed at the same time, sharing the available resources, without interfering with each other. All mainframe, most minicomputer, and some PC operating systems support multiprogramming. OS/400 supports multiprogramming for the AS/400.

Multitasking

Multitasking allows a single program to be split into several independent streams of instructions (tasks) that appear to execute concurrently. Operating systems provide facilities to create/attach tasks, communicate between tasks, and synchronize access to resources shared by two or more tasks. The AS/400 supports multitasking via the separation of an application into pieces.

Real Storage
The term *real storage* refers to physical processor memory. The terms *main memory* and *system main memory* are also seen. On the AS/400, the hardware and operating system combine to provide a single layer view of *virtual storage*. In this system, real storage is not detail managed by the system administrator, but is instead simply a hardware resource you measure and purchase more of to improve performance.

Rightsizing
See *Downsizing*.

SQL
The Structured Query Language used to access a relational database. SQL statements may be issued by an application program, and may also be packaged then invoked by name from an application program.

SQL/DS
The VSE and VM relational database management software is named SQL/DS. SQL/DS can act as a DRDA server or client for AS/400 applications.

Task
A task is a logical unit of execution. *Thread* is another term sometimes applied to a task. A task may attach other tasks. Tasks that are attached by other tasks are often called subtasks.

Virtual Storage
The term *virtual storage* is used to describe the memory seen by a program running on a computer system. This virtual memory can exceed the amount of real storage available on the computer. The architectural limitation for virtual memory is determined by the size of the processor's address register. Thus, AS/400 systems have an architected limit of 48 bit addresses and support effectively unlimited amounts (many terabytes) of virtual storage.

VTAM / Virtual Telecommunication Access Method
VTAM is the standard remote and local terminal manager for IBM mainframe operating systems. The AS/400 fully supports the LU6.2 protocol of VTAM for efficient communications.

WORM / Write Once Read Mostly
WORM drives were the first type of optical disk drive. The acronym is based upon their ability to be written one time only, then read many times.

Index

ABOUT THE AUTHORS

JESSE GAMBLE has extensive experience working with IBM's midrange systems, including the AS/400. He is a frequent conference speaker and teaches professional seminars on AS/400 performance and fine tuning.

BILL MERROW is with Legent Software, Inc., where he is director of data center management development and director of research and development working on advanced projects.